The Ebbing Tide

The Ebbing Tide

Policy and Principles of Catholic Education

James Arthur

First published in 1995

Gracewing
Fowler Wright Books
2 Southern Ave, Leominster
Herefordshire HR6 0QF

ISBN 0 85244 347 1

Typesetting by Reesprint
Radley, Oxfordshire, OX14 3AJ

Printed by Redwood Books
Trowbridge, Wiltshire, BA14 8RN

Contents

Foreword

by Professor V.A. McClelland

A cerebral definition of the meaning and purpose of Catholic education is contained in a published address to his priests by the bishop of Salford, Patrick Kelly, in December 1987. Catholic schools exist, he declared, out of a conviction that 'Jesus is not only a word from God' but *'the Word of God'*. All things were made 'through him' and 'in him all things hold together'. The consequence of this belief is that discipleship is the beginning, the context and the goal of living and, in a school, is manifested in shared vision that is clearly recognisable, lucidly formulated and exemplified in the daily lives and activities of a faith-community. Furthermore, such a school has the function of witnessing to Christianity and, by being rooted in community, makes for an education that is integrated and purposeful. Dermot Lane has carried the same concept into the political domain by envisaging the contemporary role of the Catholic school as constituting the antithesis of the 'raw and ragged' individualism propagated by the enterprise culture of that Thatcherite revolution of the 'eighties'. Entrepreneurial individualism wages conflict upon subscription to collective responsibility and social morality.

This philosophy of Catholic education, in conformity with the pronouncement of the Second Vatican Council in its declaration of 1965 on Christian education [*Gravissimum educationis*], forms a self-consistent and cohesive concept, one that is directional and pervasive. The council envisaged Catholic education as promoting 'the Christian concept of the world whereby the material values, assimilated into the full understanding of man redeemed by Christ, may contribute to the good of society as a whole' [Austin Flannery (ed.), *Vatican Council II*, I, 728].

James Arthur's study presents a challenge to the complacency of certain people, priests and prelates who are content to shelter beneath platitudinous utterance or pious sentiment. It presents abundant evidence that the Roman Catholic Church in England and Wales has failed to confront the practical implications of the educational philosophy it broadcasts. Even in the important task of the appointment of teachers to its denominational schools, perfunctory obeisance in the direction of established theological correctness is sometimes allowed to substitute for personal commitment and scholarly competence. Indeed, the broad thrust of Arthur's argument is that the Church, contained by its own ineffective structures and sometimes by criteria or ignorance, has emphasised 'quantitative goals rather than qualitative outcomes'. The pursuit of an equitable share of national resources, important as that was in terms of the effect upon school-place provision, dominated the Roman Catholic Church's educational agenda from 1870 to 1944 and beyond. This prevented that alignment of 'a critical synthesis' between the predominant culture of the day and what Rosmini described in the nineteenth century as 'the perfect unity' that ought to undergird the educational formation of an individual. Rosmini's phrase implies bringing into relationship the conservation and transmission of Divine teaching (with its transcendental values) and the missionary intent that lies at the heart of Catholic education. The latter quality necessitates the propagation of the good news of the gospel message, transforming lives in the daily service of each other. Raymond Holley sees in that measure of personal transcendence a definition of holiness.

In essence this book declares Catholic schools that only lead children to cope with the world as it encircles them are not fulfilling the theological aspirations enunciated by the Second Vatican Council. A Catholic education is not simply about personal preservation of spiritual integrity. Rather, children are to be matured in such a way that their individual commitment, their spiritual formation, their framework of belief and their desire to lead good lives, they will *confront*, *challenge* and *change* the world as they encounter it.

If the Catholic school is failing in its missionary intent today, it is so doing because it has succumbed to the values of a dominant, materialist meritocracy. It has ceased to challenge the assumptions and attitudes of the world.

V.A. McClelland
University of Hull

Preface

This book contains many criticisms, some of them severe, of the Catholic schools system in England and Wales. I hope that these will not lead the reader to think that I am an opponent of Catholic schools. I am, on the contrary, a passionate supporter of Catholic schools. I feel sure that we need them, if possible, even more than the communities which built them with such effort and sacrifice over 150 years.

It was while I was teaching in a Catholic school that I became aware of how important Catholic schools are, and how necessary it is to improve them. The more I studied, the more aware I became of how little work has been done in this area. I hope that this book will be accepted as a useful contribution to an ongoing discussion and debate.

In the course of writing this book I have been supported and encouraged by a number of friends, and to them I offer my sincere thanks. In particular, however, I wish to record my appreciation to the Rt Rev. David Charlesworth, OSB, Abbot of Buckfast, Fr Robert Ombres OP, and Dr Simon Gaine, for their valuable assistance in reading parts of the early drafts of this work and offering suggestions. I owe a special debt of gratitude to Dr Vivian Williams, Fellow of St Peter's College, Oxford, for his expert advice on educational policy matters. I have acted on much of what they have told me, but any mistakes are mine alone. I would like also to thank Barbara Hird for compiling the Index, and Dr Robin Rees for typesetting the text.

I am also doubly indebted to Professor V.A. McClelland for contributing the Foreword and I am honoured by having associated with this volume one whose contribution to Catholic education has been so singularly distinguished.

James Arthur
Canterbury
October 1995

1

Introduction

This book has been written at a time of major upheaval in the provision of schools, owing to the implementation of the reforms contained in the Education Acts of 1988, 1992 and 1993. The broad thrust of my argument is that the Church has not responded to these legislative changes by developing distinctive education policies for its schools within the maintained sector. The future shape of Catholic schooling is dependent on two factors: uncertain political developments that are outside of Church control; and the changing social and religious direction of the Catholic community itself. Many Catholics, both clerical and lay, are deeply concerned about the direction that Catholic schools have taken and have been increasingly asking for a redirection of educational effort from children to adults. In short, they believe that Catholic schools have lost their way and feel that whilst it may be too late to reform them it is not too late to disestablish them. This book aims to fuel the fire of these concerns by providing a contribution to the debate about the future direction of Catholic maintained schooling in England and Wales.

Schooling continues to be the single most expensive activity of the Catholic Church in England and Wales. The current principles on which such a schooling is founded were outlined by Cardinal Hume, in an address to Catholic headteachers in September 1988. In this address he drew attention to the fundamental 'uniqueness' or 'distinctiveness' of Catholic education and urged head teachers to be 'leaders of the Catholic school community' in building God's kingdom on earth.[1] Cardinal Hume, in common with all the other Catholic bishops in England and Wales, has consistently paraphrased the educational principles found in the Second Vatican Council's *Declaration on Christian Education* and in the Vatican's subsequent education publications. Whilst the bishops have been systematic and largely coherent in the enunciation of these educational

1

principles. I would argue that they have been pragmatic and inconsistent in the implementation of their educational policies.

The Fathers of the Second Vatican Council asserted that the Catholic school is an ideal locus of the education of Catholics. The Congregation for Catholic Education in Rome summed up these principles for every Catholic school when it stated:

> The Council, therefore, declared that what makes the Catholic school distinctive is its religious dimension, and this is to be found in a) the educational climate, b) the personal development of each student, c) the relationship between culture and the Gospel, d) the illumination of all knowledge with the light of faith.[2]

These official principles of education in schools involve the transmission of the central beliefs and values of Christian culture and the interior acceptance of these beliefs and values as part of the formation of adult members of the Church. These assertions of principle by Rome and of the English and Welsh bishops simultaneously involve policy consequences. The way in which these principles are transformed into Catholic education policies by the Catholic community is an important and legitimate subject for discussion and investigation.

This book investigates the extent to which government legislation and action has threatened or eroded the Catholic Church's influence over its schools.[3] However, such an investigation cannot simply assume that the Catholic Church in England and Wales has a clear set of educational principles which are not only distinct from those of the State but involve different policy outcomes. There is growing evidence that the Church has not given as much attention to the principles underlying its educational policy as it has to the maintenance and numerical expansion of the schools themselves; an emphasis on quantitative goals rather than qualitative outcomes. It is also the case that the nature of Catholic education cannot be determined solely by examining the Church's official documents. Official Church pronouncements may indicate what Catholic education ought to be, but they may not correspond to a reality of what a particular Catholic community has made of Catholic education. I would argue that it has become increasingly difficult to implement the 'official' principles of Catholic education. I would also argue that this difficulty arises from both the actions of Government and, equally importantly, from the changing nature of the Catholic Church in England and Wales since 1965.

The *Catholic Herald*, in a major editorial of the 10th May 1991 entitled, 'The Pillars of Catholicism under Threat', claimed that:

> In short, the Dual System is blatantly under threat....The respect which previously characterised Church-State relations is being replaced by a hollow public lip service to the idea of partnership while the government's reforms in practical terms alienate and marginalise the bishops. It is surely time the hierarchy spoke out clearly and mobilised the Catholic community in defence of our great successes, our schools.

Further support for this view has come from at least one former senior civil servant in the Department of Education and Science. John Richards, Under-Secretary at the DES between 1973 and 1977 claimed that the government since 1979 has an unambiguous record of 'eliminating, diminishing or taming sources of influence and authority mistrusted by central government.'[4] The influence of the Catholic Church on public education policy has certainly been diminished, if not mistrusted by government, in recent years. Central government action is not the only major factor that has eroded this influence. On 24th March 1995 it was reported in the *Times Educational Supplement* that the Catholic Education Service had complained that some local education authorities believed that multi-faith lessons in religious education meant that there was no longer a need for Church schools. Perceptions within the Catholic community have also changed and Bishop Mullins, addressing the Conference of Catholic Secondary Schools in 1987, observed that:

> Part of the flagging support for Catholic schools among Catholic parents is surely due to their failure to perceive any real difference between the county and the voluntary school. This is especially true at secondary level.[5]

The Vatican newspaper, *L'Osservatore Romano* of 12th August 1991, reported:

> At present not a few doubt the validity of Catholic schools or would like to see them limited to the primary level; they think that the money could be put to better use . . .

L'Osservatore Romano's report on the Catholic community in England and Wales clearly points to the changing educational perceptions of Catholics in recent years. These perceptions indicate that many Church members seek a reduction in the role of Catholic schooling within the 'dual system'. It would appear that the officially held idea of what constitutes 'Catholic schooling', as described in the Congregation's 1988 statement of principles, has become increasingly more difficult to provide in the maintained sector.

The Church recognises that:

> Today, as in the past, some scholastic institutions which bear the name Catholic do not appear to correspond fully to the principles of education which should be their distinguishing feature . . .[6]

Catholic education policy needs to be consonant with the educational principles derived from the Church's theological teaching. Yet the Church also has to set the educational policy of successive governments alongside its own specific theological insights on education. Consequently, the Church, as a provider of schools in the social and political context of England and Wales can only partially derive its policies from theological principles. Fundamental questions need to be raised concerning the role of Church voluntary schools in the context of the changing pattern of educational provision. This later point is important since the Congregation for Catholic Education stresses that:

> . . . in order to bring it into being and to maintain it the school must be able to count on the unity of purpose and cohesion of all its members.[7]

In other words, the existence of a 'faith community', a group of people united by common beliefs, accounts for the uniqueness of Catholic schools.

In England and Wales there are twenty-two dioceses whose bishops meet nationally as a Conference for purposes of consultation and common action. However, there is a degree of confusion about the authority of the statements issued by, or on behalf of, the Conference. Statements on Catholic schools are not binding on each diocese, since the Conference cannot substitute for the teaching authority of the diocesan bishop.[8] Consequently, controversies arise, more private than public, between individual bishops and the decisions of the National Conference of Catholic Bishops. Moreover, the publication of educational statements on behalf of the Conference does not necessarily constitute the official view adopted in each diocese. Discussion of a 'national policy' on Catholic education is therefore rendered problematic. So, whilst presentation of Church teaching by the bishops on education is virtually a paraphrase of Vatican statements they normally include additional material in their statements. This material generally focuses on a concern with the control and purpose of Catholic schooling, and often offers a justification for a particular type of clerical control to safeguard schools from the perceived threats to the Church from secular society. They do not normally afford specific policies that might distinguish Catholic schools from other types of school. As a result there is a major difficulty for the Catholic educator in translating general principles into policies which have practical application in schools. This helps to explain the crucial and extraordinary fact that there is no national policy for over 2,500 Catholic schools which are partially maintained by the substantial parish contributions of practising Catholics.

A further problem faces any writer on the subject of Catholic schools in that Catholic educational policy has attracted relatively little attention from educational researchers. This lack of attention is well illustrated by an extensive bibliography on educational policy and administration published by the National Foundation for Educational Research in 1980. The bibliography contains one single reference to a short article in *New Society* on Catholic schools. The continued neglect of Catholic educational policy since 1980 is also demonstrated by the Open University course on Educational Policy. In one module of the course there is a case study of educational policy in Liverpool where the scale of Catholic provision of schools in parts of the City rivals that of the local education authority. However, there is not a single reference to the role of the Church in educational policy formulation.[9] In another module on 'The Local Government of Education', there is a final section on 'What other groups are involved?', and at the end of this part there is a very brief account of the role of the Churches which is described in the following terms:

> The Churches are concerned not merely as providers, but as educators. Their diocesan organisations and their representatives, and some of their institutions of teacher training, have made distinctive contributions to the thinking and therefore policy formulation of some local education authorities.[10]

The text of this course gives no idea to what these 'distinctive contributions' to policy formulation might have been. These examples clearly indicate that there has been a neglect of the Church's role in the formulation of educational policy. There have been Catholic policy researchers, but they have followed the mainstream in their choice of topics, which has been to ignore the Catholic educational contribution. Richard Dearden, for example,

demonstrates clearly that this has been the case in the philosophy
of education.[11] Peter Hastings, writing in the 11th February 1989
issue of *The Tablet*, comments that there are surprisingly few policy
studies of Catholic education in England and Wales. In fact, educational research which is designed to inform policy decisions has
never been a priority of the bishops. It is also apparent that there
has been no major critical examination of the Catholic schools
system and there is a general dearth of published information on
the subject. Yet this state of affairs is remarkable when one considers that there is a significant and substantial network of Catholic
schools in England and Wales. The history of the Catholic community in England and Wales is characterised by a major concern for
schooling. It has invested and continues to invest time, personnel
and money in the perpetuation of a Catholic network of schools
without any serious analysis of the effectiveness of this policy.

In Chapter Two the growth of Catholic voluntary schools in the
maintained sector is considered. A major aim of this book is to
compare the institutional Church's vision of education with the
policy and principles of Catholic education as practised. It seeks
to examine and explain the various influences affecting and constraining the policies and processes of the Catholic Church's
involvement in schooling in England and Wales. Chapter Three
describes and evaluates the nature of Catholic education and
schooling as understood by official Church documents since 1965
and discusses some of the objections to specifically Catholic understandings of Catholic education. In Chapter Four an outline of
the major Catholic educational policy development since 1960 is
given. It examines the grounds on which the Church claims a right
to influence educational policy and reviews the spectrum of opinions within the Church concerning the purpose of Catholic education in schools. Chapter Five looks specifically at the role of the
Catholic community in education policy especially the degree of
lay, in particular parental, participation in schooling. It considers
the involvement of bishops in schools with their responsibilities in
Canon and civil law and examines the implications which arise
when the authority of the bishop in education is questioned by the
laity. Chapter Six contrasts policies on admissions, appointments,
the curriculum and general school control with the principles
outlined and discussed in Chapters Three and Five. It explores
these issues, raised initially in Chapter Four, in more depth. Chapter Seven discusses three possible models for understanding

Catholic education today and provides a fictional example of how a Catholic school may lose its way. I hope that this contribution to the debate on the schools question will encourage Catholics, both clerical and lay, to consider the problems with the urgency they deserve and formulate appropriate action. Another decade will be too late.

Notes

1. Hume, B., 'The Future of Catholic Schools', in *Briefing*, Vol. 18, No. 19, 30th September 1988.
2. *The Religious Dimension of Catholic Education*, Congregation for Catholic Education, Rome, 1988, para.1.
3. A Voluntary maintained school is defined as a school maintained by an LEA, but not established by it. There are three types of such schools according to the method selected for receiving financial assistance for the cost of repairs, alterations, and improvements to their buildings and, in the case of a new school, for the cost of establishing it. The three types are controlled schools, aided schools and special agreement schools. The majority of Catholic voluntary schools are either 'aided' or 'special agreement' schools since these types of school used to provide the maximum independence from LEA control. The 1988 Education Reform Act introduced the grant maintained school and there are over 140 Catholic schools in this category which completely breaks the connection with an LEA. For full details of the powers and financial implications of each type of voluntary school see Taylor, G. and Saunders, J.B., *The Law of Education*, Butterworths, London, (eighth edition), 1976, pp. 22–24 and Brooksbank, K., and Nice, D., *County and Voluntary Schools*, (seventh edition), Longman, Essex, 1989.
4. *The Catholic Herald*, 10th May 1991, p.4.
5. Mullins, D., 'Education 14–24 — The Catholic Perspective', 90th Annual Conference of Catholic Secondary Schools, April 11th–13th 1987, pp. 21–25.
6. *The Catholic School*, Congregation for Catholic Education, Rome, 1977, para. 65.
7. *Ibid.*
8. Dulles, A., *The Reshaping of Catholicism*, Harper and Row, San Francisco, 1988, p. 214 ff.
9. Open University: *The Policy-Makers: Local and Central Government*, A Third Level Course, 1986, Module 2, Part 1, pp. 7–34.
10. Open University—*Educational Studies: The Local Government of Education*, Unit 4 of the Control of Education in Britain, A Second Level Course, E222, 1979, p. 39.
11. Dearden, R.F., 'Philosophy of Education 1952–1982', *British Journal of Educational Studies*, Vol. XXXIV, No. 1, 1982, pp. 57–71.

2

Policy in Historical Perspective

Reformation to Restoration 1558–1850

Prior to the Reformation, schooling in England and Wales was under the control of a wide variety of bodies, both clerical and lay, within the Catholic Church. Educational institutions, contrary to the conclusions of some Anglican historians, were not always established by episcopal licence, nor were they generally subject to episcopal inspection. Indeed, early English councils and synods, which regulated every aspect of ecclesiastical life, hardly ever touched on schools — episcopal intervention in the affairs of schools was extremely rare.[1] Schoolmasters needed a licence from the local bishop to teach, although this requirement seems not always to have been enforced. It was only after the Reformation was well advanced that the role of teachers and schools became subject to licensing and supervision. Consequently, after the Elizabethan Religious Settlements of 1558–63, the state-created Church of England attempted to assume control over schools on the basis that the State and the Church were one.[2] Schooling was to be used as a means to suppress Catholic faith and in turn foster Anglican beliefs. Catholic schools were therefore forced out of the public domain and with subsequent penal legislation they had an intermittent and hounded existence. This is illustrated by the fact that thirty-two schools are known to have been opened in Lancashire before 1600 and Brian Cansfield, who went abroad at sixteen in 1597 to become a Jesuit, had been educated at no fewer than six different schools in Lancashire: at Lancaster, Tunstall, Blackburn, Urswick, Warton and Thornton.[3] By 1581, a scheme was devised, attributed to Lord Burghley, forcibly to remove the children of the Catholic gentry from their homes and bring them up as Protestants:

> You shall, under cover of education, have them as hostages for their parents' fidelities.[4]

9

In 1583 the Privy Council ruled that all children should be educated by the legally established Anglican Church. These rules, some of which were implemented by Royal Prerogative rather than through Parliamentary legislation, amounted to a direct violation of the natural rights of parents to educate their children in their own faith. Arthur Beales has concluded that the English Reformation constituted a cataclysm for Catholic schooling, within the space of one generation.[5] Parents who were determined in conscience to keep alive the faith of their children were forced to send them abroad. Cardinal Allen, with the Diaspora of Catholic dons from Oxford laid the foundations for a modern Catholic education system.[6] John Bossy claims that they established schools and colleges in Europe which by 1600 educated more Catholic children than did the grammar schools in England — though he provides no detailed evidence and it is difficult to evaluate his claim given that it is not known how many Catholics were being educated in schools in England.[7] Some Catholics did voluntarily attend Anglican schools, participated in prayers and supervised Church attendance. Nevertheless, their situation was not always a comfortable one: they were discriminated against at school, and on occasions Catholic priests refused them First Communion on the grounds of their attendance at Anglican institutions.[8]

As the penal policy abated, a series of Catholic preparatory schools was established, often to feed the continental colleges. These schools were inevitably small in size and many had a short existence. Only a few managed a span of more than fifty years — such as the school at Fernyhalgh near Preston, which was in existence in 1650 and continued into the next century. The exact number of schools is unknown but there were at least 120 Catholic schoolmasters in the seventeenth century rising to 135 by the eighteenth with at least 220 Catholic schools during the period.[9] Others are being discovered by further research, such as the Franciscan school at Edgbaston in Birmingham which appears to have been in existence from about 1685 to the end of the eighteenth century.[10] In 1623 the Jesuits divided England up into 12, then 14, missionary districts in an attempt to meet the educational needs of English Catholics. Few details of the schools they established survive. With the accession of James II (1685 to 1688) the Jesuits opened a total of twelve schools, some of which accepted non-Catholics, at Bury St. Edmunds, Durham, Lincoln, Newcastle, Norwich, Pontefract-York, Stapehill (Wimborne), Welshpool, Wigan, Wolverhampton, and two in London. Also during this time the administration of the Catholic Church in England and Wales was regularised by a division into four Districts, each under the charge of a Vicar Apostolic. This arrangement lasted, with an increase in the number of bishops and Districts in 1840, until the restoration of the hierarchy of bishops in 1850. By 1688 many Jesuit schools were forced to close, some were destroyed by anti-Catholic crowds, and further punitive legislation against Catholic schools effectively ended any public presence.[11] Clandestine schools did continue, even though Catholic schoolmasters could be imprisoned for life and the property of Catholic parents confiscated. It was not until the Catholic Relief Acts of 1778 and 1791 that these punitive measures were removed from the Statute Book.[12]

The first of these Acts did not allow for the establishment of Catholic schools as such, but it was interpreted permissively. In a letter from the Cardinal Prefect of the Congregation of Propaganda in Rome to the Vicar Apostolic of the Northern District we read:

> since the law now allows schools for the instruction of youth under the care of Catholic masters, this Sacred Congregation is anxious that they should be established.[13]

In fact the law of perpetual imprisonment for Catholic schoolmasters was not abolished until 1791, and then against a background of popular opposition. It is surprising therefore to find Catholics and Anglicans within a brief time engaged in a common educational purpose with 'Sunday Schools for all Denominations'.[14] In 1807 the 'Benevolent Society of St Patrick' was formed on a inter-denominational basis to provide elementary schooling for Irish immigrant children.[15] At local level Catholic lay congregations controlled much of the schooling that existed and there appeared to be a spirit of conciliation abroad, with Catholics and Anglicans participating in non-denominational schools.[16] The most important development for the future direction of official Catholic educational policy was the response of the Vicars Apostolic. Certainly, the London Vicars Apostolic seem to have discouraged lay involvement in education.[17] The sequence of events which eventually led to education, schooling in particular, becoming an enterprise led and dominated by the clergy, under the firm control of the bishops, remains obscure. As Bossy notes, the 1790s were marked by a sharp division within the English Catholic community. One party was led by the prominent noble and gentry families of the South and Midlands. This group was hostile to clerical control, and sought to

establish lay dominance over matters such as episcopal appointments. The other group was more provincial and bourgeois in
character and firmly under clerical leadership. It was identified
with the name of Bishop Milner, Vicar Apostolic of the Midland
District, who defined the issue as being whether the Catholic
Church was to be run by 'the successors of St Peter or the descen-
dants of Lord Petre' (a wealthy Catholic peer). The question of
control over schools was discussed in this context, and the eventual
triumph of the 'clerical' party was reflected in the organisation and
management of the schools.[18]

In 1838 the lay-dominated Catholic Institute of Great Britain
was set up principally to raise funds for chapels and elementary
schools.[19] It was aristocratic in composition with the Earl of Shrewsbury as its Chairman. It was also the successor to a long series of
similar lay bodies and was organised on the basis of regional
committees. The institute's immediate aim was to secure an
equitable share of the central Exchequer grants, which had been
available since 1833 for elementary school building. Catholics were
excluded from the first grants from public funds, since these
monies were specifically restricted to the then well-established
Church of England National Society and the Nonconformist British and Foreign School Society. However, it is interesting that the
first public campaign to raise funds for the building of Catholic
schools lay in character, although Lord Shrewsbury was very
much identified with the 'clerical' leadership of the Church.[20] The
first serious blow to this essentially lay organisation came when
Bishop Brown, of the newly created Lancashire district, issued a
Pastoral Letter in 1844 in which he abolished all existing fund-rais-
ing for churches and schools and replaced these arrangements with
his own district board which did not contain a single lay member.[21]
The second, and fatal, blow to lay leadership in educational matters
came with a crisis in the Catholic Institute itself.

A seemingly immutable feature of the Vicars Apostolic policy on
schools was their refusal to sanction the reading of the Authorised
Version of the Bible in Catholic schools.[22] This was the principal
obstacle to the securing of government grants. In addition, the
bishops feared the proselytism conducted by the Established
Church, especially in the light of the way the Poor Law Guardians
interpreted the Poor Law Amendment Act of 1834, which often
led to Catholic children being educated as members of the Church
of England.[23] Consequently, when the Catholic Institute expressed

some sympathy with the government proposal for the compulsory non-denominational education of factory children, to be supervised by the Church of England using the Authorised Version, the bishops moved quickly to abolish it.[24] They found little difficulty in replacing the Institute's educational work with the Catholic Poor School Committee, founded in December 1847, consisting of two laymen and eight clerics.[25] Charles Langdale who had been the Chairman of the Catholic Institute's committee on education, became the Chairman of the new bishops' body. Langdale belonged to an old Yorkshire Catholic gentry family which had been firmly on the side of Milner's party in the 1790s. He had previously achieved some success in agitating for a share in the government grant through his long correspondence with members of the government, which was followed by a deputation in 1846 and afterwards by protest meetings in the large urban centres.[26] In January 1847 the *Tablet*, the leading Catholic weekly, urged Catholics to use their vote to uphold Catholic interests.[27] These campaigning tactics have remained part of Catholic educational agitation to this day. The Catholic Poor School Committee consequently became the bishops' recognised agency for communication between the Church and the Privy Council's Committee on Education. By this time the central feature of English Catholic life was the mass Irish immigration consequent on the 1846 potato famine. This completely transformed the community into an overwhelmingly poor and ignorant group, firmly under the leadership of their priests in a strange and hostile land.

The emphasis on Catholic separatism in the provision of schools became more evident in the attitude of the ecclesiastical authorities. Some bishops began to deny parents the Sacraments for sending their children to non-Catholic schools.[28] Dr. Thomas Fergusson, the priest secretary of the education committee of the Catholic Institute, had informed the government in June 1847 that the Catholic concept of education included the fundamental idea that religion pervaded all instruction in Catholic schools. This argument formed the basis of negotiations between the government and the Catholic Poor School Committee.[29] In the negotiations leading to the first grants being given for Catholic schools, Langdale argued for the withdrawal of the regulations which required the reading of the Authorised Version as a condition of grant aid. In addition, he explained to the government that the Catholic Church would rather forgo grant aid than yield on certain fundamental principles, one of which was that the inspection of Catholic schools must be approved by the Catholic authorities.[30] He continued as Chairman of the Catholic Poor School Committee from December 1847, informing the government that his Church was opposed to lay management of schools. However, while the government finally agreed to the withdrawal of the Authorised Version clause, and to the appointment of Catholic inspectors, it insisted on the insertion of one or other of its specimen articles of management into the trust deeds of grant-aided Catholic schools. The purpose of these clauses was clearly to limit clerical control. They were designed so that trust deeds would contain clauses defining the structure of school management in such a way as to give the laity predominance. This was in conflict with current Catholic practice. As the Privy Council attempted to impose its clauses on Catholic schools the negotiations extended into 1852. The Privy Council argued that there was nothing to stop lay Catholics from implicitly deferring to the spiritual authority of the Church as individual managers of schools.[31] However, the real problem was the position of laymen in authority over Catholic schools secured by a power, the government, outside the authority of the Church. It is interesting that both Marjorie Cruikshank and James Murphy argue that the final agreed trust deed clauses on management provided for episcopal control over all Catholic elementary schools. In a more recent and detailed study of the clauses, it is argued that those clauses which were described as safeguards by the Catholic Poor School Committee were in fact concessions made to the Privy Council.[32]

Trust deeds for Catholic schools were not uniform, and some were drawn up to open the schools to non-Catholics, such as the Catholic school of St. Patrick in Carlisle established:

> for the gratuitous education of children of all denominations, more especially those born of Irish parents.[33]

This particular trust deed had no provision for the teaching of religion. Many of these trust deeds had been originally drawn up by laymen and the legal ownership of the school property belonged to lay individuals or a group of lay trustees. The Roman Catholic Charities Act of 1860 allowed many of these schools to fall under diocesan ownership, since Section Five of this Act stipulated that, in the absence of any written documents the schools and their property would transfer to whomever had operated them continuously for twenty years.[34] It was by such means that many schools, originally built and managed by the laity, passed into clerical control.[35] Since there was no substantial Catholic middle class, the government was forced to appeal to the bishops on disputed points in connection with schools and trusts.

In December 1847 the Privy Council Committee on Education passed a Minute, whilst the negotiations on the 'management clauses' continued, authorising grants to Catholic schools despite enormous opposition from anti-Catholic MPs.[36] Before grants could be given, the Government required that it be informed and satisfied that the proposed school would be 'efficiently' and 'permanently' supported. The Committee in Council also laid down a building standard and issued instructions for inspectors of schools. If these three conditions were met, maintenance grants would be provided for individual schools.[37] These conditions, however, left Catholic schools at a serious disadvantage because of the real poverty of the Catholic community, which now consisted mostly of Irish immigrants. Progress was therefore slow and the development of Catholic schools became increasingly dependent on aid from the State.

Restoration to 1902

The Catholic Church's policy of providing an extensive network of Catholic elementary schools was fully explicit by the time of the Restoration of the Hierarchy of bishops in 1850. Consequently, in 1852, at the first Synod of the Archbishop and Bishops of the Province of Westminster, it was recorded that:

> The first necessity . . . is a sufficient provision of education, adequate to the wants of our poor. It must become universal . . . to . . . prefer the establishment of good schools to every other work. Indeed, wherever there may seem to be an opening for a new mission, we should prefer the erection of a school, so arranged as to serve temporarily for a chapel, to that of a church without one.[38]

The bishops were eager that these Catholic schools should be equal in every respect to other schools, so that Catholics would send their children to them with confidence in the schools' standards. This is why the erection of many a new church resulted from the prior establishment of a school. Many of these schools not only served as temporary chapels but as centres for social work in the area.[39] The struggle for such schools largely united Catholics with a strong sense of purpose, even though they were materially poor, small in number and weak in influence. Clearly, priority was given

by the bishops to the establishment of a specifically Catholic
elementary school system for the poor.

Government financial support for Catholic schools remained
extremely limited and by 1854 the Catholic Church had only
received a total of £3,131 in contrast to the £415,000 received by
the Church of England.[40] One reason for this was the continued
suspicion by Catholics of government influence on Catholic
schools. In particular the Privy Council grant for books could only
be applied to books which it specifically approved. An indication
of this continuing suspicion of the government came when the
bishops refused to cooperate with certain parts of the enquiries
made by the Newcastle Commission.[41] Nevertheless, government
grants steadily increased and by the year ending 31st August 1867
the income of Catholic schools for England and Wales was £55,842
of which £21,591 came from the government.[42] The average income
per child for Anglican and Nonconformist schools in the same year
was £1. 6s. 9d., whilst in Catholic schools it was only 10s. 2d.[43] Only
the Ragged and Catholic schools took the poorest children, and
this proved to be a great obstacle to the expansion of Catholic
schooling.[44] The central problem was that no school received a
maintenance grant unless it provided 60% of the entire cost of
maintenance. Nor was any school given a building grant unless 75%
of the total cost of the project was forthcoming from voluntary
funds i.e. from the Catholic community itself. Nevertheless between 1850 and 1870 further, if insufficient, progress in building
Catholic schools and teacher training colleges was made, and by
1869 there were over 100,000 children in Catholic schools. The
existence of Catholic schools was the primary reason for establishing Catholic training colleges. Indeed, the first training college
for Catholic men, and the only one till 1947, was founded at
Hammersmith in 1850 as part of the Catholic Poor School Committee's policy to provide Catholic teachers for Catholic schools.
This college was later transferred to Strawberry Hill, Twickenham,
and catered for 120 students. Colleges for Catholic women teachers were founded at Liverpool in 1856 and afterwards in London,
Newcastle-on-Tyne, Salford, Hull, Southampton and Birmingham.[45]

Outlining the exact nature of Catholic education policy was the
responsibility of the Catholic Poor School Committee, on behalf of
the bishops. To this end therefore, the Chairman of the committee
sent a memorandum in 1868 to the Prime Minister.[46] The main

thrust of the statement was the determination of the bishops to safeguard Catholics against government interference in religious teaching and school management in the light of the fact that since the establishment of the Privy Council Committee on Education it had been possible for the State to espouse an education policy which it could also enforce. Therefore, it was not surprising that the government's proposal of an Education Bill in 1869 caused serious concern among the bishops. The bishops were attending the First Vatican Council in Rome when the details of the Bill were published, and this rendered opposition to the government's Bill less co-ordinated. This was made clear when Cardinal Manning, Archbishop of Westminster, indicated in discussions with the government that he was prepared to forgo the right to Catholic inspectors of the secular curriculum in schools, in return for further grant aid and a guaranteed statutory basis for denominational schooling. Bishop Ullathorne of Birmingham totally opposed this position and carried the majority of bishops with him in rejecting Manning's proposal.[47] The Catholic Poor School Committee was mandated to campaign for the retention of Catholic inspectors, but Forster, Chairman of the Privy Council Committee on Education, condemned denominational inspection as inefficient, costly and partial.[48] Only three inspectors were removed from office between 1839 and 1864 and two of them were Catholics. In addition, the Privy Council had on three separate occasions tried to prove Catholic inspectors guilty of charges of disingenuousness and falsehood. It was true that many of the inspector's reports tended to expound the argument and apologetics underlying the Catholic viewpoint in education. Bishop Ullathorne had expressed concern that while a bishop lacked the authority to secure the resignation of an inspector no longer acceptable to the Church, he also lacked the authority to protect the position of an inspector no longer acceptable to the government.[49] However, the Education Act of 1870, despite strong objections from the Catholic Church, abolished all State-supported denominational inspection. The bishops had to rely on their own clerical diocesan inspectors of religious instruction in schools, who had been appointed since 1852.[50] The bishops also decided to establish diocesan councils of education in 1869, to supervise and encourage their educational efforts.

The second main Catholic objection to the Education Bill of 1869 was the provision for School Boards. Catholics feared unfriendly local authorities, and objected to the large discretionary powers which were to be given to the Boards.[51] In particular, the proposal in the Bill to withdraw all building grants from voluntary schools caused the Catholic body to establish an education crisis fund under the presidency of the Duke of Norfolk. This fund soon amounted to £50,000, with the Duke and the Marquess of Bute each contributing £10,000.[52] The fund was aided by persistent local effort and led to an expansion of places in Catholic schools, so that by 1890 there were 964 Catholic schools with 223,645 pupils.[53] This was by any standard a considerable achievement since the Catholic community had to find all the necessary finance before being able to apply for the annual grant under the government's Code. The Revised Code of 1862 was given much greater weight by the passing of the 1870 Education Act, which extended the functions and powers of the Privy Council Committee beyond those of an agency distributing grants. The Code, revised annually, did not merely define standards and curricular matters but also contained administrative instructions regarding qualifications of teachers and building standards; it was later to be the subject of bitter and prolonged controversy.[54]

Catholics also feared that the Education Act of 1870 had begun to establish the principle that schooling was a State responsibility. The Act set up School Boards which were to supply elementary education where voluntary provision was deficient, and this is why in some areas School Boards were not set up as a result of the strength of denominational provision in those districts. Financially, the denominations had little hope of keeping pace with the School Boards, whose income was derived in part from a rate precept in boroughs and from sums collected as part of the poor rate in rural areas. Supporters of voluntary schools not only had to pay the local School Board rate but also contribute to their own schools. Catholics, with less money at their disposal, were expected to reach the same standards as rate-aided Board schools.[55] Consequently, any form of increased expenditure on Board Schools meant that Catholics had to pay the larger rate, and increase their own voluntary contributions to enable their schools to compete with the educational developments of the former. According to official figures published by the newly created Board of Education in 1884, the proportion of free admissions was greatest in Catholic schools and these schools also had the lowest receipt per pupil from fees.[56] Section Twenty Five of the 1870 Education Act permitted School Boards to pay the fees of poor children attending denominational schools. However, since Nonconformists strongly objected to this section, its interpretation and application by local School Board members varied enormously.[57]

In a letter to the Catholic Poor School Committee from the English bishops in Rome in 1870 it was explained that:

> The peculiar circumstances of England render it inevitable, that the administration of the local School Board and of the educational rate will always be in hands over which no control, sufficient to protect the children of the Catholic poor, can be exercised. This has been abundantly proved by the long and painful experience of the Poor Law Boards.[58]

Application for relief was frequently made by the poor to Anglican voluntary agencies and this often entailed a loss of the Catholic faith for the children involved. As late as 1895 Cardinal Vaughan issued a Pastoral Letter in which he complained that:

> Thousands and thousands of Catholic children have been robbed of their faith in past years . . . they have been cut off from all Catholic influence, their very names have been changed and they have been sent into the world aliens to the religion of their baptism.[59]

It was not until 1884 that the Metropolitan Poor Law Board consented to transfer the Catholic children under its care.[60] School Boards likewise were not to be trusted, especially since clause Eighteen of the Education Act 1870 gave the Boards absolute discretion to provide and supply additional school accommodation, even to the extent of providing for compulsory purchase of sites. Consequently, the government's acceptance in 1876 of an amendment to the Education Bill of that year, designed to effect a transfer of responsibility for payment of fees in denominational schools to the Poor Law Guardians, satisfied no one.[61] Catholic protest meetings in London and in other parts of the country were organised against the 1870 Bill and the Act as operated by the School Boards, and repeated representations were made by the bishops to the government.

In 1884 a movement known as the Voluntary Schools Association, the object of which was to agitate for the removal of the financial inequalities of the denominational schools, was initiated in Salford by Bishop (afterwards Cardinal) Vaughan.[62] It was organised on an inter-denominational basis despite the failed attempt at a united denominational approach the previous year. Cardinal Manning had asked for compulsory rate aid for denominational schools in a petition to Parliament of 2nd June 1883, a proposal opposed by the Church of England. Nevertheless, the Voluntary Schools Association spread throughout the country. Its first object was to ask for a 25% increase in maintenance grants immediately, and it sought the removal of four specific grievances. First, it asked for the abolition of the limit set to government grant of 17s. 6d. per capita unless the total income (per child) from other sources exceeded that amount. Second, it sought the removal of the need for Catholic parents to apply to Boards of Guardians for remission of school fees for their children when attending Catholic schools. The Association drew attention to the fact that School Boards could remit the fees of children attending their own schools. Third, it sought the abolition of the rating of voluntary schools for the support of Board Schools. Finally, it sought to end the practice of refusing to recognise the need for Catholic schools if vacant Board School accommodation existed.[63] The Catholic policy was coherent, clear and definite at this time. Its result was that the Church carried through the greater part of its building programme without the help of Parliamentary grants, but funded from weekly house-to-house collections from the poor. In addition many lay Catholic teachers willingly accepted much lower salaries than their School Board counterparts, and worked in buildings and with equipment of an inferior standard.[64]

Invariably, the bishops regarded Board Schools as Protestant establishments, scarcely different from Protestant denominational schools. Nonconformists found the teaching in Board schools, undenominational and at public expense, much to their satisfaction and began to transfer their own voluntary schools to the Boards. In many dioceses the Church of England followed suit and by 1884 about 1,000 schools had been transferred to the Boards, two thirds of them had been Anglican. Indeed, the undenominational teaching sanctioned in Board schools by the Education Act of 1870 was in complete accord with Nonconformist views, as can be seen from a Schools Memorandum of the British and Foreign School Society in 1855:

> We have often expressed our opinion and now repeat it, that the British and Foreign School Society was founded on the principle of religious equality as regarding all professing the Christian faith, that in order to carry out this principle the Scriptures were to be read in all schools, carefully excluding all catechisms and all Formularies of Faith, and that the principle was to be applied in all oral teaching, as well as to the books read.[65]

Biblical Protestant Christianity, with no catechism or particular religious tenets, was a feature of Board schools, and as such they were rejected by the bishops. It was therefore argued by the bishops that in the interests of true equality the heavy financial burden of denominational schools should be lifted.

The Cross Commission of 1886 was set up to enquire into the working of the Elementary Education Act of 1870, mainly as a consequence of denominational protests at the administration of some School Boards.[66] Cardinal Manning was amongst its members, the majority of whom were strongly denominational in character. The majority were in favour of voluntary schools and recognised the unfair financial conditions under which they worked. The recommendations of the majority report were that voluntary schools should receive rate aid for the secular instruction given in them, but no immediate action was taken by the government. Catholic claims for full and equal maintenance grew, with Cardinal Vaughan describing the way in which Catholic schools depended for survival on bazaars as *'reductio ad absurdum'*.[67] In 1891, an Education Act was passed which provided for free elementary education. Under this, Catholic schools received, for the first time, substantial aid owing to the smallness of their former income from school fees. This Act provided 10*s*. per child per annum between the ages of 7 to 15, if no fees were charged. Since the average fee per pupil in Catholic schools was 9*s*.5*d*.,[68] this was advantageous to them. The Education Act of 1891 also allowed voluntary schools to pay this money into a common fund and so assist each other. However since Catholic schools were organised on a parochial basis there is little evidence that any major diocesan response was actually made. With increasing demands from the inspectorate to raise educational standards in schools, costs soared and any advantage for Catholic schools quickly evaporated. Therefore, Catholic agitation for the redress of financial inequalities resumed.

In 1892 the Duke of Norfolk became the Chairman of the Catholic Poor School Committee and Cardinal Vaughan presented a Memorandum to Lord Salisbury, the Prime Minister, strongly deprecating the necessity for voluntary contributions for Catholic schools. In it he also requested the same support that School Boards enjoyed. Once again the Church of England, in an influential delegation to the Prime Minister, stated that they had no desire to see grants increased.[69] In the event the Education Act of 1897 was passed after a similar Bill had been aborted the previous year.

The bishops accepted this Education Act as an interim arrangement, since it provided an additional grant of five shillings per child in voluntary schools which was pooled and distributed according to necessity. This Act enjoined the voluntary schools to form associations for this purpose.[70] The Act also abolished the limit of 17s. 6d. and for the first time exempted voluntary schools from rating, and so met three of the demands of the Voluntary Schools Association. Nevertheless, the bishops strongly repeated in a joint Pastoral Letter the plea that the Catholic body could not go on paying twice for their schools. Catholic schools, they argued, despite some success, were still at a serious financial disadvantage.[71]

The bishops were not without internal critics with regard to the control they exercised over schools in this period. A number of bishops sought to restrict the freedom of Religious Orders in the operation of schools and to control further the employment opportunities of lay teachers. This inevitably led to an atmosphere of tension and mistrust between the bishops and various groups within the Church. For example the Jesuits had felt encouraged by the decree on secondary education of the Fourth Synod of Westminster in 1873, to establish a secondary school in Manchester. However, the local bishop objected to the proposed school and campaigned to have the Jesuits made subject to episcopal control in matters of educational provision. He appealed to Rome and Pope Leo XIII accepted that the local bishop could decide on such matters himself; consequently the Jesuit school was never built.[72] This Papal decision marks an important step in the expansion of episcopal power over schooling and over the educational endeavours of the Religious Orders. Another example concerns lay Catholic teachers some of whom opted to teach in Board schools in order to secure a higher salary. Catholic schools could not compete with the salaries offered in Board schools and this had an unsettling effect on Catholic teachers. In order to secure teachers for their schools the bishops issued instructions at their 'Low Week' meeting of 1875. These warned the clergy that the presence of Catholic teachers in Board schools could 'give active countenance and co-operation to a system which had been condemned in principle by the Church' and that it would 'furnish an argument that our objection to the Board school is not insurmountable' because Catholic teachers were able to teach in them. The bishops claimed that Catholic teachers were morally bound to use the skills they had acquired in the service of the Church. They therefore were

prepared to use sanctions against Catholic teachers who chose to
teach in Board schools, and even proposed the possibility of their
excommunication. Catholic teachers responded by forming an
association in 1892, the forerunner of the Catholic Teachers' Federation, which campaigned for improved salaries in Church schools.
The bishops almost banned the association and it was frequently
frustrated at local level by the clergy.[73] With regard to both the
Religious Orders and lay teachers, the bishops sought to use their
episcopal powers to ensure their control of the schools. This led to
conflict within the Church which was largely resolved in favour of
the bishops' position.

Catholic Educational Policy 1902–1944

During the passage of the 1902 Education Act the bishops kept up
their claim for rate support for old as well as new schools, whilst
the Church of England remained divided on the issue.[74] Anglican
schools had a heterogeneous school population, and the type of
'denominational' teaching in them began to vary enormously. By
contrast Catholic elementary schools had distinctive doctrinal
teaching for Catholic children only. During the debates on the Bill
some Liberal speakers observed these differences and referred to
the need for a separate settlement for Catholics. However, it was
government policy to treat all Church schools alike.[75] Nevertheless,
the Catholic claim for rate aid was met by the Education Act of
1902 in return for some specific concessions. This Education Act
abolished School Boards and established county and borough education authorities who would now control the secular instruction
in Catholic grant aided schools. In addition, they would appoint up
to a third of the managers of such schools and be responsible for
the approval of the qualifications of all teachers. Catholic schools
would still be responsible for providing the site and the buildings,
for which no grants were provided, and also for most school repairs.
These were major concessions in return for support from the rates,
but the Education Act of 1902 did not provide for equality of
treatment between county and voluntary schools.

Some Nonconformists responded to this by establishing the
'League of Passive Resistance', whose members refused to pay that
portion of the rate which they considered would be applied to the
upkeep of denominational schools.[76] The cry 'Rome on the Rates'
emanates from this period. Nevertheless, their protests were ineffective and the 1902 Education Act finally recognised the existence

of a 'dual system' and provided for the maintenance, but not the erection, of schools operated by the Church authorities, out of local rate income. With the return of a Liberal government in 1906 Catholic schools were faced with many hostile local authorities co-operating with a more exacting Board of Education, which had replaced the Privy Council Committee in 1889.[77] From its accession the new government in 1906 made a number of attempts to abolish the 'dual system' and the various holders of the office of President of the Board of Education sought to frustrate denominational schools. In response the bishops began to articulate more forcibly their educational policies. In a memorandum of the new Catholic Education Council (CEC) of 1906, the successor of the Catholic Poor School Committee, the following was declared; first, that religion is an essential factor in education; second, that parents have the right to educate their children in the tenets of their faith; third, that this right was given by God and not by the State and thus could not be denied by the State. It went on to declare that the State, if it established compulsory schooling, should not be in conflict with the parents' inalienable right to religious education and that any 'undenominational' education was in fact Protestant. It concluded that the only schooling Catholic parents could accept for their children was one which was wholly Catholic.[78]

Between 1902 and 1944 expansion of the number of Catholic schools was hindered by the absence of any grants towards the provision of new schools. In addition the Board of Education produced regulations in 1907 which restricted the establishment of denominational secondary schools and threatened denominational teacher training colleges. The Liberal government had so far failed to secure legislation abolishing aid to voluntary schools because of its inability to secure a majority of votes in the House of Lords. Instead, the government used the regulations of the Board of Education to impede denominational provision. First, the Board gave larger grants to schools which were 'undenominational', and then attempted to prevent denominational teacher training colleges from rejecting candidates on grounds of religion. These regulations seriously threatened denominational schools and colleges, and a massive public campaign of Catholic demonstrations was initiated against them. The bishops declared these regulations to be unjust and that they would strive to ignore them.[79] However, many local authorities implemented these, and further, regulations to the disadvantage of Church schools. In the West Riding of

Yorkshire a Catholic school was refused grants to pay teachers' salaries, and the local miners responded by paying the salaries out of their own weekly wages for almost two years.[80] This type of action was not uncommon among Liberal local authorities, and the 'denominational' vote was used in Liverpool and Swansea to oust such authorities in local elections.[81] However, many of these Board regulations were not finally altered until 1917 and so continued to prove a great obstacle to the establishment of Catholic schools.[82]

In 1918 the Scots achieved a 'final' settlement of the denominational schools question. The Education (Scotland) Act of 1918 provided a solution to the same fundamental issue as in England and Wales, that there should be Catholic teachers for Catholic schools. The Act of 1918 allowed the Scottish bishops a veto over the appointment of teachers in Catholic schools, and in return Catholic schools would be transferred to the local authorities with the Catholic financial burden relinquished. However, it was not until 1931 that the CEC of England and Wales declared in favour of the 'Scottish Concordat', and that Cardinal Bourne expressed a willingness to consider a change in the method of appointment of teachers.[83] In the same year, the Labour government recognised the needs of the denominational schools in the light of the reorganisation recommendations of the Hadow Report of 1926. It proposed to offer grants for all grades of denominational schools in return for local authority appointment of teachers with certain teachers being 'reserved' to the denominations. This proposal was rejected by the bishops: a Catholic Labour MP, John Scurr, carried an amendment against the government, and the proposed Bill was eventually rejected in the House of Lords.[84] It was not until much later that Cardinal Bourne declared himself in favour of considering modifications to the appointment of teachers, but it was too late. The 1936 Education Act was not as favourable to Church schools as the 1931 Education Bill would have been.

One reason for the loss of this opportunity by the bishops can be found in their 'Low Week' Declaration on Education of 1929, especially sections 6 and 7 which denied that the State had responsibility for teaching, other than that teachers should be reasonably efficient. The whole declaration was a development of the 1906 CEC Memorandum and is worthy of repeating here almost in full:

1. It is no part of the 'normal' function of the State to teach.

2. The State is entitled to see that citizens receive due education sufficient to enable them to discharge the duties of citizenship in its various degrees.

3. The State ought, therefore, to encourage every form of sound educational endeavour, and may take means to safeguard the efficiency of education.

4. To parents whose economic means are insufficient . . . it is the duty of the State to furnish the necessary means . . . from the common funds arising out of taxation of the whole country. But in so doing the State must not interfere with parental responsibility, nor hamper the reasonable liberty of parents in their choice of a school for their children. Above all, where the people are not all of one creed, there must be no differentiation on the grounds of religion.

5. Where there is a need of greater school accommodation, the State may, in default of other agencies, intervene to provide it; but it may do so only 'in default of, or in substitution for, and to the extent of, the responsibility of the parents'.

6. The teacher is always acting in *loco parentis*, never in *loco civitatis*, though the State, to safeguard its citizenship, may take reasonable care to see that teachers are efficient.

7. Thus a teacher never is and never can be a civil servant . . . whatever authority he may possess to teach and control children; and to claim their respect and obedience, comes to him from God, through the parents, and not through the State, except in so far as the State is acting on behalf of the parents.[85]

Whilst Canon 1374, of the Code of Canon Law promulgated in 1917, forbade the attendance of Catholics at non-Catholic schools and urged bishops to provide schools specifically for Catholics, it nevertheless left the bishop to decide on what circumstances attendance at non-Catholic schools would be permitted. Canon 2319 made it clear that if parents knowingly and willingly disobeyed Canon 1374, then they were open to the sanction of excommunication. It is clear from a number of commentaries on these two Canons, that for the sanction to be valid the parents would have to be bringing their children up in a non-Catholic religion.[86] Consequently, since county schools in England and Wales were not supposed to be sectarian, no excommunication would appear to be valid in their case. This would not be the case with denominational schools. The question revolved around whether or not the influence of the Church was entirely excluded from the school and whether or not Catholics attending would be exposed to dangers to their faith. Both 'non-Catholic religious instruction' and 'non-Catholic instruction' were equally worthy of the censure. The nature of the latter might be so infused with non-Catholic religious tenets that it was equivalent to the former. However, since 'non-Catholic instruction' might only be comprised, in part, of Bible reading, as was generally the case, then the parents might, at the discretion of the bishop, be given the benefit of the doubt. It would seem that the parents did not incur the excommunication of Canon 2319 if the children were withdrawn from 'non-Catholic religious instruction', and that this was the case whether or not the parents had permission from the bishop to send their children to a non-Catholic school. Nevertheless, if the parents had not sought permission from the local bishop then they had violated Canon 1374, and therefore it was open to their confessors to regard them as indisposed for absolution, unless they undertook to obey the Canon and seek the bishop's permission. In December 1929 the encyclical *Christian Education of Youth* was issued by Pope Pius XI and outlined the functions of the State in education. Together with the Code of Canon Law, they formed the basis of the English bishops' pronouncements on education during this period.

Under the Education Act of 1936 local education authorities, for the first time, were able to make contributions of not less than 50% and not more than 75% of the cost of erecting voluntary secondary schools. Teachers were to be appointed by the local education authorities, but the category of 'reserve' teachers was initiated and some local authorities allowed all teachers to be 'reserved', which meant that the Catholic governors appointed them. However, the application of this Education Act was restricted to new secondary schools, at a time when the main difficulty was with the provision of primary schools. The powers of local education authorities were discretionary, not mandatory, and only a small number of schools became 'Special Agreement' schools, as they were later called, under these limited arrangements. In another important development the Senior Public Elementary Schools Act of 1939 was passed. This dealt with the specific problem of a large Catholic population in Liverpool. The local education authority was empowered to build schools and charge rents to the Catholic authorities. Cruickshank makes clear that the Catholic Church was less concerned with the actual possession of school property than with the provision of a Catholic education.[87] This was evident from the various

proposals made by the bishops during the campaign surrounding
the 1944 Education Bill. These sought the 'Scottish Solution' of
1918, the Liverpool settlement of 1939, or an arrangement by
which the LEA assumed responsibility for Catholic schools; but if
80% of parents of a school wished the school to teach the Catholic
religion, then all the teachers appointed should be Catholic. In the
event, the government rejected all three proposals.

Catholic Educational Policy 1944–1959

It has been calculated that the Catholic view of education occupied
more time than any other issue during the passage of the 1944
Education Act.[88] The outline negotiations provided a compromise
the framework of which is still in operation today. The 'dual system'
established in 1902 had continued to produce endless complica-
tions and there was a need for a final settlement. However, at the
level of principle, the difference between the government and the
bishops appeared to be as irreconcilable as ever. In commenting on
the 1944 Education Bill, Dominic Huot remarks that:

> . . . the problem of denominational schools provides an instance
> where the policy decided upon is almost exclusively the result of
> the pressure exerted by a few sectional interests, for neither the
> political parties nor the general public seem to have had any definite
> opinion about it.[89]

Nevertheless, the leading article in *The Times* of 17th February 1940
accorded well with the Catholic position, since it stated that
religion must form the basis of any education worth the name. It
went on to condemn the fact that the then existing system of
governing elementary schools treated religious education as a mere
subsidiary subject. There was obviously significant support in
influential quarters for the continued presence of religion in
schools.

In a study of the 1944 campaign conducted by the Catholic
Church, it was demonstrated that the Catholic laity sought to
persuade the teacher unions and the local education authorities of
the need to accept the Catholic claims, or at least not to press
opposition to them with the government.[90] This left the bishops
to negotiate directly with the Ministry of Education for 100%
grants for Catholic schools; in return they were prepared to con-
cede the appointment of teachers with certain guarantees. During
the course of the negotiations, the bishops submitted a number of

proposals to the government, but the death of Cardinal Hinsley hindered these negotiations.[91] Nevertheless, the 1944 Education Act gave voluntary schools a choice of legal status. This varied according to funding either full finance under 'controlled' status, where the local education authority appointed the managers or governors; or 'aided' status where the foundation governors, appointed by a trust, were in the majority but were required to find 50% of any capital expenditure.[92] There continued to be the alternative 'special agreement' status for some schools which had been set-up under the 1936 Education Act. This category was similar to 'aided' status, but ceased to have any financial advantage after the passage of the 1959 Education Act. Catholics rejected 'controlled' status and none of their schools come under these regulations except one — and this was the result of an administrative error.

After 1944 the Church of England found itself arguing, from a position of financial weakness, for access to all State schools. Many of its own schools began to transfer to the State sector under 'controlled' status [93] with a small group of High Anglicans objecting to this development.[94] The Education Act of 1944 provided no public help for the erection of Catholic schools which were required through normal increase in population, or as a result of new housing developments in the cities. The bishops were the only group to oppose the 1944 Education Act, and never accepted its provisions. Their reaction was to enlist and mobilise massive support from parents in defence of their own policies.[95]

The aims of the bishops immediately after the legislation of 1944 were to secure its favourable administration through minor adjustments. This was achieved through the Education Acts of 1946 and 1948 which made adjustments to the 1944 Act in favour of voluntary aided schools. The 1946 Education Act in particular made it the duty of each local education authority to provide additional sites or a new site if a school had been transferred. It also modified the standards of premises of aided schools at the discretion of the Minister of Education when insistence upon them was considered unreasonable. Worship could also now be conducted outside the school building, e.g. in the local parish church. It was soon realised by the bishops that the organisation to defend the interests of Catholic schools needed to be strengthened, both at local and national level, in order to deal with questions of law, building grants and the many technical negotiations with the

Minister.[96] In order to achieve this, the Association of Diocesan
School Commissioners was founded on 29th March 1949.[97] This
was necessitated by the preparation of development plans en-
trusted to the local education authorities after the 1944 Education
Act. The development plans submitted to the Ministry of Education by local authorities included aided schools. Under the provisions of the 1944 Act, governors and managers were given six
months, after the completion of local authority development plans,
in which to apply for aided status. If the application was not made,
or if the Minister was not satisfied that the managers or governors
were able and willing to meet the costs involved, the schools would
automatically become 'controlled'. The Ministry distributed Form
18, which was to be endorsed by the diocesan authorities, and
which could be understood as committing them to the costs of
building or making alterations to existing schools as contained in
the relevant local authority development plan. The bishops were
alarmed at the financial commitments that were being asked to
make and sought further negotiations with the government. As a
result the government removed the threat of 'controlled' status in
Form 18, but rejected any further assistance to Catholic schools.[98]

A number of dioceses began to centralise funds, and many
diocesan education funds came into existence; but this solution
was not uniformly adopted throughout the country. At national
level the CEC was still, theoretically, representative of all the
dioceses in the country but it had limited funds and was unable to
employ a full-time secretary. Consequently, discussions during the
passage of the 1944 Education Act were left to a few dominant
clerical personalities. Cardinal Griffin, with the support of the
other bishops, decided to reform the CEC in September 1949 and
appointed a full-time lay secretary. The CEC was set up in its own
premises, with Bishop Beck as Chairman and an Ecclesiastical
Assistant, to co-ordinate the flow of information to and from the
dioceses. Previously the Chairmen of the CEC had always been lay
men drawn from the upper classes, the last being the Earl of Perth
in 1949. Both the Diocesan organisations and the CEC continued
to be firmly under the control and direction of the bishops. The
CEC, in particular, began to play a more vital role, with its work
during the 1950s being expanded to include involvement in direct
negotiations with government, and provision of advisory services.
Bishop Beck organised an Action Committee and brought a greater
degree of professionalism to the Council's work.[99] In many dio-

ceses, from the late 1940s onwards, the bishops encouraged the formation of the Catholic Parents' and Electors' Associations, which questioned Parliamentary candidates on educational matters. The tiny majority enjoyed by the 1950 to 1951 Labour Government rendered it particularly vulnerable to pressure, especially from its own 'natural' supporters in urban areas such as Liverpool and Leeds.

An article in the influential *Clergy Review* in March 1949 signalled the bishops' determination to seek a change to the 1944 Education Act, in order to achieve full financial assistance for aided schools.[100] The claim for full financial assistance was formally placed before Parliament by David Logan, a Catholic Liverpool Labour MP, in July 1949 and marked the official registration of the Catholic case, which was promptly refused by the Minister.[101] The bishops responded by initiating a public campaign and issuing a Memorandum[102] in November 1949. This called for the 'Scottish Solution', or a complex procedure by which new schools could be built with government grants and then leased to local authorities — the rents were intended to cover the repayment of loans and interest charges. This amounted to a demand for full financial assistance from the public purse. The whole thrust of the Catholic campaign has been well analysed by Butterworth:

> The kinds of argument used in the course of the campaign may be roughly divided into two categories. The two main categories were first, arguments concerned with obtaining marginal concessions within the meaning of the 1944 Act and with the invention of devices to overcome the provisions of the Act and, second, arguments which were directed towards upsetting the provisions of the 1944 Act by advocating theories and principles contrary to those established in the settlement.[103]

The Case for Catholic Schools, published by the reformed CEC in 1951, is a classic example of this form of argument. It was produced for the 1951 General Election in an attempt to seek sympathy from Parliamentary candidates and it was an intensely political document. On the eve of the election the bishops were about to declare the negotiations with the Labour government unsatisfactory.[104] The Labour Party were holding their Annual Conference in Scarborough at the time, and felt uneasy about the 'Catholic vote' in the industrial towns. It responded by making a proposal to the bishops through the Ministry of Education on 5th October 1951, indicating that the government was willing to consider sympathetically

certain financial changes to the operation of the 1944 Education
Act which would be to the benefit of voluntary aided schools. This
move by the Labour government caused a sharp reaction from the
Conservative Opposition, and Bishop Beck, the Chairman of the
CEC, wrote to Churchill on the 8th October assuring him that the
bishops did not wish to appear to be interfering in political matters
by encouraging their people to vote for one party and against
another. On 15th October a group of bishops met with Winston
Churchill and Richard Butler, who gave them their personal assur-
ance that a future Conservative government would not be less
generous than the Ministry of Education had recently proposed to
be. The bishops issued a statement published in *The Times* on 19th
October which welcomed the response of all three political parties
(the Liberals also agreed to assist aided schools) and recognised
that the proposals by the parties could bring considerable relief to
the financial difficulties over school buildings that the Church was
experiencing. However, the statement also emphasised that the
proposals by the three political parties had only dealt with the
alleviation of some of the more immediate problems — the fundamental problems of finance were still unresolved. In short, the
bishops had succeeded in modifying the attitude of the three major
political parties in the Church's favour.[105] This was especially noted
by an editorial in *Education* of 12th October 1951 which represented
the views of many teachers and local education authorities:

> In short, education legislation in this country is not a matter of party
> political difference . . . We regret therefore that the question of
> particular amendments, apparently designed to please particular
> interests, should be the subject of an announcement at the start of
> an election campaign.

The editorial also resented the fact that its own recommendations
had been ignored by all the parties.

The eventual Education Act of 1953, carried by the new Conservative government, proved to be an immediate help to the
Catholic authorities who faced the problem of building schools in
new towns and in housing estates. The campaigns by the bishops
during the 1950 and 1951 General Elections were not entirely
successful, since their proposals were not implemented in full.
Nevertheless, there were significant gains. During the General
Election in 1955, a new campaign was initiated by the bishops
whose aim was to secure support in Parliament. No specific proposals were advanced, although *The Case for Catholic Schools* was

revised and a further publication, The *Cost of Catholic Schools*, written by Bishop Beck, was produced. The interviewing committees of the Catholic Parents' and Electors' Associations, which had been used by the bishops in the 1951 General Election to put the Catholic case to Parliamentary candidates, were less aggressive in 1955.[106] The long-term perspective was taken. By mid-1955 there was a national financial crisis developing, and costs of building and maintaining schools soared. This prompted the Church of England to ask for further financial assistance.[107] In a Memorandum of the CEC in 1957, the bishops again proposed the 'Scottish Solution', or the more simple proposal of 75% grant. There was some discussion among the Catholic side whether or not to propose this as a permanent settlement to the voluntary schools question, but in April 1957 the bishops objected to the use of the phrase 'permanent settlement' and inserted 'long-term' instead of 'permanent' into the Memorandum.[108] With the Church of England claim for additional aid, the bishops began to consult more widely in an attempt to engender good relations with other denominational interests. However, Free Church opposition to the Catholic claims was still very much in evidence, and this left the bishops generally isolated from the other denominations. Catholic negotiations with the Church of England, which had begun as early as 1950, came to very little, despite early hopes.[109]

The 1959 Education Act was passed because, *inter alia*, the government recognised the financial strains on voluntary schools. The new Act provided 75% building grants for new aided secondary schools, needed wholly or mainly to match voluntary aided primary schools of the same denomination. Clearly, the 1953 and 1959 Education Acts allowed aided schools to maintain their existing numbers, but they did not allow for any expansion. Nevertheless, these Acts did influence the direction and interpretation of the general principles on which the 1944 Education Act rested. As Huot says:

> . . . the campaigns organised by the Roman Catholics at the 1950 General Election appear much more successful than one might have thought at the time. Because of this campaign, the Roman Catholics secured, at the eve of the 1951 election, assurances from both the Labour and Conservative parties, which led to the 1953 Act, and a few months before the 1959 election not only assurances but another Act — and an Act introducing much more substantial changes than the 1953 Act.[110]

The sheer persistence of Catholic pressure and educational claims was responsible for many of the gains made, as was the ability of the bishops to mobilise the support of the Catholic community in mass campaigns such as those between 1906 and 1908 and between 1950 and 1951.

Summary

The direct participation of the Catholic Church in the organisation of schooling in England and Wales has both an historical and a philosophical foundation. At the onset of the Reformation, Catholic teaching was proscribed and teachers were made the agents of an anti-Catholic policy. Early attempts at providing schools for the small Catholic population were fraught with serious dangers and were often short lived. Nevertheless, Catholic schooling was never completely ended, despite the severity of the sanctions against it. The strains of the late eighteenth century had been resolved by the triumph of the clerical party within English Catholicism, a triumph which was formalised in regard to Catholic schools in 1847. Previously the leading laity had enjoyed strong influence over schools, and had favoured the maintenance of a decentralised system of Church power which placed less emphasis on the prerogatives of the local bishop. However, the insecurity of the Irish immigrants, who faced social and religious discrimination, led them to invest their power and decisions totally in the hands of the clergy. As education became the focal point of religious controversy between the government and the Church, the bishops initiated and controlled the separate elementary school system whose purpose was the defence and preservation of the Catholic faith in a hostile environment. In 1870 Cardinal Manning wrote in a letter to the Prime Minister, Mr. Gladstone, pointing out that:

> . . . the integrity of our schools as to (i) Doctrine, (ii) religious management, and the responsibility of the Bishops in these respects, cannot be touched without opening a multitude of contentions and vexations.[111]

Catholics lacked a well established tradition of local political action in support of their newly formed and clerically dominated central organisation, the Catholic Poor School Committee. Whilst internal tension arose between Catholics on organisational matters, they were united behind the cause for a doctrinally based education and were also agreed on what that doctrinal content should be. The period 1847 to 1870 is one in which the Catholic community, led by their bishops, agitated for a share in government building and maintenance grants. There was division among them over whether Catholics should work with the State and accept conditions which might ultimately prove to be incompatible with the Catholic philosophy of education. Bishop Ullathorne in particular was concerned about the State's discretionary powers with regard to schools and argued strongly that neither agreements nor laws favourable to Catholic education bound succeeding governments. It is worth noting that the rival to the Catholic Church in schooling is identified as the State and not the other Christian denominations. Between 1870 and 1902 the Catholic claim was for rate support combined with full maintenance. The financial disabilities that Catholic schools suffered were due in part to the social composition of the Catholic body, but also to the rigid regulations for State aid and the refusal of the government to sanction further assistance. Catholics objected first to the use of the Authorised Version, and also to the proselytising activity of Anglican schools. In evidence to the Cross Commission, Thomas Allies, secretary of the Catholic Poor School Committee, expressed the Catholic position on the notion of religion in education:

A total rejection to the principle that religion and education, either for the poor or for the rich can be severed.[112]

This was, and still is, the central issue and justification for continuing Catholic agitation in the matter of schools.

From 1902 to 1959 the Catholic demands progressively increased to achieve equality of treatment between county and voluntary schools. Whereas the number of Church of England schools steadily dwindled from 1902, Catholic schools increased not only in numbers but also in importance and influence. Catholic educational pressure operated mainly at a administrative and executive level and sought to use political parties as 'support' for its campaigns, especially at the time of General Elections and in Parliamentary debates. The Catholic laity fully supported this position and joined with one another in a strong sense of common purpose. Nevertheless, before 1944 the Catholic school system was a completely uncoordinated and loosely organised one. Catholic diocesan authorities also largely accepted the educational system found within their boundaries. They were most successful as a pressure group in obtaining concessions for Catholic schools, despite the decline in popular support for the Churches and the policy of the Church of England to increase its influence in county schools rather than retain a large separate school system.[113]

Catholic educational policy was successful during this period as a result of enormous sacrifice on the part of the laity and Religious Orders, and through the ability of the bishops to secure compromises from the government. The bishops compromised on the composition of governing bodies of schools, on the appointment of teachers, and over curricular matters. As a body the Catholic Church in England and Wales conducted its educational campaigns alone, and usually without the support of other denominations and often in the teeth of their opposition. As a result Catholic educational policy evolved and became more articulated. None of the Education Acts of 1870, 1902, 1936, and 1944 was acceptable to the bishops and, although they sought compromises, sometimes on fundamental principles, there was a feeling that practical politics dictated the solutions. Government grants to schools and the corresponding need to inspect, the separation of religious education and secular subjects for inspection, and the establishment of LEAs as major secular employing authorities contributed to the gradual surrendering of the autonomy of Catholic schools. Cardinal Bourne's comment on the 1902 Education Act typifies the attitude of the bishops for the whole period: 'There was no bargain; we had to accept what we could get.'[114]

The bishops consistently emphasised parental rights and duties and demanded social equality and financial justice for Catholics in education. After the passing of the Education Act of 1944 a sense of mission in education was declared, or as Alan McClelland calls it:

> . . . a crusade for the preservation of the faith itself in the teeth of increasingly hostile, secular and materialist attitudes.[115]

The principal religious opposition to the 1902 and 1944 Education Acts inside Parliament came from the Catholic Church. The basic weakness of the legislation in the period was the lack of a clear definition of the duties and powers of the trustees of voluntary schools. In the Catholic sector these trustees were, and are, the bishops and one or two of their senior clergy in each diocese. In addition, the Education Act of 1944 lacked any coherent framework to govern the relationship between parents, governors, local authorities and central government. Moreover, the financial position of Catholic schools, as far as the bishops were concerned, was still unresolved in 1959. Glover observed a twofold pattern in Catholic negotiations with the government after the Education

Acts of 1953 and 1959.[116] First, he saw a period of 'prolonged gestation', with the bishops raising the possibility of amending legislation immediately after each of the two Acts. The second pattern he terms the 'pro-active stance', by which the bishops initiate discussion with the government and its agencies. He cites as evidence the fact that the bishops between 1950 and 1953 had some 38 meetings, and between 1957 and 1959 a further 36 meetings between themselves and government ministers, civil servants and prominent MPs with large Catholic populations in their constituencies, such as Harold Wilson. The campaigns for administrative and financial equality for its schools which the Church was forced to mount, successful though they were in part, may also have led to a serious neglect of the philosophical and religious justification for their separate existence. Bishop Beck observed of the English Catholic community in 1950:

> It seems to be generally admitted that the influence of the Catholic community in England on public life is by no means commensurate with its size, and there seems to be a good case for arguing that, at least until very recent years, this influence has been throughout the greater part of the century declining.[117]

This judgement has its confirmation in the extent to which the claims on the State of Catholic educational policy have been met in the period from 1960 to 1990.

Conclusion

The Catholic Church in England and Wales has accepted as self-evident the belief that the Catholic school is the most effective agency for Catholic education. Consequently, Catholic schools were established as the result of great personal sacrifice within the Catholic community: the dedication and commitment of Catholic school teachers, the efforts and determination of Religious Orders, and the loyalty and support of priests and their parishioners. The overwhelming majority of Catholics freely chose to pursue the specific principles of Catholic education articulated by their bishops, who were recognised by the government as the official leaders of the Catholic body in matters of education policy. These principles were unambiguous and the Church was prepared to forgo any monetary gain in order to uphold them. The Catholic body clearly desired an education to take place within the perspective of the Catholic faith, so that believing children of believing parents could

be taught by believing teachers in Catholic schools. Catholics
viewed religion, in particular the Catholic faith, and education as
inseparable. However, parental participation in the control and
administration of Catholic schools was minimal and wholly dependent on the clergy. Open criticism of Catholic schools from
within the Church was seldom voiced, and when it surfaced the
bishops denied the criticism as being disloyal and without foundation. Overall, the Catholic community found the *raison d'être* of
Catholic schooling convincing, and concentrated their efforts on its
continued maintenance and expansion under clerical leadership.

Notes

1. Brown, C.K.F., *The Church's Part in Education*, National Society /
   SPCK London, 1942, p. 2 in his introduction he states that educational institutions prior to the Reformation were established by
   episcopal licence and were subject to episcopal control. More recent
   research by Orme, N., in *English Schools in the Middle Ages*, Methuen,
   London, 1973, pp. 142–143 and in his collection of essays *Education
   and Society in Medieval and Renaissance England*, London, 1989, he
   disputes this assertion by Brown. In Hulme, A., *School in Church and
   State*, St Paul Publications, London, 1959, a list of the different types
   of lay schools prior to the Reformation is provided. See also Glover,
   D., *Roman Catholic Education and the State*, University of Sheffield,
   PhD, 1979, p. 26 who argues that the influence of the Church over
   education in pre-Reformation England had already begun to be
   challenged by the laity. Unfortunately, like Brown, he provides little
   in the way of historical evidence for this position.
2. Cruickshank, M., *Church and State in English Education 1833–1941*,
   Macmillan, London, 1963, p. 1.
3. Beales, A.C.F., 'Struggle for the Schools' in Beck, G.A. (ed.), *The
   English Catholics*, Burns and Oates, London, 1950, p. 365. See also
   Lawson, W., 'Education Under Penalty', *The Month*, December 1963,
   pp. 353–359.
4. Beales, A.C.F., *Education Under Penalty : English Catholics from the
   Reformation to the Fall of James II*, University of London, The Athlone
   Press, London, 1963, p. 58.
5. *Ibid.*, p.VII Preface.
6. Beales, A.C.F., *The Tradition in English Education*, pp. 7–12 published
   by the Catholic Education Council, 1963.
7. Bossy, J., *The English Catholic Community 1570–1850*, Darton, Longman
   and Todd, London, 1975, p. 165.
8. *Ibid.*, p. 166. See also Beales, A.C.F., *Education Under Penalty: English
   Catholics from the Reformation to the Fall of James II*, University of
   London, The Athlone Press, London, 1963, p. 85 who cites some
   evidence that attendance at Protestant schools led to apostasy.

9. Beales, A.C.F., 'Struggle for the Schools', *op. cit.*, also Lawson, W., *op. cit.*

10. Whitehead, M., *English Catholic Education: the beginnings of a system 1789–1850*, Catholic Record Society Conference Lecture, November 1989.

11. *Ibid.*

12. Murphy, J., *Church, State and Schools in Britain 1800–1970*, R.K.P., London, 1971, p. 3.

13. Gaine, M., 'The Development of Official Roman Catholic Educational Policy in England and Wales', in Jebb, P., *Religious Education: Decision or Drift*, Darton, Longman and Todd, London, 1968, p. 147.

14. Connolly, G., 'The Transubstantiation of a Myth: towards a New Popular History of Nineteenth Century English Catholicism in England', *Journal of Ecclesastical History*, Vol. 35, No. 1, January 1984, pp. 78–104.

15. Gaine, M., *op. cit.*, p. 149.

16. Holmes, J.D., *More Roman than Rome*, Burns and Oates, London, 1978. p. 205.

17. Bossy, J., *op. cit.*, p. 348.

18. *Ibid.*, p. 333. See McClelland, V.A. '*Sensus Fidelium*: The Developing Concept of Roman Catholic Voluntary Effort in Education in England and Wales', in Tulasiewicz, W. and Brock, C. (eds), *Christianity and Educational Provision in International Perspective*, Routledge, London, 1988, pp. 61–88.

19. Beales, A.C.F., 'Struggle for the Schools', *op. cit.*, p. 366.

20. *Ibid.*, pp. 366–367, and Bossy, J., *op. cit.*, p. 349.

21. Bossy, J., *op. cit*, p. 350.

22. Murphy, J., *op. cit.*, p. 14.

23. Feheney, M., 'Towards Religious Equality for Catholic Pauper Children 1861–1868', *British Journal of Educational Studies*, Vol. XXXI, No. 2, June 1983, pp. 141–153.

24. Bossy, J., *op. cit.*, p. 350.

25. *Reports of the Catholic Poor School Committee 1848–1852*, 1848, p. 30 f. The bishops requested that the Catholic Institute hand over all educational monies to the CPSC, and issued a joint pastoral letter which called for all future educational collections at parish level to be sent to the CPSC; see p. 32 of the 1848 Report for full details.

26. Gilbert, J., 'The Catholic Church and Education' in Various, *English Catholics 1829–1929*, Longmans, London, 1929, p. 50.

27. *The Tablet*, January 2nd 1847. In June 1847 the 'Association of St Thomas of Canterbury for the Vindication of Catholic Rights' was formed and urged political action among Catholics — that candidates at elections should be asked to support Catholic claims. see Norman, E., *The English Catholic Church in the Nineteenth Century*, Clarendon Press, Oxford, 1984, p. 167.

28. Holmes, J.D., *op. cit.*, pp. 208 and 251.

29. Gaine, M., *op. cit.*, p. 162.

30. Murphy, J., *op. cit.*, p.35.
31. See *Reports of the Catholic Poor School Committee* 1849, pp. 121–139, and 1850, pp. 72–89, *Appendix K*, for full details of the draft management clauses and the negotiations between the Privy Council and the CPSC. In 1849, the CPSC claimed that it had negotiated with the Privy Council 'without yielding a particle of principle', 1849, p. 8 ff.
32. Holland, M.G., *The British Catholic Press and the Educational Controversy 1847–1865*, Garland Publishing, New York, 1987, p. 161 and Cruickshank, M. *op. cit.*, p. 9, Murphy, J. *op. cit.*, p. 36, and Norman, E., *op. cit.*, p. 168. The Catholic Poor School Committee framed a model trust deed for Catholic schools to use when applying for grants known as the 'Kemerton Trust'. Bishop Ullathorne in his 'Notes on the Education Question', 1857, had been highly critical of the terms upon which Catholic schools had accepted maintenance grants from the State – see Norman, E., *op. cit.*, p. 166. See *Reports of the Catholic Poor School Committee*, 1852, pp. 103–116, for details of the 'Kemerton Trust' deeds.
33. Reported in the *The Tablet*, 7/9/07, pp. 393–394.
34. Roman Catholic Charities Act 1860 Section 5.
35. Bossy, J., *op. cit.*, p. 348, for a discussion of 'trusteeism' see Norman, E., *op. cit.*, pp. 75–77 and of charitable trusts, pp. 188–192.
36. Gilbert, J., *op. cit.*, p. 50 and Murphy, J., *op. cit.*, p. 35.
37. Chartered Institute of Public Finance and Accounting Publications Volume 20 Education, September 1983, 20.01.11.
38. Guy, R.E., *The Synods in English*, Stratford Upon Avon, St Gregory's Press, 1886, p. 268 ff.
39. Beales, A.C.F., 'Struggle for the Schools', *op. cit.*, p. 375.
40. Gilbert, J., *op. cit.*, p. 51.
41. Holland. M.G., *op. cit.*, p. 186, for details of the grant for books see *Reports of the Catholic Poor School Committee* 1852, p. 12.
42. Gilbert, J., *op. cit.*, p. 52.
43. *Ibid*.
44. Cruickshank, M., *op. cit.*, p. 9.
45. Carrigan D., *The Catholic Teacher Colleges in the United Kingdom 1850–1960*, PhD, Catholic University of America, 1961, see also Gilbert, J., *op. cit.*, p. 53, also pp. 71–72.
46. Carrigan, D., *op. cit.*
47. Selby, D.E., *The Work of Cardinal Manning in the Field of Education*, PhD, University of Birmingham, 1974. Also McClelland, V.A., *Cardinal Manning*, OUP, 1962. Norman, E., *op. cit.*, p. 284 disputes McClelland's contention that Cardinal Manning failed to consult with the other bishops before he made his proposal to the government. He cites a meeting called by Manning whilst in Rome to discuss the Education Bill.
48. Selby, D.E., *op. cit.* See also Leese, J., *Personalities and Power in English Education*, Arnold and Son, Leeds, 1950, p. 95 — there were a

number of complaints about Catholic inspectors made in the House of Commons concerning their alleged irrelevant and inaccurate reporting. This referred to their comments about religious ethos and the advantages of Catholic education. For a detailed study of the private attitudes of HMIs in their visits to Catholic schools, see McClelland, V.A., 'The Protestant Alliance and Roman Catholic Schools 1872–1874', *Victorian Studies*, December 1964, Vol. 8, No. 2, pp. 173–183. Also, Whitehead, M., ' "Briefly, and in Confidence": Private Views of Her Majesty's Inspectors of English Catholic Elementary Schools, 1875', *Recusant History*, October 1991, Vol. 20, No. 4, pp. 554–562.

49. Holland, G.M., *op. cit.*, p. 333.
50. *Reports of the Catholic Poor School Committee* 1848–1856, 1853, p. 264.
51. Cruickshank, M., *op. cit.*, p. 27. For a fuller account of the consequences of the 1870 Education Act for Catholics, see McClelland, V.A., *Cardinal Manning*, OUP, 1962, pp. 61–86.
52. Gilbert, J., *op. cit.*, p. 53.
53. *Ibid.*, p. 54.
54. Holland, M.G., *op. cit.*, pp. 318–332, and pp. 337–338.
55. Gilbert, J., *op. cit.*, p. 54.
56. *Ibid*.
57. Cruickshank, M., *op. cit.*, p. 41.
58. The instructions sent by the bishops from Rome to the CPSC are published in the *Reports of the Catholic Poor School Committee* 1870, p. 21 ff, and details of the meetings of the CPSC on the Education Bill are on pp. 4–5 and p. 58.
59. Brentwood, Bishop of, in Various, *English Catholics 1829–1929*, Longmans, Green and Co, London, 1929, pp. 171–172.
60. Selby, D.E., *op. cit*. The 'rescuing' of Catholic children from workhouses had also been a particular and repeated concern of Cardinal Manning, see McClelland, V.A., *op. cit* ., pp. 33–37.
61. Parliamentary Debates 3rd Series Vol. CCXXX, Col. 518, see also Cruickshank, M. *op. cit* ., p. 43.
62. Gilbert, J., *op. cit.*, pp. 56–57.
63. *Ibid.*, pp. 56–58.
64. Cruickshank, M., *op. cit.*, pp. 52–53.
65. Beales, A.C.F., *Struggle for the Schools, op. cit.*, p. 369.
66. Cruickshank, M. *op. cit.*, p. 58 ff.
67. Beales, A.C.F., *op. cit.*, p. 383.
68. Gilbert, J., *op. cit.*, p. 57 also Education Act 1891 Sections 6 and 7.
69. Gilbert, J., *op. cit.*, pp. 57–58.
70. Education Act 1897 clauses 1 and 3.
71. Gilbert, J., *op. cit.*, p. 58.
72. Rafferty, O.P., 'The Jesuit College, Manchester, 1875', *Recusant History* Vol. 19, 1990, pp. 291–304.
73. Selby, D.E., 'The Catholic Teacher Crisis 1885–1902', *The Durham and Newcastle Review*, Vol. 37, Autumn 1976, pp. 33–47.

74. Cruickshank , M., *op. cit.*, p. 71.
75. *Ibid.*
76. Gilbert, J., *op. cit.*, p. 60.
77. *Ibid.*, p. 60 ff.
78. Reported in the *The Tablet*, 21st December 1907.
79. Regulations reprinted with commentary in *The Tablet*, 13th July 1907 by the Catholic Education Council and also in *The Month* by Smith, S.F., 'Mr McKenna's Anti-Conscience Clauses', August 1907, No. 518. The delegation to the Prime Minister to inform him that the Catholic Church would do its best to ignore these regulations was made in July 1907 and fully reported in the *The Tablet*, 13th July 1907, p. 130.
80. Reported in the *The Tablet*, 31st August 1907, p. 352.
81. Reported in the *The Tablet*, 23rd November 1907.
82. Gilbert, J., *op. cit.*, p. 65.
83. Beales, A.C.F., *Struggle for the Schools, op. cit.*, p. 392. For full details and commentary on the Scottish Education Act 1918 see Findley, I., 'Christianity and Educational Provision in Scotland', Tulasiewicz, W., *op. cit.*, pp. 17–37.
84. Cruickshank, M., *op. cit.*, p. 130.
85. Davis, H., *Moral and Pastoral Theology*, Vol. II, Sheed and Ward, London, 1943, p. 87.
86. *Code of Canon Law*, 1917 edition, Polyglot Press, Vatican, 1917. The conditions for Catholics attending non-Catholic schools with regard to the Code are explained by E.J. Mahoney in the *Clergy Review*, Vol. XXIV, No. 4, April 1944, p. 186, and also in a commentary by the same author in *Questions and Answers*, London, 1949, pp. 28–31. See also the commentary by P.C. Augustine, in *A Commentary on the New Code of Canon Law*, London, 1921, Volume VIII, p. 297 ff, and Volume VI, p. 414 ff.
87. Cruickshank, M., *op. cit.*, p. 157.
88. Canon, C., 'The Influence of Religion on Education Policy 1902–1944', *British Journal of Educational Studies*, Vol. 12, May 1964, pp. 143–160.
89. Huot, D., *Denominational Schools as a Problem in England and Wales 1940–1959*, DPhil, University of Oxford, 1961.
90. Butterworth, R., *The Structure of Catholic Lay Organisations*, DPhil, University of Oxford, 1959.
91. Cruickshank, M., *op. cit.*, p. 158.
92. Education Act 1944, Section 9.
93. Cox, E., *Possibilities in Religious Education*, Hodder and Stoughton, London, 1983, pp. 6–7.
94. Leeson, S., *Christian Education Reviewed*, Longman, London, 1957, p. 40.
95. Cruickshank, M., *op. cit.*, p. 161 ff, see also Davis, H., *op. cit.*, p. 90 in which it is claimed that 'It is sinful [for Catholics] to vote for the enemies of religion or liberty . . . outside the limits of legitimate

freedom of opinion, Catholics should be guided by their ecclesiastical Superiors in their choice of candidates to represent them', especially in regard to schools.

96. Beck, G.A., *Progress Report*, Catholic Education Council, 1963, p. 14.
97. Huot, D., *op. cit.*
98. Beck, G.A., *op cit* ., p. 15.
99. Beck, G.A., 'The Schools Question', *Clergy Review*, Vol. XXXVI, No. 4, October 1951, pp. 209–230. Cardinal Manning first raised the the issue of centralising diocesan educational efforts at national level in 1866. Unfortunately, according to McClelland, 1962, *op cit.*, pp. 37–38. Manning faced opposition from members of the Hierarchy who sought to keep under their personal control all diocesan matters, including the provision of schools.
100. Wood. W.J., 'The New Education Act: Counting the Cost', *Clergy Review*, Vol. XXXI, No. 3, March 1949, pp. 145–149. Wood, W.J., 'New Education Act: The Cost of the Schools', *Clergy Review*, Vol. XXXV, March 1951, pp. 151–159. Canon Wood was an influential cleric in the diocese of Westminster.
101. Huot, D., *op. cit.*, p. 213.
102. Memorandum of the Bishops of England and Wales entitled 'The Catholic Voluntary School: The Problem and the Possible Solution', reprinted in the *The Tablet*, 3rd December 1949.
103. Butterworth, R., *op. cit.*, p. 191 also in an article by Grimley, B., 'Our Schools — Are We Satisfied', *Clergy Review*, Vol. XXXIII, No. 4, April 1950, pp. 240–246 in which Grimley observes 'our official policy has moved far from the previously recognised minimum standards laid down for acceptable Catholic education'.
104. Huot, D., *op. cit.*, gives an account — see also the *Clergy Review*, Vol. XXXVI, No. 4, October 1951, and Vol. XXXIII, January 1950, for a detailed account of the setting up of the Catholic campaigns and of the Catholic organisational responses to the Education Act 1944.
105. Huot, D., *op. cit.*
106. The interviewing of Parliamentary candidates by Catholics became more systematic and widespread from the 1885 election when Cardinal Manning urged Catholics to question their MPs, which Cruickshank, M. *op. cit.*, p. 157 says had a strategic importance for the outcome of the election. See especially McClelland, V.A., 'The "Free Schools" Issue and the General Election of 1885: A Denominational Response', in *History of Education*, Vol. 5, No. 2, 1976, pp. 141–154. Henry Pelling in his *Social Geography of British Elections 1885–1910*, Macmillan, London, 1967, p. 16 mentions the importance of the education question for Catholic voting behaviour. Huot, D., *op. cit.*, p. 91 also details cases in which the Catholic vote was decisive as in the Bradford City Council when a motion for the approval of the TUC's opposition to denominational schools was eventually defeated through the setting up in September 1942 of

Associations of Catholic Electors in each of Bradfords's twelve
Catholic parishes. It was soon after this that Catholic Parent Electors Associations were established all over the country and these are
mentioned in the *Nuffield Election Studies* for 1950 and 1951 as
significant.

107. Huot, D., *op. cit.*
108. *Ibid.* — the case for further assistance had already been asked for in
     Parliament by Wing Commander Grant Ferris — House of Com-
     mons Vol. 560, Col. 453–456, November 1956.
109. Huot, D., *op. cit.*, p. 334. See also Phillips, F.R., *Bishop Beck and English
     Education 1949–1959*, Edwin Mellen Press, Lampeter, 1990 for de-
     tails of the negotiations between Catholics, Anglicans and the Free
     Churches, pp. 39–47, and 176–182.
110. Huot, D., *op. cit.*, p. 331.
111. McClelland, V.A., in Tulasiewicz, W., *op. cit.*, p. 67.
112. Cross Commission, First Report, 1886, cc. 4863 XXV, pp. 328–362.
113. Canon, C., *op. cit.*
114. Beales, A.C.F., *Struggle for the Schools, op. cit.*, p. 384.
115. McClelland, V.A., in Tulasiewicz, W. *op. cit.*, p. 87.
116. Glover, D., *Roman Catholic Education and the State*, University of
     Sheffield, PhD, 1979.
117. Beck, G.A., *The English Catholics*, Burns and Oates, London, 1950,
     pp. 602–603.

3

The Goals of Catholic Schools

Introduction

In attempting to define the term 'Catholic education' one is faced with extraordinary difficulties, since no body of scholarly literature exists in which the term is used with any consensus. In the past, religion gave legitimacy to the values and institutions of society and any question of the relationship between religion and education would not have made sense. Prior to the Reformation, two basic assumptions were more or less universally held: first, that all human beings were recognised as having a spiritual dimension and a supernatural destiny; second, that life only found its meaning and fulfilment in obedience to the moral and spiritual demands of the Christian vocation. These assumptions found their proper focus in membership of the Catholic Church. Although this consensus was a living influence in education, there was no necessity for discussing or articulating a concept of Catholic education as such. However, with the division and fragmentation of Christianity, and the rejection, explicit or otherwise of these basic assumptions, the need for a clear articulation of the Catholic idea of education has become more urgent.[1] Some have doubted whether the conditions for an authentic understanding of Catholic education are still present.[2]

Although, the purpose of this chapter is not to offer a typology of all the competing models or visions of Catholic education today, it does however present and discuss three central issues. First, the nature of authoritatively Catholic goals and objectives for schooling; second, the response of the bishops in England and Wales to official teaching from Rome; and third, the principal philosophical objections to Catholic education in England.

The Religio-philosophical Context: A Preliminary Note

Catholic schools are essentially an expression of the Church's salvific mission, since the Church is the context for all Catholic education.[3] This identification with the Catholic Church, its mission and character, remains the principal grounding for the existence of Catholic schools. The salvific mission by which the Church interprets and directs its experience is also the mission upon which the aims and objectives of the Catholic school are based. Consequently, in order to interpret these aims and objectives it is necessary to understand what might be called the Catholic philosophy of life.

The Catholic philosophy of life originates in the Catholic faith. This faith is belief in the living God, and in Jesus Christ in whose life God was made known and present in a unique way. More abstractly, Catholic faith claims to be in possession of a body of truths, revealed by God and taught by the Church, which explains our place in creation and reveals our relationship to the Creator.[4] This relationship is in and through Christ Himself, whose life and work can alone lead us to God with Whom we have an eternal destiny. The life of faith on earth is both preparation for that destiny and, in a mysterious way, a participation in it; both preparation and participation are constituted by the life of prayer and sacraments which forms the heart of Catholic faith.

What are the implications of Catholic faith for Catholic education? The most important is that, according to Kevin Nichols, Catholic education is an enterprise concerned with, carried on in, and justified by Christian faith.[5] Faith is not the result of Catholic education, since faith is a gift from God, but it is its presupposition. As with Catholic faith, so with Catholic education, the life and work of Jesus Christ is the indisputable focal point; for in Christ we are revealed to ourselves in our earthly life and eternal destiny. It can be said then, that Catholic education above all is about communicating the life and work of Christ.[6] It is faith in Christ, the life of Catholic faith, which guides and inspires the Catholic educationalist's search for principles and values on which to build a distinctive Christian view of education.[7] The Church has said that the practice of Catholic education will require:

> ... the utilisation of philosophical concepts which provide 'a solid and correct understanding of man, the world, and God' and can be employed in a reflection upon revealed doctrine ... It is the theologian's task in this perspective to draw from the surrounding culture

those elements which will allow him better to illumine one or other aspects of the mysteries of faith.[8]

The elements mentioned here will include thinking about education, philosophy, history, the social sciences and so on. But it is important to note that it is revealed doctrine, the content of what is believed by Catholic faith, which provides the criterion necessary for the evaluation and use of these elements. The implication for Catholic education is clear: faith and human knowledge need to be integrated so that religious truth informs the whole of life and understanding.[9] Education is not simply the application of secular knowledge to a secular world; on the contrary, the Church insists that truth and human knowledge are in profound harmony, so that all knowledge and understanding is touched and transformed by the truths about human beings and God which are taught by faith.[10] The embodiment of this vision is the purpose of Catholic education.

Neither can an understanding of the requirements to be met by an account of Catholic education neglect the teaching of faith or the effects of original sin. These effects make the intellect less ready to attain to what is true, the will less ready to seek what is good. In short, human nature is damaged: and this damage cannot be thought of as simply ignorance or immaturity. Thus, Catholic faith rejects any view of education which concerns it as being merely the right adjustment of the individual to his environment by the application of human skills and intelligence. For the Catholic, the restoration and transformation of human nature is achieved by the redeeming work of Christ, the fullness of which comes only through Catholic faith:

> ... changed by grace into a new creature, the Christian sets himself or herself to follow Christ and learn more and more within the Church to think like Christ, to judge like him, to act according to his commandments and to hope as he invites us to.[11]

This is the Church's vision of humanity restored and renewed, and it is for the completion of this work that the Church exists and exercises her mission. Catholic education is an essential part of that mission, and must seek to minister to people in a way which is co-ordinated with the whole truth about human beings as revealed in faith; his creation by and dependency on God, the damaged condition of his humanity, the coherence of religious truth with every aspect of his life on earth and the supernatural vocation he has uniquely in Christ. Modern educational theories which are

founded on a denial of one or more of the elements of this picture
can have no place in an account of Catholic education.[12]

Catholic Educational Goals and Objectives:

In its understanding of Catholic education, the Church makes a
distinction between primary and secondary aims. Primary aims are
constants, grounded in revealed truths about our nature, our origin,
and our destiny. Secondary aims are variables and involve educational theories, methods of teaching, administration and other
techniques. Secondary aims reflect the changing conditions of
society, while primary aims are unchanging and independent of
social conditions. Primary aims are normative rather than descriptive, since they express, not a pragmatic conception of how things
actually are, but a vision of what is intended to be, John Redden
and Francis Ryan make clear this distinction in aims:

> The primary aim of education is to form an individual so that he will
> be both fitted and determined to strive constantly towards moral
> perfection, unto the attainment of his eternal salvation ... It should
> not be concluded however, that Catholic education seeks to achieve
> this primary objective only. To limit educational activity to this end
> alone might result in a one-sided, exclusive type of education.
> Hence, secondary or proximate aims ... The purpose of the secon-
> dary aims is to supply those essentials which help to achieve the
> primary aim of education. These secondary aims imply conscious
> efforts so to form a youth by instruction, guidance and discipline
> that he will be well fitted and determined to carry out his life's work
> with interest and zeal in conformity to unchanging moral principles.[13]

The whole of our nature, body, mind and soul, is to be fully
developed, and not simply the spiritual to the neglect of the mental
and bodily. The aim of Catholic education concerns our call to
eternal life, while the secondary involves the essentials or means
employed to this end. The secondary aim therefore embodies an
appropriate educational *milieu* within which it is possible to give
first place to the things of the spirit, and in which Catholic faith is
fostered and strengthened. Together, then, primary and secondary
aims reveal the identity of Catholic education; but this identity
must be discovered, developed and applied. Because Catholic faith
is both a preparation for and in part a participation in our supernatural destiny, Catholic education must fit pupils for life on earth
as well as for eternity. Authoritative statements by the Church on

education have continuously sought to provide guidance for Catholic educationalists engaged in this process.

In 1929 Pius XI issued his encyclical on the *Christian Education of Youth*.[14] This document sets the framework within which the identity of Catholic education can be constructed. It taught that there are three necessary societies established by God; the family, the State and the Church. The Church has the right to select the means suitable for the education of its members. Schools are viewed as institutions auxiliary to the family unit, the insufficiencies of which it complements in unison with the teaching of the Church. The State's role is to defend and protect the rights of the family to choose a Christian education, and to provide financial assistance for this from taxes levied on the family. It certainly must not promote a form of education which is contrary to the religious one. For Pius XI, the rights of the State are clearly limited by the prior rights of the family and the superior rights of the Church. The State's educational rights are subsidiary, understood as assisting the educational rights of the family. Many have interpreted this declaration exclusively in terms of the argument about whether State, Church or parents should control education.[15] This would be a narrow interpretation, for the declaration's main focus is the identity of Catholic education. The Pope makes clear that Catholic education is for the person, whole and entire; body, mind and spirit. The primary aim of education is a person's salvation and everything else is subordinated to this end, including the content of education. He argues that only Catholic education is capable of leading us to our eternal destiny.

The Second Vatican Council (1962–1965) enunciated certain basic principles of Christian education which are intended to be applicable to the Catholic school. A *Declaration on Christian Education* was approved, which substantially reaffirmed the central arguments of Pius XI's encyclical letter. However, this came as a disappointment to a number of 'progressive' commentators at the Council, who have consequently not viewed Vatican II's statement on education as one of its major achievements.[16] The Council was clearly conciliatory in tone, avoiding narrow sectarianism and insularity. But this has prompted some Catholic educators to look beyond this declaration for the more progressive vision of Catholic education which they require. They claim, with some justification, that it would be a mistake to see the conciliar declaration as all the Council had to say on education. In particular, they have urged

Catholic educators to follow the message found in other documents of Vatican II, like *The Church in the Modern World*, to arrive at
a better understanding of the role of the Catholic school.[17] In
addition, many have developed in a radical way the declaration's
recommendation that national groups of bishops should formulate
appropriate national educational statements applicable to their
local situations. As a result of the complexities inherent in education and the vast differences in educational conditions between
countries around the world, Pope Paul VI created the Congregation
for Catholic Education which he charged with developing the
authoritative development of the Council's work on education.
This Post-Conciliar Congregation has to date produced four major
statements; *The Catholic School* (1977), *Lay Catholic Teachers* (1982),
Educational Guidance in Human Love (1983), and *The Religious Dimension of Catholic Education* (1988). These documents attempt to set
out and establish significant objectives for the Catholic school, but
leave the practical means of their implementation to local circumstances. (The Congregation's name was changed, soon after the
publication of its last major statement, by the Apostolic Constitution *Pastor Bonus* of 1988. The Congregation is now called the
Congregation for Seminaries and Other Institutes of Study. However, the use of 'Congregation' in the present discussion refers to
the pre-1988 Congregation).[18]

It is clear from the *Declaration on Christian Education* that the
bishops designated the school as an indispensable component of
the Church's commitment to education.[19] During the debates on
the drafts of the declaration, not all the bishops had the same
priorities for the future identity of Catholic education. Some
wanted a more ecumenical approach, some a more missionary
approach, whilst others sought a more specific definition which
would include a firm statement of the end of Christian education,
which they saw as the development of a deep personal faith.[20] The
final declaration was in many respects a compromise between
these various groups. Thus, whilst within the declaration there is
clear continuity with past teaching, there is also a significant shift
towards increased dialogue with modern educational thought. As
the drafts developed, emphasis was increasingly placed on service
to the community, involvement with the secular world, the dignity
of persons, and religious freedom. These concepts are presented
in the final declaration in a general and abstract way which leave
many questions in need of future clarification.

The identity of Catholic education in the wake of Vatican II has therefore been a centre of controversy between competing conservative and radical interpretations. For an entire understanding of the sixteen documents of Vatican II, recourse to a theologian is certainly necessary. Nevertheless, it should also be recognised that in the Catholic Church full teaching authority on doctrinal and moral matters rests with the bishops. The relationship between the roles of bishop and theologian is clarified in the Vatican's statement on the *Ecclesial Vocation of the Theologian*, where it is stated that both have ultimately the same goal — 'preserving the people of God in the truth' — and that the bishop 'authentically teaches the doctrine of the apostles' whilst the theologian 'strives to clarify the teaching of revelation with regard to reason and gives it finally an organic and systematic form'.[21] So the teachings of the bishops at Vatican II, including the *Declaration on Christian Education*, without omissions or arbitrary changes, give the authoritative identity of Catholic education. No one, including the theologian, can on his own initiative make a selection of what he considers important in Catholic education and reject the rest. This point is essential in trying to discuss the authoritative identity of Catholic education in the light of the documents of Vatican II.

The first paragraph of the declaration speaks of the inalienable right, shared by all, to an education. It goes on to list the specific aims of Christian education in terms which accord with the language of modern educational theories. First, Catholic education must be holistic; it seeks the integral formation of the whole person and concerns itself with the development of physical, moral and intellectual endowment. (Indeed, it can be said that Catholic education was holistic long before the term became popular in educational jargon.) Second, it must be developmental, taking account of the changes and growth which children and young people experience. Third, it must be social, because far from being individualistic, Catholic education must aim at the common good of society, and insists on a refined sense of responsibility and the right use of freedom for an active participation in the life of the human community. Finally, Catholic education strives for the formation of the human person, in the light of their eternal destiny, which is life with God. In short:

> . . . true education aims at the formation of the human person in view of his final end; at the same time its purpose includes the good

of those societies of which man is a member, in the duties of which he will share as an adult.[22]

Most secular educationalists see no objection to the first three aims, for they fit well with a secular understanding of what it means to become fully human. The fourth aim, with its explicitly religious dimension, would not command such widespread agreement.

The philosophical writing of Jacques Maritain had a tremendous influence on the Second Vatican Council as a whole, but more especially on the subsequent Congregation for Catholic Education established in 1965. In his social and political philosophy he decries the bourgeois individualism which he sees as characteristic of modern people, and which fosters the notion of the self-sufficiency of human beings. Maritain saw two serious misconceptions in modern educational theories; first, a disregard for ends; and second, false ideas concerning ends. Means in education, he argued, are cultivated for the sake of their own perfection, and whilst Catholic education can agree in many respects with the practical methods of progressive education, it cannot accept the supremacy of means over ends. The means are not in themselves contrary to Catholic education, but may be such as to cause us to lose sight of the end. The second misconception that he criticises is the often incomplete ideas we have concerning the nature of this end. He draws a distinction between the basic philosophical position on which theories of education depend and the more practical questions of methods in education. Since education presupposes an anthropology, he answers the resulting question of 'what is man?' with:

> ... man as an animal endowed with reason, whose supreme dignity is in the intellect; and man as free individual in personal relation with God, whose supreme righteousness consists in voluntarily obeying the law of God; and man as a sinful and wounded creature called to divine life and to the freedom of grace, whose supreme perfection consists in love.[23]

The chief goal of Catholic education is to develop a consciousness of God as a reality in human experience and a sense of personal relationship with Him. It must also develop an ability and disposition to participate constructively in the world, embodying the ideals of the fatherhood of God and the brotherhood and sisterhood of men and women. By attempting to offer a Christian interpretation of life, Catholic education seeks to develop an ability to see God's purpose in it for each individual's existence. This accords with Vatican II, for it maintains that a religious and spiritual education is superior to a wholly secular one. The Church continues to reject theories which look for the perfectibility of humankind and society through our own unaided efforts. In maintaining a Christian identity and combining the aims of understanding and commitment, Catholic education's focus is more properly the religious formation of the Church's members, and its ultimate goal is their preparation for union with God. Consequently, this education assists the child with the obligations placed on him at baptism. These obligations include a vital social dimension, since Catholic education can never be an education for power, wealth or even success, but rather must direct itself to service and responsibility for others.[24] Catholic education therefore needs to encourage the fulfilment of social obligations for the welfare of the whole community. The Church gives no sanction to an education in which the spiritual aspect is cultivated and the mind, body and senses neglected, for the formation of the human person is seen in its totality. For men or women to attain their full formation or completeness their education needs to be directed towards their whole nature, the physical, mental and the spiritual. So whilst education can be defined loosely as a preparation for 'complete living' and be widely accepted as such, the Christian will object if the word 'complete' leaves out preparation for eternal life. Maritain's principal criticism of modern educators is that they ignore the spiritual and consequently start from a false philosophy of humankind, ending with false educational ends which educational methods are made to subserve.[25]

Vatican II accorded supreme importance to the sacredness of the human person. It gave emphasis to the value of all persons and stressed the personal development of each individual. Catholic schools are urged to help their students:

> ... combine personal development with growth as the new creatures that baptism made them; in the end, it makes the message of salvation the principle of order for the whole human culture, so that the knowledge which pupils gradually acquire of the world, of life, and of man, is enlightened by faith.[26]

By stressing the value of each individual person in the sight of God, Catholic education attempts to unfold itself as a distinctive concept. The Catholic Faith does provide a framework within which this insistence upon the value of the individual person is intelligible and defensible. It states that God created man and woman in

his own image and loves all of them equally no matter how weak
or insignificant in human terms they may be. All human beings are
therefore irreducibly valuable in the Christian perspective. Catholic schools are committed to the development of the whole person
which is a task they share with the family and the wider Catholic
community. They endeavour to integrate the whole person within
the Catholic faith. This was clearly asserted by the Congregation
for Catholic Education in Rome when it proclaimed:

> Future teachers should be helped to realise that any genuine edu-
> cational philosophy has to be based on the nature of the human
> person, and therefore must take into account all of the physical and
> spiritual powers of each individual, along with the call of each one
> to be an active and creative agent in service to society. And this
> philosophy must be open to a religious dimension. Human beings
> are fundamentally free; they are not the property of the state or of
> any human organisation. The process of education, therefore, is a
> service to the individual students, helping each to achieve the most
> complete formation possible. The Christian model, based on the
> person of Christ, is then linked to this human concept of the person
> — that is, the model begins with an educational framework based
> on the person as human, and then enriches it with supernatural
> gifts, virtues, and values — and a supernatural call.[27]

Consequently, since Vatican II, it has been consistently declared
by the Church that what makes the Catholic school distinctive is
its religious dimension, for Catholic education is based on the
belief that to be human is to be religious. An examination of the
Church's documents on education indicates that this religious dimension is to be found not only in the Catholic idea of the 'person',
but in three central areas — the curriculum, community and the
climate of the school — all of which are interrelated.

In the curriculum, Catholic education is concerned to integrate
the person around love of God and of neighbour. This necessarily
involves a more integrated view of all that is learnt in schools, a
position advocated by the Post-Conciliar documents. Catholic
schools therefore should be committed to attempting a proper
synthesis of religion and culture; faith and life.[28] The main quality
that differentiates the Catholic school from the secular is the
importance it attaches to religion. As the Congregation of Catholic
Education's publication of 1977, *The Catholic School*, states:

> Complete education includes a religious dimension. Religion is an
> effective contribution to the development of other aspects of a

personality in the measure in which it is integrated into general education.[29]

This document asserts that the Catholic school must be concerned with intellectual values, but that it must also be specifically Catholic. Therefore, it adds:

> A school is not only a place where one is given a choice of intellectual values but a place where one is presented with an array of values which are lived.[30]

Religion must permeate all other areas of the curriculum, for as Pope John Paul II has said:

> The special character of the Catholic school, the underlying reason for it, the reason why Catholic parents should prefer it, is precisely the quality of the religious instruction integrated into the education of the pupils.[31]

According to this view, religion cannot be separated or divorced from the rest of the curriculum, nor can religious education be seen as the only *raison d'etre* of the Catholic school. If it were so, then it would be contrary to the basic premise of unity between revelation and other sources of knowledge and would ignore the view that all subjects in the curriculum need the light of the Gospel for their delivery. From the Catholic point of view, God is the source of all knowledge and in creating human beings He has endowed them with a desire for knowledge and a freedom to pursue it.

Therefore, simply teaching religious education does not qualify a school as Catholic. In addition, while teaching religious education is certainly part of the school's concern, it must not allow other subjects to become mere adjuncts nor allow itself to become submerged by the rest of the curriculum. The central point is that a school cannot be truly Catholic unless religion and its values are diffused into the entire curriculum, methods and organisation of the school. Cardinal Manning, near the end of the nineteenth century in a Pastoral Letter on the subject, declared:

> Christian training (education in its truest form) . . . may not be taken in doses once a week, nor even once a day, but like the salt that seasons our food, it must be in the food at every meal . . . It must be in history, geography, reading lessons, in the manners and examples of the teachers — in his or her very eyes.[32]

In order to facilitate the integration of religious truth and values with the rest of life, Catholic educators need to discern what is valuable in current curriculum theories and incorporate those

aspects into their schools. Nevertheless, some modern educational
approaches to the curriculum, such as the pragmatic and the
utilitarian, are hostile to the Catholic view. In particular, these
approaches think of education almost exclusively in terms of curriculum structure and course content, which inevitably treats
knowledge as a product for consumption. The Catholic Church's
position is that knowledge has a value and significance irrespective
of its usefulness, and it warns that:

> Education is not given for the purpose of gaining power but as an
> aid towards a fuller understanding of, and communion with man,
> events and things. Knowledge is not to be considered as a means of
> material prosperity and success, but as a call to serve and to be
> responsible for others.[33]

In considering the curriculum, the attitudes and values which
underpin its factual content need to be consistent with the Catholic vision of the person and society. The Catholic school, according
to Vatican II, also has a serious obligation to resist any policies
which might tend to maintain the privileged status of a few people,
thereby contributing to the perpetuation of injustice and alienation.

The first priority of Catholic education is the maintenance of
the Catholicity of the school curriculum. However, since many
Catholics at all levels are so immersed in current theoretical
approaches in education, there is a danger of this priority being
impossible to implement. As Francis Bottomley says:

> If there is a Catholic education or even Catholic views about
> education we should expect to see them manifested in Catholic
> organisations which were significantly 'other' than their secular
> counterparts and it is difficult to see that this parochial school (or
> the Catholic public school) characteristically reflects more than the
> values of the society in which it is embedded or is more loyal to the
> values of the Gospel than to the ill-considered aims of the system.
> We are committed to a sort of elitism if the evangelical remarks
> about salt and leaven are to be taken seriously, yet it is a very curious
> kind of elitism which involves service, sharing and love.[34]

Since the Church has become committed in principle as well as in
practice to a variety of educational efforts, it would seem natural
that it should have its own unique and distinctive contribution to
make — a contribution centred on the life and teaching of Christ
in the Gospel. The Church has given emphasis to this point in
declaring that:

Intellectual development and growth as a Christian go forward hand in hand. As students move up from one class into the next, it becomes increasingly imperative that a Catholic school help them become aware that a relationship exists between faith and human culture. Human culture remains human, and must be taught with scientific objectivity. But the lessons of the teacher and the reception of those students who are believers will not divorce faith from this culture; this would be a major spiritual loss. The world of human culture and the world of religion are not like two parallel lines that never meet; points of contact are established within the human person. For the believer is both human and a person of faith, the protagonist of culture and the subject of religion.[35]

The first assertion made is that the integration of learning and living in the light of Christian faith should be a distinguishing feature of the Catholic school's curriculum. However, a second point can be detected here, since the Catholic school is ideally a 'community of believers'.

One of the principal themes of Vatican II was an understanding of the Church as 'People of God'. The communal and personal aspects of the Church were reaffirmed and the Catholic school was urged to contribute towards the fulfilment of the mission of the People of God. By stressing the idea of the Church as the People of God, Vatican II helped shift an understanding of the school from 'institution' to one principally of 'community'.[36] However, it was a definition of 'community' seen not as a sociological term, but primarily as a theological concept. In addition, this definition of the Church and school favoured brotherly service over juridical and authoritarian structures. Catholic thought began to emphasise and rediscover the integral place of the 'community of faith' in the religious education process. Robert Malone has distinguished three factors which he considers are essential to the formation of a faith community in schools. They are first, that each individual's uniqueness should be respected by all; second, that all within the community should have a sense of belonging; and finally, that the rights to freedom of conscience should be respected.[37] For the Church, these conditions for establishing a faith community are achieved within a shared perspective of meaning. The individual Christian's need for belonging and social interaction, for clarification and interpretation of their life's experiences and for their responsible participation in adult roles should be met by the local Church — the community of believers. This happens essentially through scripture, creeds, liturgy, and the sacraments, but also through Catholic schooling, which together represent a concrete religio-philosophical system wholly absent in secular schools.[38] However, the Catholic school needs also to reconcile the tensions which arise between the curriculum and the faith-community. Harold Buetow sees the school community of faith as living, conscious and active, a genuine community, not just academically orientated, but one which enables its members to adopt a Christian way of life. The tension he sees developing here is the over-emphasis that can be given to the academic content of the curriculum.[39] Buetow places more importance on the people who make up the community. He writes:

> As a major agency for the transmission of Christian values for living, the Catholic school, being the centre of the educative Christian community, promotes a faith relationship with Christ, in whom all values find fulfilment. This faith is principally assimilated through contact with people inside a community.[40]

Again, there has to be a total commitment to Christ at the centre of this faith community.

There are, however, some apparent contradictions in Vatican II's teaching on the educative faith community, at least so far as its implications at the practical level are concerned. Vatican II and its subsequent Education Congregation saw that:

> The activity of a Catholic school is, above all else, an activity that shares in the evangelising mission of the Church.[41]

Further that:

> Christ is the foundation of the whole education enterprise in a Catholic school. His revelation gives new meaning to life and helps man to direct his thought, actions, and will according to the Gospel, making the beatitudes his norm of life. The fact that in their own individual ways all members of the school community share this Christian vision, makes the school Catholic.[42]

Consequently, it follows that what makes the school Catholic is the extent to which the pupils share the Christian vision. However, Vatican II also recognised the presence of non-Catholics in Catholic schools and applauded this along with its development of further ecumenical dialogue as well as a more positive attitude towards the secular State. For Vatican II, the Catholic school was, in certain areas, open to all; and the 1977 Congregation's statement on *The Catholic School* went much further by declaring that:

In the certainty that the Spirit is at work in every person, the Catholic school offers itself to all, non-Christians included, with all its distinctive aims and means, acknowledging, preserving and promoting the spiritual and moral qualities, the social and cultural values, which characterise different civilisations.[43]

This appears to contradict previous statements and, significantly, there has been a conspicuous absence of this point in subsequent Vatican statements on education. 'Preserving' and 'promoting' other spiritual and moral qualities does not fit easily with a unitary Christian vision. The 1988 Vatican statement does however reinforce the point that the Catholic school is open to all, but recognises that it might not then be possible for it to fulfil its evangelising mission, and even in the context of full Catholic admissions it uses the phrase, 'pre-evangelising'.[44] In England and Wales, voluntary-aided Catholic schools have not been universally open to non-Catholics. In regard to the Catholic school's mission to evangelise, the advisers to the bishops have published, with official approval, the statement that Catholic schools must no longer assume faith in the children they admit.[45]

Michael Winter has outlined three models of what it can mean to be a Catholic teacher, which help explain the various views on this theme. The first is the 'presumption' model, which presupposes that the child has made a definitive act of faith and all the teacher needs to do is provide the theological content. The second model he calls 'conscious detachment', which presents Catholic doctrine like any other subject with no element of personal commitment required. The third he terms 'elected silence' by which the teacher transmits Catholic values by silent witness — by a sort of osmosis.[46] He rejects the first two and advocates the third, but in doing so he rejects the active evangelisation which is part of the model of 'presumption' and also part of official Catholic practice. However, his 'presumption' model is rigid, and does not accommodate the fact that teaching can take place in an atmosphere of commitment, for the teaching of Catholic dogma is not an 'education' in pre-cast conclusions. In his third model he provides no substance to what should be transmitted. A combination of an amended model one and a more explicit model three would appear to characterise the model which Vatican II has in mind.

The 'climate' of the school is the third area which requires some clarification. Whilst much educational thought stresses the importance of an appropriate climate within schools, there is little in the way of practical definition given to this elusive term. Padraig Hogan

has offered three models of what Catholic school ethos or climate
may entail, these models being named 'custodial', 'accommodation' and 'dialogue'. The custodial approach to ethos views the
school authorities as custodians of a set of standards which are to
be preserved, defended and transmitted. The 'accommodation'
approach seeks to 'accommodate' the demands of various interests,
and aims for an expedient settlement in areas of uncertainty or
conflict. Both the 'custodial' and 'accommodation' models resist
any fundamental questioning of the *status quo* which they seek to
maintain. The final model, and the one which is recommended by
Hogan for Catholic schools, is the 'dialogue' model which sees
ethos as the natural outcome of what actually goes on in schools.
It involves criticism, listening to others, and is not limited to being
a strategy for resolving crises at meetings.[47] The idea of dialogue in
education here originates from Martin Buber's work, but like
Hogan he does not develop the concept, and it is left rather vague
as to what concrete application it could have for schools. Indeed,
Buber speaks of the child being 'preserved and guarded in a
dialogue' with its parents 'which never breaks off'.[48] There is much
that corresponds to the 'custodial' model in Buber's thinking. The
ideal Catholic ethos or climate would seem more accurately to
reflect a combination of all three models, with the reservation that
whilst no healthy school climate can be static, it does need a firm
framework or background in which to develop. This framework, for
the Catholic school, can only be the set of standards presented by
the Gospel and Church Tradition.

Schools develop unique climates and lives of their own, created
by means of a great many influences which affect the quality of
relationships and the process of learning within them. All official
Church statements agree that a Christian atmosphere or tone
within the school can act as a profound formative influence on the
development of the pupil's faith. However, while these notions are
among the most pervasive, potent and provocative of concepts, the
realities they signify are difficult to measure or even identify. On
entering a Catholic school it is said that one:

> ... ought to have the impression of entering a new community, one
> illuminated by the light of faith, and having its own unique charac-
> teristics.[49]

In order to follow the consequences of the Catholic school's unique
characteristics, there is a need to have a clear realisation of its
identity and *raison d'être*. Pius XI made this point when he said that:

For the securing of a perfect education it is essential that the whole environment of the pupil should be in keeping with the end to be attained.[50]

The sum of this environment has since been defined as being that:

. . . everyone agree with the educational goals and cooperate in achieving them; that interpersonal relationships be based on love and Christian freedom; that each individual, in daily life, be a witness to Gospel values; that every student be challenged to strive for the highest possible level of formation, both human and Christian.[51]

Conditions which threaten the health of a school climate are: undefined aims; excessive concern for academic achievement; impersonal relationships; isolation of the school from the local Church; and authoritarian methods.[52] The emphasis on the distinctive 'Catholic atmosphere' in a school has become a central theme on which Catholic educational policy is still founded. It is a policy which is intended to ensure that there is some form of unity of attitudes and values between the school and the home. However, the same criticisms that have been made about the idea of 'faith community' can be applied here also. In particular, the values and attitudes of teachers and pupils in a Catholic school cannot be the product of an arbitrary agreement between people who have been thrown together. There is a 'Gold Standard' to which the school community can relate their views and behaviour — it is the standard of the life and teachings of Christ. Catholics can provide a figure of general validity and so answer the question 'to where, to what, must we educate'? Above all, teachers and pupils need to join together voluntarily in creating and sustaining a climate which is directly intended and shared. It is precisely the configuration of attitudes, values, and beliefs held in common by members of the community which effectively sums up the total pattern of life within the Catholic school. Whilst the climate in schools will differ, as a result of local traditions and successive intakes, it is what they ultimately share in belief that makes them a 'community of faith' rather than another kind of community. An adequate basis for understanding the nature of Catholic education cannot be provided by a loose combination of religion and secular subjects taught in a 'religious atmosphere', but by a proper integration of climate and community. Thus, the climate, curriculum, and the communal nature of the school are integral to Catholic education, and give the school its distinctive character.

In concluding its commentary on the formation process in a Catholic school the 1988 Vatican statement on education said:

> We need to think of Christian education as a movement or a growth process, directed toward an ideal goal which goes beyond the limitations of anything human. At the same time the process must be harmonious, so that Christian formation takes place within and in the course of human formation. The two are not separate and parallel paths, they are complementary forms of education which become one in the goals of the teacher and the willing reception of the student.[53]

However, whilst official Church statements recognise that the Catholic school must: 'fulfil its own educational goals by blending human culture with the message of salvation into a co-ordinated programme'.[54] It also points out that this needs to be achieved within culture. In addition, the Catholic school has to obey the laws and regulations of the State, which can lead to tension and conflict, for it is unlikely that they will both seek the same educational ends. The situation is made more problematic since, apart from the attempt made in this discussion, it is no easy matter to discover any modern philosophy of Catholic education in England and Wales. This is despite the fact that the Catholic Church is to a very large extent an educational institution and community. The response of the bishops in England and Wales to Vatican pronouncements on education needs to be reviewed in this connection.

The Response of the Bishops

The Catholic Church in England and Wales does not confine its objectives to a narrow set of religious goals, but includes educational aims and procedures. These procedures therefore require a clear and conscious purpose in the minds of those engaged in them. Since the bishops are the leaders in enunciating these aims, they have been concerned with establishing and maintaining a Catholic Christian identity among the young. Their overall aim has remained the spiritual growth and development of all Catholics through an education which includes preparation for a fuller life in eternity. In this they have consistently reflected the stand from Rome, as can be seen from their Declaration in 1929 which was a restatement of Pius XI's encyclical of that year.[55] The view of Catholic education held by Henry Evenett in the 1940s was that the hierarchy of values taught by Catholicism is one which runs directly counter:

... to much modern social and moral ideology ... Death and original sin are the constants in the light of which the Catholic Church surveys humanity. Life is a preparatory stage and its values are secondary ... if education is what remains after we have forgotten all we learnt at school, the quintessential left by a Catholic education is a lasting consciousness of the fact and meaning of death.[56]

This was restated by Bishop Beck on behalf of the bishops in 1951 as their official view.[57] However, this position has been challenged by a number of Catholic critics who bemoan the lack of any well-formulated philosophy or theory in support of Catholic education.[58] Nevertheless, in 1951 and again in 1955 the bishops felt confident not only to repeat Evenett's aims of Catholic education but to declare:

> We Catholics are the only body in the country consistently concerned with the content of education; we are the only body which have clear ideas on what education is for, and how its whole purpose is to be achieved. More than that, we find that those others who are at all deeply concerned with these questions not only agree with us but demand of the educational system of this country what, in fact, the Catholic part of it is alone providing. In that sense we are very really educational leaders at the present time.[59]

This statement has never been repeated, nor has the Church been so confident of its own primacy in education. In 1961 Bishop Beck gave a public lecture at Manchester University on the 'Aims of Education: Neo-Thomism' which largely presented the views of Maritain and spoke of the traditional thinking on Catholic education.[60] He concluded that the true teachers were the Saints, who more than anyone else, have had the final end in sight. In 1964 he made an intervention on behalf of the English and Welsh bishops at the Second Vatican Council which spoke in similar traditional terms; that the promise of complete and absolute fulfilment was to be found in eternity and that the fulfilment of this aim in education could be only partially realised here on earth.[61] It is difficult to conclude that the bishops had anything new to offer the Council Fathers, since they largely repeated the content of Pius XI's encyclical.

Vatican II produced a set of principles on education and then asked the local bishops in each country to produce their own statements of application. This has been a key feature of the Congregation for Catholic Education's policy, which leaves the adaptation of its guidelines to local circumstances as judged by diocesan bishops. Consequently, a number of bishops in different countries have produced their own particular view of Catholic education based on the documents of Vatican II. In 1972, for instance, the bishops of the USA published a major statement on their schools called *To Teach as Jesus Did* which outlined three central objectives for the American Catholic school. First, the document placed emphasis on the 'message' of salvation, secondly on the idea of 'community of faith' and thirdly on Christian 'service' to all. The aim espoused by the document is that schools are to teach the Gospel message of Christ with authentic Christian doctrine, they are to build an active and living school community of faith, and are to help people grow in the service of others. The content of 'message', 'community' and 'service' has helped focus American educators on the direction Catholic education in schools should take, and has expressed at the same time the leadership of the bishops.[62] The document also advocated the establishment of a research centre in Catholic education as one of its priority recommendations, and the USA has a number of such centres today. In contrast, the English and Welsh bishops have produced no major declarations on Catholic education, although they have made some brief statements on the subject which have occurred as a result of specific areas of concern at the time. For example, the 1974 statement on the *Appointment of Teachers* showed concern at the number of non-Catholic and non-committed teachers in Catholic schools. Another brief statement in 1978 merely endorsed, rather than elaborated, on the Vatican statement issued the previous year.[63]

Nevertheless, in the autumn of 1972 the Education Commission of the Bishops' Conference circulated a letter in which they expressed the intention of making a 'study of the theology of Catholic education in the light of the teaching of the Second Vatican Council and, with the help of experts in the various branches of education' of making 'a full enquiry into the present educational needs of the Catholic Church in England and Wales'. Later in the same year the bishops asked twelve theologians to write a paper on Catholic education.[64] However, whilst conferences were held in 1973 and 1974, little was produced except for a collection of papers on *Education and Theology* which was published by the Association of Teaching Religious after their Easter 1974 conference at the University of Kent at Canterbury. Their main conclusion was that there could be no question of the emergence of a definitive theology of education, and that uncertainty and confusion in educational policy should not be resolved pragmatically.[65] In 1977 the bishops did establish a study group chaired by Bishop Konstant 'to review the principles of Catholic education and to make recommendations'.[66] The group did not confine itself to school education, but rather saw education in its broadest sense, and their report was published in May 1981. By attempting to tackle everything, including adult education and religious education, this commission produced a report which was vague and generalised. There were no research findings underpinning the report, nor did the commission conduct any new research of its own. Its principal conclusions, as far as the Catholic school was concerned, were basically traditional, i.e. that education must be based on religion. However, the report offered little in the way of concrete direction and it appears to be more a collection of diverse ideas which have now been largely forgotten. Its only achievement, it seems, was to give emphasis to adult Christian education.

The closest the bishops have come to enunciating their own ideals in Catholic education has been through their national advisers on religious education. Whilst these have been concerned primarily with religious education, the three successive occupants of this post have influenced our understanding of Catholic education more generally. The period since Vatican II has seen a great ferment in the field of catechesis and religious education, but the most controversial event in the history of Catholic religious education in England and Wales during recent years must surely be the adoption of *Weaving the Web* as the framework for the religious education in Catholic schools of pupils between the ages of eleven and fourteen. Two dioceses (Birmingham and Salford) went so far as to discourage the use of this programme. *Weaving the Web* grew out of the work of the National Project of Catechesis and Religious Education, the initiation of which was endorsed by the bishops. It was published by the Project during 1987–1988 as a framework for the development of school curricula, and has been widely criticised for its alleged lack of doctrinal content and presentation of all religions as being of equal value. One possible response to these criticisms appears to have been that its critics mistook the programme for 'catechesis', whereas it is in fact 'religious education'. And in the *Teachers' Book* it is stated that 'religious education should be non-inclusive'.[67] Thus religious education is aimed equally at all pupils of whatever religious conviction or none; faith is presupposed neither in teacher nor in pupil. Religious education is geared towards learning about and from various religions; though it is admitted that pupils may be challenged to deepen their own faith-commitments, whatever they might be, religious education is not primarily concerned with developing Christian, or any other, faith. This approach is a form of liberal theology which has a corresponding way of understanding and practising Catholic education; the approach also renounces much of the former dogmatic quality of Catholic education's content.

The principles behind the National Project were furnished by Fr. Patrick Purnell SJ in his book *Our Faith Story*. Religious education in a Catholic school, in Purnell's approach, is not concerned with the maturation of faith and the handing-on of various aspects of religious tradition, but with the imparting of knowledge so that the pupil might be able to make a mature commitment to, or rejection of, a faith-tradition. Not only is evangelisation excluded, but the school is not seen as the normal setting for catechesis, since the latter presupposes faith. If believing pupils happen to receive religious education as catechesis and non-believing ones as evangelisation, this is seen as a kind of by-product — such responses are neither the purpose of religious education nor the intention of the teacher. In justification for this approach Purnell recognises that the Catholic school had been part of the local faith-community in the past, but sees this as now no longer the case. The dominant theme is the experiential approach, with its focus on the life experience of the learner and his or her 'dignity and freedom'. It would appear inevitable that as religious education becomes less confessional in character, denominational schools become increasingly anachronistic and perhaps even less desirable. But, whilst agreeing with Purnell's observations of where our secondary schools are today, it does not follow that Catholics therefore should ascribe some legitimacy to this approach in religious education. It is rather curious that the committed Catholic parishioner is expected to pay for a school which does not offer committed Catholic pupils, in Purnell's words, 'faith-sharing' because the school has admitted other pupils who need to be protected from such overt 'faith-sharing' in the classroom.

In Pope John Paul II's Apostolic Exhortation, *Catechesi Tradendae* of 1979, (chapter IV section 34), there is approval given to children being taught about other religions in an objective way. However, this section refers to religious education in State schools, and teaching about other religions is not considered catechetical for it lacks 'both the witness of believers and an understanding of the Christian mysteries and of what is specific about Catholicism'. The National Project viewed religious education in a broader way than catechesis, and detailed its function as an attempt to appreciate the spiritual dimension of religious life. Religious education in this understanding does not presume faith, and is addressed to all pupils irrespective of whether they are from committed Catholic homes or not, or even whether they practise or not. The function of catechesis is defined as being addressed to those who have expressed some commitment to the Catholic faith already. The difficulty is that the National Project's religious education programme uses many of the same aims as the *Agreed Syllabus* which is applicable to the LEA school. In this respect, and in the idea that catechesis is primarily for adults, the National Project does not follow the Pope's Exhortation. In paragraphs 18 and 19 of this Exhortation the Pope's treatment of the topic is clear and incisive. It is recognised that initial evangelisation has often not taken place before children participate in religious education or catechesis. Therefore, since the Catholic school is part of the evangelical mission of the Church, catechesis may have to concern itself with arousing faith. Religious education in a Catholic school which is only implicit or indirect is to be reprobated, for the Pope states that 'education in the faith . . . especially the teaching of Christian doctrine . . . ' should be 'imparted in an organic and systematic way'.

Section 81 of the *General Catechetical Directory* of 1971 recognises that questions are sometimes raised about the appropriateness of giving catechesis to children from families who do not practise the faith. However, the *Directory's* answer is clear; for it states that 'catechesis is certainly not to be omitted for such children'. The Catholic school has to be openly and consistently committed to the Catholic faith through catechesis, and therefore its frame of reference should be service in and on behalf of the Church. In a sense the Catholic school is given the missionary task of evangelising itself. However, no consensus exists on the current usage of the key terminology in religious education, and consequently there is no clearly defined purpose for religious education in Catholic schools. The use of the phrase 'religious education' by the National Project in a non-confessional sense has led to ambiguity, and out of this ambiguity has grown misunderstanding and confusion about the aims of Catholic education.

The bishops have in a recent statement on education restated the Vatican's position that education must be concerned with personal growth rather than with what might be useful or simply of passing value.[68] The statement is simply reactive to government intentions, this being a main feature of the bishops' responses. The bishops have failed to establish any solid base from which to criticise government education programmes. They have produced no major authoritative statement on education for the country as a whole, but rely on repeating statements from Rome which are often too general, and when used in England can seem like mere rhetoric. Consequently, Catholic principles in education have been largely reactive to, rather than anticipatory of, the questions and policies set by the government and local education authorities. A paper of the bishops' entitled *Evaluating the Distinctive Nature of the Catholic School* did make a brief attempt at providing the main goals of Catholic education for teachers. The full text of these goals is as follows:

> The Church sees education as part of its mission to proclaim God as Creator, Christ the Redeemer and the Holy Spirit as Indwelling Inspirer of all that is good in human living. The Church believes that the created order speaks of God, that human relationships are redeemed by Christ's saving death and resurrection, and that real human advancement and achievement testify to the Holy Spirit at work in humanity enabling everyone to grow and develop. God is at work in his world and can be discovered in our daily living, drawing us to himself in love, inviting us to grow in a relationship with him as the most perfect fulfilment of our lives. This means that, despite our sinfulness or shortcomings, every person's life is charged with God's presence and every human experience presents us with the opportunity to deepen our knowledge and love of Him. Therefore, the process of education, teaching and learning, is a holy act and, since the world in which we live is God's, all teaching and learning is somehow related to Him. Everything connected with human living, and the means by which we understand and come to terms with it, is part of the process of God's self-revelation to humanity, whether those engaged in it are conscious of it or not.[69]

The difficulty here is that these goals are given no elaboration. Teachers are given no concrete aims or objectives so as to ensure that their teaching and learning become ever more holy. No real attempt has been made to provide teachers with a clear set of Catholic aims in education based on the holistic educational goals promoted by the Second Vatican Council and the Congregation for Catholic Education.

There have been some very limited and individual attempts among the bishops to discuss the goals of Catholic education for schools. Cardinal Hume, repeating the traditional Catholic philosophy of education, says that the Church does not see education as a means to an end, but as an integral part of its mission to evangelise and that this is a matter of 'immense importance' in England and Wales. However, he recognises that many Catholics are unclear about the role of the Church in education and of the distinctive character of Catholic schools.[70] In his book, *Towards a Civilisation of Love* he says:

> Without renewed understanding and increased support on all sides, the unique Catholic contribution will inevitably suffer.[71]

He adds:

> We have a coherent philosophy and vision of education that we believe to be of universal significance.[72]

The claim is not only that the Catholic Church has a coherent philosophy of life and education but that it has a universal significance. The main thrust of the Cardinal's argument in this book concerns the assertion that the bishop is the focus of unity in a diocese and that parents and governors of schools should cooperate with his leadership. Leadership requires a clearly articulated vision which is understood and assented to by the followers. Indeed, the Catholic philosophy of education cannot be separated from the Church without losing its whole meaning. The principal requirement of a full Catholic education is that those who receive it should have faith in Christ within his Church. In England and Wales, schools have been established in communities which did have shared convictions and values and which need a shared vision clearly perceived and presented in order to continue. Bishop Kelly of Salford underlines this point when he says:

> We are implicitly undermining our case for Catholic schools if we simply think that those who are not Roman Catholics can find a fitting place in our schools as long as they are not expected to be involved in the formal Roman Catholic aspects.[73]

He repeats the view that the religious dimension is not an adjunct or something parallel to the whole enterprise for faith and life, and that therefore the whole of formation is bound together. It would appear more accurate to say that Catholic education is properly suited for people of faith in Christ as understood by the Catholic Church. Clearly there is some confusion in presenting a coherent case for a philosophy of Catholic education in England and Wales, and very little attempt has been made to do this. In such a situation, the Church has faced formidable criticism and opposition to its claims.

Criticisms of Catholic Education

Contemporary educationalists, some of considerable influence, implicitly exclude Christianity from any general consideration of the aims and purpose of education. Modern educational language favours a commitment to pluralism, and consequently strongly opposes the imposition of any particular religious system on society as a whole. Moreover, many educational pluralists hold that society is too heterogeneous to have any conception of a common good. Some of these educationalists are also relativists, since for them there is no absolute objective truth, 'truth' being only relative to a particular individual, group or culture. Moreover, in a free and democratic society many religious ideas, whether ultimately true or false, are often considered to be of equal value and the search for meaning and truth in these circumstances has largely become a private individual affair. Indeed, this can be seen among many Catholics themselves for a vague 'spirit of Christianity' often takes the place of the authoritative creed. Since it is impossible to agree on precise definitions of this 'spirit', whatever a new generation declares education to be may well depend upon the relative and subjective nature of the definitions of the needs of that age. This leads to all sorts of individualistic ways of viewing education, and finally to the adoption of the dominant theory and methods prevalent at that time. In such a situation some Catholics could easily be in danger of merely accepting the normal school system and over-stamping it with the label 'Catholic'. It is partly against this background that critics of the Church's role in education have found its claims to a supernaturally-based education unacceptable. The work of Richard Pring and Paul Hirst requires examination, in order to assess the principal criticisms put forward about Catholic education.

Richard Pring was the first to attempt to apply the methods and philosophical analysis developed by Richard Peters to the ideals and processes of Catholic education. In a collection, *Catholic Education in a Secular Society,* edited by Bernard Tucker and published in 1968, he contributed an article with the title 'Has Education an Aim?'. Tucker's collection of articles was clearly a radical departure

from previous Catholic thinking on education since they found the
whole justification for a separate Catholic school system question-
able. Tucker admits that this was a 'minority view' within the
Church. Pring's article dealt specifically with three important areas
for education; moral education, freedom and authority. In his
discussion of moral education, he states that Church education
cannot attach meaning to a system issuing from a 'discovered aim'
of education whether the source is religious or not.[74] This would
appear to deny Christian revelation's role in assisting with the
formulation of the aims of education. He does recognise later in
the article that the relationship between revelation and education
needs to be studied in greater depth. However, his chapter does
not really explicate the meaning of the educational terms used by
the Church, nor does it examine their linguistic and conceptual
basis. He does say that it is not his intention to deal with the
theological aspects of education in such a short space, but these
are essential in any treatment of how the Church understands its
role in education. Instead, he calls for the Church to accept the
basic framework of language and ideas which informs the current
debate about education. He sees the value of what the Church has
to offer as being understood and justified within the scheme of
ideas and values which underpin the total educational system. How
the Church could possibly make a contribution in such a scheme
of things remains obscure, especially as Pring himself states that
the Church speaks a 'different language' which is ludicrous to many
in and outside the Church. It is important to recognise at the outset
that many analysts inevitably operate on the basis of certain tacit
philosophical assumptions which include the rejection of the supernatural.

Since Pring is a Catholic it can be firmly assumed that he does
not reject the supernatural and its role in human life, including its
contribution to the aims of education. In an article in the *British
Journal of Educational Studies* of June 1995 he significantly modifies
his 1968 approach to Catholic education. Nevertheless, the 1968
chapter is of more than passing interest, since it was the first to
address the question of Catholic educational aims from a post
Vatican II perspective. In the chapter he adopts the language of
Peters and views education as human-centred and concerned with
the development of human potentialities. Education's main fruit
is a spirit of criticism, which accepts nothing as being beyond
questioning. Children are not to be taught *what* to think, but rather

how to think. It follows from this view that Christian beliefs, values
and attitudes should not be passed on through formal teaching, but
that children should be free to develop their own. However, the
Church has always inducted its members, who include children,
into given sets of religious beliefs and has used its own distinctive
view of education to assist it. For Pring, at least in 1968, this could
not be considered as 'education' *per se*. He appeared to assume that
there are only two ways of viewing education in the Catholic school:
either it is teaching set dogmas which are closed to discussion, or
it involves teaching *about* Catholicism. Since the former does not
meet his criteria of what constitutes education, it is unacceptable
— and so he favours teaching *about* Catholicism. For Pring education is an initiation into certain ways of thinking and conceptual-
ising, and he concludes that this is the only tenable analysis of what
education really is. He makes this clear when he says:

> To propose an education programme of which the first principles
> are a privileged revelation of the Church, (and thus outside rational
> questioning), and the details of which are simply a question of
> logical deduction, (and thus necessary truths not open to dispute),
> is tantamount to the suppression of healthy criticism of the basic
> principles underlying educational decisions.[75]

Consequently, in order for Catholic education to be acceptable in
Pring's view it may need to suppress the importance of the 'revelation' element.

Pring's principal point concerns the question of truth, which is
also central to the Church's view of education. He found that:

> Since truth is concerned with what is the case and with the reasons
> and evidence for believing that something is the case, the role of
> authority would seem confined to the limited function of initiating
> the pupil into the adult world of rational enquiry. Anything else
> could not be counted as education where matters of truth are
> concerned.[76]

He adds:

> . . . the Church often seems like an alien body in a world which
> assumes, almost as an axiom, the relativity of truth.[77]

Since the pursuit of truth lies at the heart of the Christian enterprise, there is a need to clarify this in the light of Pring's early
criticisms. The traditional philosophy of Catholic education has
been essentially a philosophy of Realism, since truth is viewed by
the Church as an objective value. Truth, for the Church, is an

objective value not created by the mind, but rather consists in the conformity of the mind with reality. In other words, the objects of a person's knowledge have an existence independent of the person having knowledge of them. There are, however, a number of positions which challenge this concept of 'truth'. Some say clearly that there is no objective truth, whilst others accept objective truth but limit it to matters of 'empirical' fact — thereby excluding religion and morality. Another position is that there are objective moral truths, but that these have no relation to the supernatural. Finally, it is argued that there are, or may be, supernatural truths but that we cannot know them for they are 'above reason'. The implications for Catholic education of some of these ways of viewing truth need some elaboration.

Maritain, has argued that total or absolute truth has the divine qualities of infinity and transcendence.[78] Specific truths, such as those in the disciplines of a school curriculum, are only fragments of truth. These fragments are not static, for they are open to development. New truths can be discovered at the level of human knowledge. However, by way of an answer to Pring's criticism of the Catholic view of education, Maritain makes clear that absolute truths are not equivalent to pre-packaged truth. The quest for truth in the disciplines opens the mind rather than closes it, and any charge of indoctrination therefore does not apply. Since Catholic education is dedicated to truth-seeking, it must liberate the individual. As Maritain says, a person is free when he is equipped for the discovery of truth and capable of enjoying it for its own sake. At school level this means 'to cultivate, and liberate, form and equip' natural intelligence.[79] Nevertheless, Gospel truths, according to Maritain, unify the partial truths discovered in the several subjects of the curriculum, and so primacy is given to the religious dimension of the curriculum. Other philosphers, such as Mortimer Adler and Robert Hutchins, do not give such primacy to theology, but emphasise the study of Mathematics and the Humanities, which they claim also exhibit the absolute truths of the universe.[80] However, Maritain warns teachers in a Catholic school that they must not regard the truths of the Gospel as pre-cast conclusions which dispense them and their pupils from any further intellectual effort. In other words, nothing is outside rational enquiry and everything within a faith-orientated education is open for healthy discussion. By this view, it is no part of Catholic education to present ready-made formulae to be received in a passive way, or 'knowledge' without understanding or meaning. Moreover, St Thomas Aquinas viewed education as a lifelong process of self-activity, self-direction and self-realisation. Freedom, he says, must be respected and the pupil should be the principal agent in the education process, with the teacher acting as the essential mover. The pupil is the primary agent in the education process with the teacher secondary.[81] This was expounded many centuries before John Dewey made 'discovery learning' popular. Pring's early objections to Catholic education counting as 'education' are partially answered by Aquinas and his followers such as Maritain, who assert rationality and the primacy of truth in the educative process.

Nevertheless, Catholic education is still accused of emphasising passivity in education with students learning by rote under authoritarian teachers. Whilst these practical characteristics have been historically observed as part of Catholic education they are neither its purpose nor necessary to it. It would be a distortion to equate these stereotypes with the official teaching of the Church, for its statements, since Vatican II, have encouraged the creative and free expression of children. Catholic education is not about coercion or manipulation. The object of Pring's criticism of Catholic education is perhaps the widely perceived authoritarianism within the educational structures of the Church in the 1960s. Pring spoke about pressure being brought to bear on individuals, and the way diocesan authorities attempted to exercise control over the education debate in the Church. He strongly warned against authoritarianism, and on this point there was much to be concerned about within the Church when his article was written.[82] Nevertheless, Pring's main philosophical point in 1968 was that the aims of education cannot be discovered or deduced from theological premises. The Catholic Church teaches that the aims of education are partially deduced as a practical consequence of what it means to be fully human in the light of Christ's revelation. In other words, in order to develop desirable human potentialities it is important to know what these are. This will depend on our conception of human nature. Consequently, for the Christian, these human potentialities will be sought in the light of Christian teaching. Human experience and observation will also have a contribution to make so that the Catholic aims of education are not based exclusively on theological premises. A second, and more fundamental, criticism has been that the Catholic view of education has led to an overly intellectualistic approach to Faith.

Basil Mitchell has argued that the systems of belief in Christianity are not purely intellectual, and that their importance is not exclusively intellectual. He says:

> They matter because they affect, at the deepest level, our conception of what it is to be a human being. They profoundly affect our emotions, character and attitudes. Whatever education is given to develop moral, aesthetic and spiritual capacities must to some extent be pre-rational and sub-rational. However much we may have as our ultimate aim a high degree of autonomy, no one can ever achieve it completely, and no one can even begin to achieve it who had not first been reared in a firm tradition in the first place.[83]

Pring's objections are given an answer in that autonomy can be reached through a Christian education. In addition, Mitchell does not accept that the distinction between what to teach and how to teach can be sustained. Quite simply he argues that the only way in which you can teach people how to think is by showing them how it is done:

> One learns to be a good historian by seeing a good historian arrive at the conclusion he does, and one will not learn this from someone who refuses to come to any conclusions at all.[84]

Teachers in a Catholic school therefore need to view their teaching more broadly, for whatever is said or done, or indeed not said or done, is in fact teaching. Within this, all good teaching requires fidelity to the phenomenon being taught, for the pupils will only really learn about something through some empathetic identification with it. Education can occur within a community of faith, for educational criteria do not rule out that teaching and learning can co-exist in a climate of commitment.

Paul Hirst is another influential educationalist who denies the possibility of constructing a useful relationship between Christian faith and education. Indeed, he has gone so far as to say that Christianity has no contribution to make to an understanding of education and that it would be illegitimate to apply it in this way. He explains that the very search for a Christian philosophy of education is a 'huge mistake'[85] and that:

> . . . there has now emerged in our society a concept of education which makes the whole idea of Christian education a kind of nonsense.[86]

Hirst distinguishes between two concepts of education: primitive and objective. The former is concerned with passing on customs

and rituals, whilst the latter is concerned with truth and reason.
For Hirst the primitive idea of education cannot be recognised as
'education' at all. He says that when it comes to rational, sophisti-
cated education, 'dominated by a concern for knowledge, for truth
and for reasons',[87] then there can be no such thing as Christian
education. However, Hirst seeks an accommodation with the individual Christian, but exclusively on his own terms. He suggests
that his view of education should be acceptable to the Christian
who adopts a rationally coherent system of thinking about education, by beginning with basic premises which are self-evident to
reason:

> . . . it seems to me it is precisely the concept of education an
> intelligent Christian must accept.[88]

Hirst develops this position and then argues that:

> Just as intelligent Christians have come to recognise that justifiable
> scientific claims are autonomous and do not, and logically cannot,
> rest on religious beliefs, so also, it seems to me, justifiable educa-
> tional principles are autonomous. That is to say that any attempt to
> justify educational principles by an appeal to religious claims is
> invalid.[89]

The Christian Hirst has in mind is presumably one who will accept
his view of education in so far as he is 'intelligent'; but Hirst's idea
of a Christian is not coherent, since Christianity pursues a rational
wholeness and cannot accept an argument that seeks to isolate
truth from truth. If religious beliefs are logically and existentially
irrelevant to education, how can they be intelligibly combined with
relevant and intelligible secular concepts as the Christian vision
demands? The Christian who accepts Hirst's position is in fact
thinking irrationally; any Christian must insist that religious belief
does have something to contribute to education and so must refuse
to go along with Hirst's totally secularist position. His argument
for an accommodation with Christianity appears unconvincing,
since it simply begs the question against the truth of Christian
beliefs.

The thrust of Hirst's arguments is towards the irrelevancy of
religious beliefs especially dogmatic Catholicism, for an understanding of education. Clearly the secularisation of modern
thought has resulted in the decline in the use of religious concepts,
and theology is no longer considered by many to be necessary for
an understanding of education. Religion has become a private

concern with various individual beliefs current in a pluralist society.
Hirst argues that religion must never be allowed to determine or
influence public issues, and must accept the purely private status
it is offered.[90] For him, the school must be neutral; but it would
seem that this can only be a theoretically constructed neutrality,
since the majority of schools in England and Wales are not neutral,
being properly described as secular and pluralist, despite the
religious education provisions of the 1988 Education Reform Act.
These schools require a consensus at their core, and involve a
commitment to values which make society possible. These values
form a basic social morality, and are pragmatically justified. They
include respect for persons, property, the right to hold differing
opinions, equality and tolerance etc. These elements can be clearly
seen in school-based personal, social and moral education courses.
Consequently, the notion of 'neutrality' for schools is not sustain-
able, for as Harvey Cox says:

> . . . when we rely as a society on the values which safeguard but do
> not nurture the symbolic affirmations in which they are anchored
> we have no evidence that the values themselves will continue to
> flourish. Our commitment to pluralism and secular education thus
> seems in some measure contradictory.[91]

Christopher Dawson has pursued this argument in more detail in
his book *The Crisis of Western Education*.

The progress of secularisation has not eliminated the religious
element from education completely, but it has attempted to approach religion from a secular basis such as is advocated by Hirst.
Richard Dearden, in a review of British philosophy of education in
the period 1952 to 1982 observed that there had been no development of Catholic educational philosophy in England and Wales.[92]
Whilst there had been British Catholic philosophers of education,
he noted that these had followed the mainstream in their choice
of topics and methods. However, some Catholic educationalists
since 1982 have presented a case for Church schools which can be
defended on philosophical grounds.[93] Nevertheless, the line of
development taken by many modern educationalists is to argue
that Church schools should cease to favour any particular religious
tradition and its associated values. A number of Catholic educationalists have followed this line, and have placed religion in a more
broadly based context, centering their teaching around knowledge
about world religions, with all the different faith traditions presented as being of equal value. This has been accompanied in

recent years by a clear movement from Realist categories in Catholic education towards a more phenomenological approach. In addition, there have been attempts, mainly in the U.S.A., to open Catholic education up to non-Realist philosophies, such as classical idealism and Christian existentialism, with varying success.[94]

In answer to Hirst's denial that Christianity has anything to offer education, and that this primitive way of looking at education is dead, John Hull says:

> The Christian view of man is that, like the education view, he is unfinished; the Christian context of that process is that the image of God is being daily renewed in us. Christian anthropology, therefore, goes hand in hand with a developmental view of human personhood. As for authority *vs.* freedom, we must distinguish between two concepts of authority; the authoritarian and the authoritative. The authoritarian person contains no criteria and offers no reasons: he is right because he says so. The authoritative person, on the other hand, has his authority because of specific reasons, gives specific criteria based on research or the quality of arguments. Catholics believe that God's authority is authoritative. He and His Church do not, like frustrated parents, shout, 'Do as you're told.' . . .[95]

In regard to Pring's belief that the Church in education lacks an openness essential for the educative process, Hull helps explain the Christian view in the following terms:

> . . . the highest realms to which we are called in Christian spirituality do not call for the mere passive obedience of easily led sheep, dependent children who are to take up our cross and not our syllogism. Christ calls us to be disciples, learners . . . constantly challenged by Christ's question to the apostles, "What do you think?" We are to have a spirit of critical openness — not the proud spirit of complacency that sometimes characterises the academic, but the humble attitude of one who knows that he has much to learn.[96]

Consequently, whilst Catholic education must keep pace with advancing secular thought, it needs also to cultivate personal religious life if it is to remain true to its goals. This is what makes the goals of Christian education distinctive, for it attempts to provide a specifically Christian alternative to purely humanist values. Robert Nowell has encapsulated what Catholic education is about, emphasising openness and critical assimilation in saying that its purpose:

... is to make it considerably more probable that when in later life
the time comes for the pupil to make a choice, or to reaffirm his
commitment to Christ, that choice will be the Christian one ...
That this choice must be free rules out the easy and tempting
solution of conditioning; but for the choice to be free the person
making it must also know ... what that choice and its various
alternatives entail.[97]

The principles which educationalists have used to attack the
Church in education have not always been consistent. Often their
ideological predispositions and inclinations intrude into their work,
and this tends to distort their presentation of what the Church
means by education. There is also a failure by the Church's critics
to distinguish between the basic philosophical issues on which
theories of education depend and the questions of a more practical
nature which bear on the concrete application and techniques in
education — emphasis being placed on means rather than ends.
Christian education is a lifelong process that continues long after
formal schooling is over. Every experience in life is potentially an
opportunity for acquiring a deeper knowledge about what God has
revealed, for the Christian and indeed for all humankind. Edward
Hulmes accurately sums up the main features of Christian education when he says that:

> Christian education would appear to have three essential features.
> To begin with, it establishes faith in Jesus Christ as the foundation
> and guide for correct thinking and right action. Second, it is inte-
> grative, in that it serves to harmonise elements which may otherwise
> tend to be fragmented in individuals and in society. It is thus
> concerned with human beings 'whole and entire', and at each
> succeeding stage of life. Third, it enables individuals to decide for
> themselves whether they will believe or not, by exercising their
> capacity for reason as well as for faith.[98]

This summary of the goals of Christian education is the one which
represents a close approximation of the official Catholic view of
education presented in this chapter. The ideal of Catholic education must be all-embracing, co-terminous with life and based upon
a clear notion of our supernatural end. Religion must not only find
a place in this view, but have first place and be the norm by which
other truths are measured. A Catholic schooling, more specifically,
promotes knowledge and understanding of Catholic beliefs and the
free acceptance of these beliefs. This school-based initiation
should also promote a sense of belonging to a community of faith,
and a sense of responsibility to others.

Summary

The work of the Second Vatican Council clearly strengthened the argument for the retention and development of Catholic schools. Consequently, the Congregation for Catholic Education in 1988 encouraged the Catholic Church across the world 'to examine whether or not the works of the Second Vatican Council have become a reality'. The Congregation urged that this 'reflection ... lead to concrete decisions about what can and should be done to make Catholic schools more effective in meeting the expectations of the Church'.[99] Cardinal Baum, the Prefect of this Congregation at the time, had earlier given some indication of the central problem involved in this process of reflection when he addressed the Synod of Bishops in 1983:

> The basic problem of the Catholic school is that of being what it ought to be. Hence, not only a school of high quality, but a Catholic school, in the full meaning of the term.[100]

The Congregation has consistently expounded the view that the Catholic school is an educational setting within which a critical synthesis should occur between culture and the Catholic religious vision. In claiming to be Catholic the school needs to commit itself to pursuing the meaning, values and truths specific to the Catholic Church. Without this the Catholic school has no reason for existing since the Catholic school is within the Church and must proclaim and live the Catholic faith. This would appear to be the key to an understanding of the Catholic school's cohesiveness and intelligibility. Its specific character must reside in the possibility of teachers, pupils and parents uniting as a school community around a Catholic conception of school life and all its expressions in reference to the Church and Gospel.

Prior to the Second Vatican Council the theory of Catholic education was clearly drawn from dogmatic Church teaching. Scholastic thought provided the framework which gave Catholic education a strong sense of identity and established principles upon which a philosophy of Catholic education could be developed. However, the post-conciliar statements on education have had to face the ecclesial revolution which has changed many of the theological and philosophical assumptions on which Catholic education had rested. Consequently, while the Church continues to promote the search for an explicit philosophy of Catholic education, no all-embracing Catholic philosophy has emerged undergirding the post-conciliar developments. There are in fact many differing interpretations of Catholic education current. It would appear that just as there is a lack of consensus in the general philosophy of education, this is paralleled by disagreement in the philosophy of Catholic education. Nevertheless, Catholics, precisely as Catholics, are not free to accept or reject the essential postulates of Catholic education. These include the Church's understanding of our nature, the nature of truth, sin, grace, revelation, and our supernatural end. Questions of method in teaching are of secondary consideration. The most widely influential statements in the philosophies of education have been dominated by concepts arising out of the behavioural sciences and secular education. The Congregation in Rome used similar modern language in an attempt to bridge this divide. However, the truth is, as Dearden has observed, there has been no development of a specifically Catholic alternative to the dominant concerns of secular education. In fact, those engaged in educational studies continue to question the role of religion in helping to determine educational theory and practice.

In England and Wales, Catholic education has been synonymous with Catholic schooling. As a consequence, discussion of the philosophical foundations for Catholic education tends to be interwoven with justification for the existence of the schools. Little attention has been given to the roots of the problem, and arguments from the practical and expedient have been favoured. There appears to have been a strong assumption among many involved in Catholic education that the goals have already been given and that they need only to be achieved. This view does not take account of the serious neglect of a rationale for Catholic schools. This neglect has made it easier for professional educationalists to be critical of, or more commonly ignore, Catholic education. Many single out one aspect or another of Catholic educational practice, and, by excluding other aspects, they render them incoherent and useless for the purposes of understanding education. The idea of deferred values — that which is done or sought in the light of eternity — which is so central to Catholic education, has no meaning for secular educationalists. Liberal approaches to education which have strongly influenced modern Catholic educational thought, are fully committed to the notion of the individual as a rationally autonomous agent in a pluralist society. Consequently, some Catholics have sought compatibility with these liberal demands and proposed a dualism in Catholic education. This has involved education and

religious nurture being separated and distinguished both conceptually and practically. As Terry McLaughlin says, these are distinguished in the aims and rationale of the school, its structures,
practices and teaching, but especially in the minds of the pupils.[101]
This view of Catholic education is however not based on the
authoritative teaching of the Church, which accepts only an holistic conception of Christian education integrating both the religious
and secular in the school — a critical synthesis between culture
and the Catholic religious vision. Any attempt at analysing Catholic
education in practice needs, therefore, to be based on the characteristics of Catholicism, on what the bishops say about it and on
the individual mission statements of schools. Ultimately, the
Catholic school 'finds its true justification in the mission of the
Church . . .'[102] Rosemary Haughton has argued that Catholicism has
been the attempt to 'integrate the whole of human life in the
search for the Kingdom of God'.[103] This fits well with the official
vision of Catholic education, which aims at the integration of
Catholic education into the whole pattern of human life in all its
aspects; social, vocational, personal, academic, religious and spiritual.

Conclusion

This Chapter has established that Catholic schools are required by
the Church to be different from largely secular institutions in their
philosophy, mission and actions. The Church recognises that
Catholic schools will differ from each country and from school to
school. However, the Church maintains that there are general
principles which reflect the universality of the Church and which
should form the basis of a Catholic education. For example, Catholic schools must be engaged in 'the formation of the whole person'
by emphasising the central place of Christ in their work. The
Catholic school needs to be imbued with a Catholic theological and
philosophical basis of education, and of life. This foundation allows
schools to serve the Community, the Church, and, through them,
Christ. This chapter's analysis of Church documentation on education, which was selective rather than exhaustive, indicates that
the fundamental problems in Catholic education are theological in
nature. Whilst the main objectives of any school will be reflected
in the curriculum, for the Catholic school the ethos and composition of the school community will play significant parts in influencing the way in which teaching and learning take place. Catholic
schools need to examine their own policies and practices in the

light of the Church's vision and philosophy of education. It can be concluded that, in the context of England and Wales, the articulation of the essential, timeless, non-negotiable aspects of Catholic education as compared with the circumstantial, contemporary and adaptable aspects have been neglected by the Catholic community, and that criticisms of traditional Catholic understandings of education are being strongly voiced by some from within the Church itself.

Notes

1. Cox, H. G., 'The Relationship between Religion and Education', in Sizer, T.R. (ed.), *Religion and Public Education*, University of America Press, 1967, pp. 99–111.
2. Dawson, C., *Enquries into Religion and Culture*, Sheed and Ward, New York, 1937, and *The Crisis of Western Education*, Sheed and Ward, London, 1961.
3. *The Positive Value of Catholic Education*, Statement by the Catholic Bishops of Scotland, 1978, based on their commentary on *The Catholic School*, Congregation for Catholic Education, Rome, 1977, para. 7.
4. Abott, W. M., 'The Dogmatic Constitution on Divine Revelation', in *The Documents of Vatican II*, Collins, London, 1966.
5. Nichols, K.F., *The Basis of Catholic Education*, Catholic Education Council, London, 1969.
6. *The Catholic School*, Congregation for Catholic Education, Rome, 1977, para. 33.
7. *Catechesis in Our Time*, Encyclical of Pope John Paul II, Rome, 1979.
8. *Instruction on the Ecclesial Vocation of the Theologian*, Congregation for the Doctrine of the Faith, Rome, 1990, Section 10.
9. *Instruction on the Ecclesial Vocation of the Theologian*, Congregation for the Doctrine of the Faith, Rome, 1990, Section 10. Brady, B.J., *The Congregation for Catholic Education, The Catholic School and the Thought of Jacques Maritain*, EdD, Columbia University Teachers' College, 1979.
10. *The Religious Dimension of Catholic Education*, Congregation for Catholic Education, Rome, 1988, para. 100.
11. *Catechesis in Our Time, op. cit.*, para. 20.
12. Cf. *Veritatis Splendor*, Encyclical of Pope John Paul II, Rome, 1994
13. Redden A.M., and Ryan, F.A., *Catholic Philosophy of Education* , Bruce, Milwaukee, 1956, p. 133.
14. Pius XI., *Christian Education of Youth*, Encyclical, Rome, 1929.
15. Douglas, A., *Church and School in Scotland*, St. Andrew's Press, Edinburgh, 1982.

84   The Ebbing Tide

16. Malone, R.J., *The Roman Catholic Secondary School as Faith Community: Educational Development and Theological Considerations*, PhD, University of Boston, 1981.
17. See especially a speech by Cardinal Hume to the Conference of Catholic Colleges in 1979 entitled *The Catholic School*, and reprinted in *Signum*, 9th November 1979, Vol. 7:18. In addition, the religious education advisers to the bishops have made strong advocacy of this approach as have many others — see Davies, M., 'The Church's Role in Education', *The Tablet*, 8th October 1983, pp. 975–977.
18. *Acta Apostolicae Sedis Commentarium Officiale*, Rome, 28th June 1988, Vol. LXXX, p. 841 ff.
19. Pohlschneider, J., 'The Declaration on Christian Education, in Vorgrimler, H., (ed.), *Commentary on the Documents of Vatican II*, Burns and Oates, London, 1969, Volume IV, pp. 1–48.
20. Ryanne, X., *The Third Session*, Faber and Faber, London, 1965, pp. 225–228.
21. *Instruction on the Ecclesial Vocation of the Theologian*, Congregation for the Doctrine of the Faith, Rome, 1990, Section 21.
22. *Declaration on Christian Education*, Rome, 1965, para. 1.
23. Maritain, J., *op. cit.*, pp. 2–4.
24. *The Catholic School*, Congregation for Catholic Education, Rome, 1977, para. 58.
25. Maritain, J., *op. cit.*, p. 3.
26. *Declaration on Christian Education*, Rome, 1965, para. 8.
27. *The Religious Dimension of Catholic Education*, Congregation for Catholic Education, Rome, 1988, para. 63.
28. *The Catholic School*, Congregation for Catholic Education, Rome, 1977, para. 49.
29. *Ibid.*, para. 19.
30. *Ibid.*, para. 32.
31. Catechesis in Our Time, *op. cit.*, para. 69.
32. Wenham, J., *The School Manager in Denominational Schools*, St Anselm's Press, London, 1892, p. 213.
33. *The Catholic School*, Congregation for Catholic Education, Rome, 1977, para 56.
34. Bottomley, F., 'New Directions for Catholic Education', *The Cergy Review*, January 1974, pp. 42–52.
35. *The Religious Dimension of Catholic Education*, Congregation for Catholic Education, Rome, 1988, para. 51.
36. *Declaration on Christian Education*, Rome, 1965, para. 6, and *The Religious Dimension of Catholic Education*, Congregation for Catholic Education, Rome, 1988, para. 31.
37. Malone, R.J., *op. cit.*
38. *Ibid.*
39. Buetow, H., *The Catholic School*, Crossroad, New York, 1988, p. 225.
40. *Ibid.*

41. *The Religious Dimension of Catholic Education*, Congregation for Catholic Education, Rome, 1988, para. 101.
42. *The Catholic School*, Congregation for Catholic Education, Rome, 1977, para. 34 and para. 53.
43. *Ibid*, para. 85.
44. *The Religious Dimension of Catholic Education*, Congregation for Catholic Education, Rome, 1988, para. 108.
45. The three national advisers and their major work to date are: Nichols, K., *Cornerstone* St Paul Publications, Slough, 1978; Nichols, K., *Orientations*, St Paul Publications, Slough, 1979; Purnell, A.P., *Our Faith Story*, Collins, London, 1985; Gallagher, J., *Our Faith Our Schools*, Bishops of England and Wales, London, 1988; Gallagher, J., *Guidelines*, Bishops' Conference of England and Wales, London, 1986.
46. Winter, M., *Whatever Happened to Vatican II?*, Sheed and Ward, London, 1985, p. 103.
47. Hogan, P. , 'Ethos in Schools', *The Furrow*, November 1984, pp. 693–703.
48. Buber, M., *Between Man and Man*, Fontana Library, Collins, London, 1971, p. 125. See also, Cohen, A., *The Educational Philosophy of Martin Buber*, Associated University Press, London, 1988.
49. *The Religious Dimension of Catholic Education*, Congregation for Catholic Education, Rome, 1988, para. 23.
50. Pius XI, *op. cit.*, para. 83.
51. *The Religious Dimension of Catholic Education*, Congregation for Catholic Education, Rome, 1988, para. 103.
52. *Ibid.*, para. 104.
53. *Ibid.*, para. 98.
54. *Ibid.*, para. 100.
55. *Declaration on Catholic Education*, Bishops' Conference of England and Wales, 1929.
56. Evenett, H.O., *The Catholic Schools of England*, CUP, 1944, p. 124.
57. *The Case for Catholic Schools*, Catholic Education Council, London, 1951.
58. Tucker, B. (ed.), *Catholic Education in a Secular Society*, Sheed and Ward, London 1968 and Jebb, P. (ed.), *Religious Education*, Darton, Longman and Todd, London, 1968.
59. *The Case for Catholic Schools*, Catholic Education Council, London, 1955, p. 1.
60. Beck, G.A., 'Aims in Education: Neo-Thomism', in Hollins, T.H.B., (ed.), *The Aims of Education*, Manchester University Press, 1964, pp. 109–132.
61. Beck, G.A., 'The Rights of Parents: an address at the Second Vatican Council', *Catholic Education Journal*, Vol. 8, No. 2, March–April 1965, p. 5.
62. *To Teach as Jesus Did*, USA Bishops' Conference, 1972.
63. *Memorandum on the Appointment of Teachers*, 1974, *Statement on Catholic Schools*, 1978, Bishops' Conference of England and Wales.

64. Nichols, K.F. (ed.), *Theology and Education*, St Paul Publications, Slough, 1974, p. ix.
65. *Ibid.*, p. xiii.
66. *A Report of the Bishops of England and Wales, Signposts and Homecomings: The Educative Task of the Catholic Community*, St Paul Publications, Slough, 1981, p. 1.
67. *Weaving the Web* was rejected for use in the Archdiocese of Birmingham and the Diocese of Salford by their respective bishops.
68. *The Education Reform Bill — A Commentary for Catholics*, produced by the Bishops' Conference of England and Wales, 1988, and the most recent statement 'A Joint Pastoral Letter from the Bishops of England and Wales for Education Sunday on Catholic Education', 27th January 1991.
69. *Evaluating the Distinctive Nature of the Catholic School*, Bishops' Conference of England and Wales, 1988.
70. Hume, B., *Towards a Civilisation of Love*, Hodder and Stoughton, London, 1988, pp. 104–105.
71. *Ibid.*, p. 105.
72. *Ibid.*, pp. 105–106.
73. Kelly, P. , *Catholic Schools*, Diocese of Salford, 1987, p. 11.
74. Pring, R.A., 'Aims of Education', in Tucker, B. *op. cit.*, pp. 98–146.
75. *Ibid.*
76. *Ibid.*, p. 100.
77. *Ibid.*, p. 126.
78. For a full commentary on Maritain's view see Brady, B.J., *op cit.*
79. *Ibid.*, p. 10.
80. Peterson, M.L., *Philosophy of Education*, Intervarsity Press, Leicester, 1986, pp. 45–46. A classic exposition of Thomism and education is given in Donlon, T.C., *Theology and Education*, W. M. Brown, Dubuque, Iowa, 1952.
81. Mayer, M.H., *The Philosophy of Teaching of St Thomas Aquinas*, Bruce, New York, 1929.
82. See Mays, J.B., *Education and the Urban Child*, Liverpool University Press, 1962, and *Growing Up in the City*, LUP, 1964. Mays's study of education in Liverpool in the early 1960s found that Catholic schools were dominated by the clergy and that they placed emphasis on conformity to authority and dogma.
83. Mitchell, B., *What is Christian Education?*, Bloxham Conference Paper June 1981.
84. *Ibid.*
85. Hirst, P., *Moral Education in a Secular Society*, University of London Press, 1974, p. 77 ff.
86. *Ibid.*, p. 77.
87. *Ibid.*, p. 80.
88. *Ibid.*, p. 85.
89. Hirst, P., 'Religious beliefs and educational principles', *Learning for Living*, No. 15, 1976, pp. 155–157.

90. Hirst, P., *Moral Education in a Secular Society*, University of London Press, 1974, p. 81.
91. Cox, H. G., 'The Relationship between Religion and Education', in Sizer, T.R. (ed.), *Religion and Public Education*, University of America Press, 1967, pp. 99–111.
92. Dearden, R.F., 'Philosophy of Education 1952–1982', *British Journal of Educational Studies*, Vol. XXX, No. 1, 1982, pp. 57–71.
93. Haldane, J., 'Religious Education in a Pluralist Society', *British Journal of Educational Studies*, Vol. XXXIV, June 1986, pp. 161–181. 'Metaphysics in the Philosophy of Education', *British Journal of the Philosophy of Education*, Vol. 23, No. 2, 1989. 'Chesterton's Philosophy of Education', *Philosophy*, Vol. 65, No. 251, 1990, pp. 65–80.
94. Buetow, H., *op. cit.*, pp. 54–64.
95. Hull, J. M., *op. cit.*, pp. 198–205.
96. *Ibid*.
97. Nowell, R., quoted in W. Glynn, *Aims and Objectives of Catholic Education*, Catholic Teachers' Federation, London, 1980, p. 14.
98. Hulmes, E., *Education and Cultural Diversity*, Longman, London, 1989, p. 86.
99. *The Religious Dimension of Catholic Education*, Congregation for Catholic Education, Rome, 1988.
100. Baum, W., 'Vatican Report on Catholic Education to the Synod of Bishops in 1983', *Origins*, 17th November 1983, pp. 391–395.
101. McLaughlin, T.H., *Parental Rights in Religious Upbringing and Religious Education within a Liberal Perspective*, PhD, University of London, 1990, p. 212. These ideas are almost identical to the ones proposed in De Ferrari, T.M., 'American Catholic Education and Vatican Council II', *Catholic Educational Review*, November, 1965, Vol. LXIII, No. 8, pp. 532–541.
102. *The Religious Dimension of Catholic Education*, Congregation for Catholic Education, Rome, 1988, para. 34.
103. Haughton, R., *The Catholic Thing*, The Catholic Book Club, London, 1979, pp. 15–16.

4

Catholic Education Policy
and Provision 1960–1990

Introduction

In the 1960s the Catholic Church in England and Wales still had a number of coherent educational policies which were driven by definite religious principles. During this period the Catholic Education Council (CEC) aimed to remain aloof from party political considerations, whilst ensuring that Catholic schools gained fully from government policies. Catholic education policy had to consider the changing priorities of successive governments. Maurice Kogan, writing almost a decade later, claimed that the CEC in developing and presenting its educational policy had become 'a minority group which has become party to a continuing and relatively undisturbed consensus.'[1] His observations are based on the assumption that power is distributed within the whole educational system and that 'policy-making' is a 'partnership' between the providers of schooling, which includes the Catholic Church. However, Catholic influence on educational developments at national and local level since the late 1970s is hard to detect and the direction of central government policy since the 1980s has led, as argued by me in this book, to less consultation with the Catholic Church. It has also become commonplace in educational policy literature to refer to the 'breakdown of consensus'. This renders Kogan's comments about the 1970s less appropriate for the 1990s. The development of official Catholic educational policy needs to be examined in response to the changes that have taken place in the Church and in society.

The Social Context: A Preliminary Note

The ethnic Irish numerically constitute the largest strand in contemporary English Catholicism. It has been calculated that between one-fifth and one-quarter of English Catholics are either
first or second generation Irish immigrants. Another third of English Catholics have an Irish ancestry which originated three or more
generations ago. In addition to the Irish there are also the old
English families from the recusant period and in more recent times
immigrants from Europe and the Commonwealth. Converts represent around 8% (which includes their children). Michael Hornsby-
Smith has claimed that it is important to 'demythologise the past',
for he rejects any idea that there had been a golden age in English
Catholicism and goes on to say:

> ... one cannot uncritically assume that the Catholic Church during
> the nineteenth century and up to the 1950s was a cohesive, tightly-
> knit body, sharing the same values and beliefs, substantially united
> under a clerical leadership, and manifesting an absence of divisive
> conflicts.[2]

This is an interesting comment, given the widespread critical
assertion that pre-Vatican II English Catholicism had a 'ghetto
mentality'. It was certainly the case that the recusants and Irish
immigrants differed in both national identity and social class. In a
Gallup Omnibus survey of 1978 around 11% of the adult population
of England and Wales claimed to be Roman Catholics.[3] Including
children, this indicated that there were 5.4 million English Catholics. Catholics on average were slightly younger than the general
population and had a tendency to be 'working class' and to vote
Labour. The survey also suggested that around 40% of Catholics
attended Mass each week and that this compared with around 8%
of the rest of the population attending other religious services. The
number of Catholics regularly attending Sunday Mass in 1991 was
1,292,312 and this number has continued to decline. In addition,
the worshipping Catholic community, from whom the funds for
Catholic schools are raised, would appear to have a strongly ageing
profile. Hornsby-Smith concluded from his research that the
Catholic Church in 1987 can be regarded 'as a domesticated
denomination unlikely to rock the boat of British complacency to
any marked extent, content with the *status quo*'.[4]

The influence of the Second Vatican Council on the Catholic
community had major implications for future attitudes towards

Catholic education. In particular, the Council affected the way some perceived the government and control of schools. As Michael Winter says:

> One change has taken place which is irreversible. It is not in the area of institutions but belongs to the realm of attitudes, and I refer to the arrival of free speech in the Church.[5]

Today it is possible for Catholics to behave and express themselves publicly in ways which, before the Second Vatican Council, required considerable courage. The Catholic Church no longer, it appears, exacts a high price for deviation. Secular determinants of values and attitudes which were once transcended by Catholicism are now commonplace. Before the Second Vatican Council the bishops spoke unambiguously and authoritatively and Catholics responded positively, at least in public.

Bill McSweeney identifies the emergence of three strands of Catholicism after the Second Vatican Council. They are: political, charismatic and traditional Catholicism, and all are organised within the Church. Political Catholicism seeks to transform Catholicism into a movement for the elimination of social and political injustice more or less along socialist lines. Charismatic Catholicism seeks to renew the Church by renewing its liturgical life, and the origins of this movement lie in an evangelical approach. It is characterised by a distinctive style of worship — enthusiastic, spontaneous and given to speaking in tongues. Traditional Catholicism's main focus is the liturgy and opposition to change.[6] McSweeney proceeds to say that the existence of these different theologies and organisations is not pluralism, but individualism, an individualism which threatens the survival of the religious community for it has a tendency to fragment that community. He concludes:

> Before the Second Vatican Council, Catholicism was united by common beliefs in the sense that the Pope and his Curia enjoyed legitimate authority and, through the episcopacy, controlled the faith of Catholics, successfully preventing public challenge to the Roman definition of orthodoxy. After the Council, Catholics began to demonstrate their religious freedom for the first time and to express their emancipation from clerical and Roman authority.[7]

Much of this can be seen in England and Wales by the proliferation of dissent on fundamental questions of authority and principles as relating to Catholic schools. There appears to be no identifiable continuity with a recognisably Catholic educational tradition, as

Catholics appear no longer to be united by common beliefs and practices. More pointedly, McSweeney says:

> Modern Catholicism, deprived of the means of controlling the beliefs and values of its adherents and ensuring a degree of consensus necessary for it to claim political significance and moral authority, is rapidly becoming an association of disparate groups and individuals whose affiliation to the Church is an expression of common origin rather than common commitment.[8]

McSweeney's claim does not appear to take account of the common commitment involved among Catholics in their acceptance of the Creed, Mass and Sacraments. Nevertheless, with regard to the 'consensus necessary for it (the Church) to claim political significance', an assessment of education policy during the last thirty years provides some justification for his claims.

Phase One: Stability and Expansion 1960–1970

In 1960 the Catholic school population stood at 681,000 children in 2,700 primary and secondary schools in England and Wales. Within this figure 73,000 places were in 590 Catholic independent schools, which had 41,000 non-Catholics compared with only 9,000 in the whole of the Catholic voluntary-aided sector.[9] In percentage terms the Catholic Church had a disproportionate share of the independent sector compared with its overall membership, but its independent schools were generally small, and they had a majority of non-Catholics on their rolls. Baptisms, the criterion by which the Catholic authorities choose to predict future school provision, had stood at 90,000 per annum in the mid-1950s, rising to their peak of 137,000 in the mid-1960s. This represented 16% of all births in England and Wales, and to this must be added immigrants from Ireland and elsewhere, and converts with children.[10] Up to the 1959 negotiations for increased capital grant aid for schools, the Catholic Church had planned to spend around £80 million on school buildings compared with the Church of England's £40 million.[11] The Catholic Church continued to give priority to its schools over all else, and with the expanded numbers, schools became overcrowded with an average ratio of 33 children per teacher compared to 26.8 in Church of England schools. Staffing problems were also more acute in Catholic schools and from 1960 there was a significant increase in the number of non-Catholic teachers employed in them. Indeed, the pressure for new provision led to the establishment of a National Catholic Building Office in Manchester to co-ordinate the expansion of school places.[12] The Catholic school system, as shown by diocesan directories, became noticeably more systematic and planned from this period since there was a move away from the parochial system of oversight towards diocesan organisation. It was said of this period that the Catholic school system was the only one which was permanently expanding at the base.[13] It was not surprising that an article in the October 1961 edition of *Education* predicted that the Catholic Church would reopen the debate about the level of grant support to aided schools.[14]

At the major political party conferences in September 1961 the religious aspects of education, including the position of aided status, were not discussed. The Labour Party had banned discussion of Church schools from conference agendas as far back as 1911 as a result of the divisive effect it had on the Party. However, at the annual conference of the Catholic Teachers Federation in December 1961, a resolution was passed which read:

> That Conference views with deepest concern the serious shortage of Catholic school provision, which is aggravated by the rising Catholic school population, and urges the Minister, in the spirit of the Education Acts, to open discussions with the Catholic Education Council with a view to alleviating, by increased financial aid, the intolerable burden placed upon Catholic education.[15]

A few months later, the Secretary of the CEC, Richard Cunningham, published an article in the influential *Dublin Review* which said: 'The size of the financial burdens still confronting Catholics must before long compel them to seek new legislation.'[16] This policy became fully explicit in the Memorandum sent to the Ministry of Education by the Chairman of the CEC in 1963. In it Bishop Beck argued for further financial assistance, especially for new primary schools as a result of the increasing growth and movement of the Catholic population.[17] The 1944 Education Act had envisaged a static situation for aided schools which the Memorandum claimed was unrealistic and unfair. Soon afterwards, a meeting was held between the CEC and the Ministry of Education in which the Minister said that no legislation would be possible during the existing Parliament, and advised the Catholic body not to press for it.[18]

Pressure for new legislation mounted from the CEC, especially with developing proposals for the raising of the school leaving age, the publication of the *Newsom Report* in 1963, and more particularly the reorganisation of secondary education which had become official Labour Party policy. Indeed, it is within the context of comprehensive reorganisation policies that the claim for increased financial support to aided schools must be viewed. The official Catholic attitude to comprehensive reorganisation was favourable from the outset. Catholics, it was stated, could have no objection to comprehensive schools on religious grounds,[19] and the Chairman of the CEC observed that:

> There were many who held that the comprehensive pattern was more in keeping with the general Christian philosophy of the equality of all men before God.[20]

More importantly, he made explicit the Catholic policy to follow, as far as possible, the local pattern of reorganisation adopted by LEAs. There appeared to be a real desire on the part of the Church and the government to ensure that financial problems should not hamper co-operation on the part of voluntary schools in local plans for reorganisation of secondary education.[21] The Church's position was that since Catholics had paid to create the present system, they should not have to pay again to alter it. In an article in the *Times Educational Supplement*, Bishop Beck wrote that Catholic schools should not be 'financially worse off if they decided to fall in with the [Comprehensive] scheme'.[22]

At the time of Labour's victory in the General Election of 1964, there were already in existence eleven Catholic aided comprehensive schools with some 5,514 pupils.[23] A quarter of all local education authorities had made major changes in their selection procedures between 1960 and 1964 and the National Foundation for Educational Research had found evidence that there was a new readiness to accept the comprehensive solution in 1964. It claimed that 71% of all local authorities had, or intended to establish, some form of comprehensive education.[24] However, any reorganisation of the Catholic sector would entail expenditure by the Church of a full quarter of the capital costs in order to implement government policy. Thus, Bishop Beck in January 1965 once again called for financial assistance.[25] The Catholic Teachers Federation also called for 100% of the capital costs for all aided schools.[26] In a House of Commons debate on 21st January 1965, which Bishop Beck attended, both the Labour government and the Conservative opposition agreed that voluntary schools should be protected against additional costs of proceeding with comprehensive schemes.[27] The general mood of the opponents of comprehensive reorganisation in the Church was one of caution, rather than outright opposition.

The *Catholic Herald* accused the CEC of proposing wholesale comprehensive patterns. This was formally denied by the Council in October 1964 and the Secretary wrote to the *Catholic Herald* to explain its position.[28] In February 1965 the Bishop of Salford complained that:

> . . . some of the reasons for the suggested changes are not educational at all and that does introduce a little note of hesitancy on our part.[29]

Bishop Beck had announced that Catholics should not commit themselves to an idea 'which had no guarantee of permanence'.[30] His real policy was outlined in a Pastoral Letter, which read:

> There is no common Catholic view on the merits or demerits of comprehensive secondary education. Some Catholics are in favour of the system. Some are opposed to it . . . The Catholic bishops have taken the view that in any given area the pattern of Catholic secondary education should follow broadly the pattern adopted by the local authority. It would be unfortunate and would lead to tension and strain if, for example, the local authorities pattern of secondary schools would seem to be in competition and this could well lead to a clash of loyalties, particularly for Catholic parents whose children may have failed to obtain admission to a grammar school.[31]

This policy was defended around the country by diocesan school commissioners.[32] The CEC believed that the political climate was favourable to pressure for further legislation especially since their claim was linked completely with the government's educational policy. The confidence in this stance was expressed by Cardinal Heenan at a Mass in Westminster Cathedral in March 1965, at which the Prime Minister and members of the Cabinet were in attendance, when he said:

> Legislation on Church schools is no longer a controversial issue between religious denominations or political parties.[33]

There had been a degree of rapprochement between the denominations, especially between members of the Free Churches and Catholics. However, any proposed legislation on Church schools, contrary to what Cardinal Heenan had said, was still a controversial issue among politicians at local and national level. Archbishop Beck, having become the new Archbishop of Liverpool in 1965, made it clear that even without comprehensive reorganisation it would take the Catholic body between twenty and thirty years to pay for existing schools.[34] By January 1966 the bishops reported that:

> If Catholics are to participate fully in comprehensive reorganisation, government financial aid is essential — representations made by Catholic bodies are now being considered by the Government.[35]

On 14th February 1966, the Secretary of State for Education and Science announced to the House of Commons his intention to bring forward a Bill to extend grants to voluntary schools. The proposed increase was to 80%, rather than the 85% of capital building grants which the Catholic Church claimed was essential for it to implement the reorganisation schemes resulting from Circular 10/65. The Secretary of State, in this circular, requested all LEAs to submit for his approval schemes of reorganisation designed to eliminate selection at eleven plus and to provide education for all levels of ability in comprehensive schools. Various ways in which this might be achieved were outlined in the circular and included all through schools for children aged 11 to 18, first schools for children up to the age of 8 or 9 years, middle schools for children aged 8 or 9 to 12 or 13 years and upper schools for older pupils, schools for children aged between 11 and 16 followed by education either in a sixth form or a college of further education. Some of these schemes involved substantial capital expenditure on the part of the Catholic authorities.

An additional difficulty faced by the Catholic Church was that the boundaries of each diocese did not fit easily into local government boundaries. Consequently, children were often sent to schools outside the local authority areas in which they resided. For example, Archbishop Beck's own Archdiocese of Liverpool had 400 schools in 1965 which were shared among eight local education authorities.[36] Therefore, for the Catholic system it was desirable that there should be a degree of uniformity in the type of comprehensive reorganisation between neighbouring authorities. In the absence of uniformity, the Catholic policy was to fix, as far as possible, their own catchment areas irrespective of local authority boundaries.[37] The age of transfer between schools was certainly a problem between some dioceses and LEAs. In 1966 Luton LEA adopted a sixth form college scheme for its 16–18 age range, whilst the Catholic schools in the town retained their 11–18 provision, since it was not financially viable for them to establish a voluntary-aided sixth form college. Since Catholic schools were generally small outside urban areas, it was hard to see how many of them could support the range of abilities the orthodox model of a comprehensive school required. As a result Catholic schools often found themselves with no satisfactory alternative to falling in with a scheme that they had played little part in formulating and had found it difficult to influence. Indeed, Archbishop Beck admitted that many of the changes at local level were dictated by necessity. It was inevitable that tensions and conflict between parents, local authorities and Church authorities would arise. James Murphy has remarked that social considerations and class or political solidarity often carried more weight than advice or instructions from Church leaders from this time onwards.[38] At the inaugural meeting of the Association of Voluntary Aided Schools, which had a number of Catholic members, it was announced by the Chairman that voluntary-aided status made it possible to resist or delay reorganisation plans.[39] At the philosophical level, Arthur Beales spoke of 'social equality' being an 'optimism which in the given circumstances is but superstition', and he went on to say that many Catholics appeared to assume, wrongly, that social equality through comprehensive reorganisation would hasten personal salvation.[40] Whilst a number of articles appeared in the Catholic press supporting comprehensive schools, there was mounting criticism of Catholic educational policy from radical groups within the Church.

Two books which questioned the high priority the Church had given to providing denominational schools were published in 1968. *Religious Education*, edited by Philip Jebb, and *Catholic Education in a Secular Society*, edited by Bernard Tucker, made some devastating criticisms of Catholic policy on schools. The latter opened with:

> There is a growing minority in the Church which finds the common Catholic position on education questionable.[41]

From this critical opening it went on to list a number of objections to Catholic schooling and concluded that the Catholic school had failed. It was argued that the 'ghetto mentality' which was responsible for educating Catholics in a minority culture was wrong and that the financial commitments to maintain the schools were too high.[42] In 1966 the Union of Catholic Students published *The Case for Catholic Schools*, in which it was claimed that there was no accurate knowledge of the extent of the Church's financial commitments to its educational policy. It further stated that there was no rigorous educational philosophy and no plans for research into the effectiveness of Catholic policy. This student document caused much discussion at the time in the Catholic press, but official reaction tended to dismiss it.[43] Anthony Spencer, who had previously worked for the CEC, spoke of the Catholic policy on schools as an 'untested and failing orthodoxy'.[44] This resulted in a scathing attack from the Secretary of the Council who said of Spencer that it was unfortunate that he should advocate research, but at the same time provide the benefit of his results in advance.[45] In Philip Jebb's collection of articles it was argued that official Catholic policy relied on *a priori* argument and an appeal to inherited wisdom. It was further argued, without much evidence, that there had been no continuous policy of denominational education in the Catholic Church in England until the close of the nineteenth century. It was claimed that non-denominational education might have been the norm, and Michael Gaine claimed that existing Catholic education policy could not be justified by an appeal to its historical origins.[46] By dismissing the *a priori* and historical arguments, the critics turned the argument on policy into a debate about empirical questions, founded on socio-religious research studies.

These sociologically based empirical studies, conducted by various individuals into Catholic schooling, were used in support of a wide and not always consistent range of views. It was argued by Monica Lawlor that a specifically Catholic-oriented education should only be given to children between the ages of 9–12. This was based on the 'observation' that adolescents were less likely to accept information on any topic second-hand and that they needed to 'restructure and test out the reality and validity of what they have learned'.[47] The central Catholic policy in providing a distinctive ethos for Catholic children in Catholic schools which assisted with their religious formation and complemented the home and parish was severely criticised on a number of grounds. It was regarded as being too nebulous a concept on which to base a respectable educational argument. In particular it was pointed out that independent schools had always had large numbers of non-Catholics in them and this was used as an example of the gap between what the policy-makers said about Catholic atmosphere, and what actually happened in schools.[48] The reasons why young Catholics lapsed from the practice of their religion was due, it was claimed, to the over-protective influence of a Catholic school and therefore on meeting the outside world they promptly lapsed.[49]

Mass attendance figures were used to demonstrate that there was no connection between Catholic schooling and future attendance at Mass. Spencer, using studies from America, claimed to find similar results in England and Wales — that the family home atmosphere was a more important factor in determining future religious behaviour than the Catholic school.[50] Another academic critic claimed:

> There are some historical grounds for believing that a common school, in which the children of Christians of various kinds together with the children of 'pagans' are educated side by side, would be a means of breaking out of the cultural ghetto constructed by and for Catholics since the sixteenth century.[51]

This claim contradicts Gaine's argument that Catholic schooling was a more recent policy of the bishops.

Between 1965 and 1970 the opposition from within the Church to existing Catholic educational policy was intense. The opponents were generally liberal, but a number of them were Marxists. This radical movement was confined to a small elite of Catholic intellectuals who published a journal called *Slant* between 1965 and 1970 to give expression to their views. One of its leaders was Terry Eagleton, a Fellow of Wadham College, Oxford, who wrote:

> Most people who have gone through the process of Catholic education and emerged with some salvaged awareness won't need to be told that there is something badly wrong with our schools.[52]

Another 'Catholic Marxist', Michael Hennessy, wrote that Catholic educational policy was enforced by threats of eternal damnation and mortal sin. He went on to say that these pressures had been unchallenged since the Church, meaning the clerically dominated Church, had been able to present its own policy to central and local government and to other Churches with no reference to the growing body of Catholics who questioned the schools policy. As might be expected Catholic private education was attacked and he concluded:

> The fundamental question of the necessity for and role of the Catholic school and college are suppressed beneath the policies of the hierarchy to maintain control over the education of Catholics.[53]

Slant saw the basic problem in the world as that of the growing gap between the rich and poor and saw the Church's role as one that made a contribution to the solution. The articles in *Slant* argued that the Church could begin its contribution by the abolition of all

Catholic private schools and the integration of Catholic voluntary
aided schools into the county system. None of these radical ideas
was ever entertained by the bishops nor did they feel the need to
make any official response to them. *Slant's* ideas remained confined
to a small vocal group of intellectuals.

More moderate criticism was voiced by Anthony Spencer who
called for a moratorium on new school building until official policy
had been fully evaluated.[54] Arthur Beales, one of the great defenders of Catholic schools, whilst rejecting most of the attacks on
them, called for fewer schools of better quality.[55] He was critical of
the expansion programme during the 1960s. However, the bishops
continued to expand the school system despite these criticisms,
and the CEC *Reports and Handbooks* during the 1960s never referred
to any opposition to the policy of the bishops. By 1968 the number
of Catholic schools had risen to 3,042, with a further 30 opened by
1972. Reorganisation along comprehensive lines was slow but
steady: 56 Catholic comprehensive schools in 1968 with 34,644
pupils rising to 157 comprehensive schools by 1972, with 102,384
pupils which amounted to 38.5% of Catholic-aided secondary
school provision in January 1972.[56] The number of Catholic independent schools declined during the 1960s, some of them becoming voluntary-aided, but this arose less from deliberate policy and
was more attributable to the lack of manpower among the Religious
Orders. The Education Act of 1967 was a practical source of
financial relief to the Catholic school system. It increased the
capital grants to voluntary-aided schools from 75% to 80%, and
removed the limitations on the cases where grant was not previously payable. The Act provided 80% grant in all cases where the
need for a school could be demonstrated and where the project
secured a place in an LEA building programme. The measure
commanded all-party support and was a major boost to Catholic
schools.

Phase Two: The Emergence Of Policy Issues 1970–1979

The position of direct-grant schools in the Catholic Church was
never one of exalted status as was often the case with non-Catholic
direct-grant schools. In 1966 there were 34,831 pupils in Catholic
direct-grant schools with 23,380 pupils in Catholic grammar
schools.[57] The report of the Public School Commission, normally
referred to as the *Donnison Report*, showed that, by the late 1960s,
86% of all places in Catholic direct-grant schools were paid for by

local education authorities.[58] All direct-grant schools received 30% of maintenance costs from the State and could raise the rest from fees. However, 25% of places in the year of entry in these schools had to be reserved for local authority use; the local authority could claim an additional 25% of places, all of which were given without charge to the parents. Moreover, local authorities in negotiation with the school could agree even larger numbers of free places above the 50% they were entitled to, and this is what happened in many Catholic direct-grant schools and accounts for the large number of free places in them. In the north of England there were 67 Catholic 'grammar' schools of which 42 were direct-grant.[59] Comprehensive reorganisation threatened Catholic direct-grant schools and the Catholic proportion of them was one third of all direct-grant schools. In addition these schools faced particular problems, since the majority of them were owned and operated by Religious Orders and were single-sex establishments. Reorganising Catholic schools into a comprehensive system raised fundamental questions on the educational and technical level. Nevertheless, few of these schools transferred to voluntary-aided status during the 1960s, and between 1964 and 1974 their number stood constant at 56. The number of Catholic independent schools continued to decline in the same period from 590 to 347.[60]

However, in March 1975 the Labour Government announced its intention to abolish all direct-grant schools. It was planned to cease grant aid from September 1976, unless each direct-grant school signed, by the end of 1975, a declaration of intent to seek voluntary-aided status as a comprehensive. While 48 of the 51 existing Catholic direct-grant schools signed, the other three in Lancashire, an area of relatively high Catholic population, became independent schools. No objection was made by the bishops or their agency, the CEC, to this government policy, but a Catholic direct-grant Action Committee was established among the parents of the schools in an attempt to save them. The CEC did not promote their case, but discussed the financial arrangements with the government concerning the transfer of schools to voluntary-aided status. The main concern appeared to be the building debts and how these might hinder their successful transfer to comprehensive status.[61] It is significant that Bishop Emery, the new Chairman of the CEC, in a meeting with the Department of Education and Science drew attention to the concern that would be felt by Catholics to any proposal to withdraw charitable status from the independent schools.[62] Significantly, he defended the Catholic independent sector even though these schools did not fall under the CEC's auspices, nor under direct diocesan control. The main reason for this defence may have been that there were no Catholic voluntary-aided boarding schools. Bishop Emery was concerned that essential boarding provision would be lost to the Catholic sector. Roy Hattersley had formerly, as Labour's opposition spokesman on education in 1973, attacked the independent schools and threatened to abolish them under the next Labour government.[63] The CEC claimed that it was not concerned with independent status as such, but rather with the preservation of the religious character of these schools. The early 1970s saw comprehensive schools increase to 218 by January 1974 out of a total of 518 Catholic voluntary-aided secondary schools.[64]

In *The Tablet's* leading article of July 1975, entitled 'The Hierarchy and Our Schools', reference was made to the fact that some Catholics, without naming names, were indignant with the bishops for falling in with government policy. Nevertheless, after criticising the CEC for its secret negotiations and lack of consultation with the laity (at the time the CEC and the government were discussing the possibility of a further rise in the level of capital grant aid to voluntary schools), the editorial made clear that the bishops lacked the resources to adopt any other pattern than the State system.[65] This was certainly true of Catholic direct-grant schools, most of which were not in a position to enter the independent sector. Pressure was being applied on the Church by government departments, and Circular 4/74 of 16th April 1974 provided an important indication of the government's view of the role of voluntary schools. The circular noted that, while in many instances diocesan authorities and governors of voluntary-aided schools had responded constructively in the matter of reorganisation plans, there were some cases in which governing bodies had resisted the wishes of the LEAs to achieve a full comprehensive system in the area. The CEC handbook for 1974 had commented on Circular 4/74 and claimed that it was mainly non-denominational schools which had frustrated attempts at reorganisation, and thus disproportionate attention was being given to Catholic schools which had changed status or were in the process of doing so.[66] Nevertheless, the circular invited governors of aided schools to reconsider their position, and threatened to withdraw financial support if they did not co-operate with their LEAs. The Secretary of State for Education and Science further announced that he would use his full powers under the Education Act of 1944, and might seek further legislation, to ensure compliance with his wishes. The 1976 Education Act gave the Secretary of State power to require the governors of voluntary-aided schools to submit proposals for comprehensive reorganisation where this had not already been done.

In 1972 it appeared that the CEC had recognised that school expansion had come to an end with the number of pupils in Catholic schools standing at 899,240.[67] By 1974 this had reached its peak of 944,536, due largely to the raising of the school leaving age. Building costs had doubled between 1964 and 1974, and sites had become more costly. Interest rates were only 8% in 1966, but had risen to 15% in 1974. Between 1953 and 1973 the Department of Education and Science records show grants to diocesan authorities of £112,796,505 and loans in the order of £22,387,371. The total of Catholic building liabilities stood at £70 million.[68] The Education Act of 1975 provided some relief, with the rate of capital grant increased to 85%, as requested by the bishops in 1967. This measure applied to work begun on or after 6th November 1974 which was the date of the First Reading of the Bill in the House of Commons. The exact details of the negotiations between the Government and the Catholic body remain confidential. Nevertheless, Catholic school provision increased, despite cuts introduced by the Government. According to annual statistics the proportion of Catholic State secondary-school provision had expanded from 2.9% in 1949, to 4.4% in 1959, to 7.9% in 1969, to 8.8% in 1979 and reaching 9.8% in 1988.[69] Relative expansion continued, even with immigration from Ireland reduced to a trickle and a lower birth rate, which was especially marked among Catholics in the 1970s. There were other factors, such as the rapid increase in the number of non-Catholic pupils, which helped explain the increase in pupil enrolments. With the election of the Labour Government, 1974–1979, the first signs of the erosion of voluntary school autonomy are discernible in the areas of admissions, the curriculum, teacher training, and the management of schools.

By 1975 the number of Catholic baptisms had fallen to 75,000 per annum.[70] Future admissions policy needed to be clarified in view of the continuing decline in the number of Catholic children. The 1976 CEC report discussed the contribution which Catholic schools could make to the nation as a whole and especially to other denominations.[71] However, the more fundamental point appeared to be the viability of schools threatened with closure, and how far they could be retained with a wider admissions policy. In 1974 the non-Catholic intake had increased to 14,000 for all maintained Catholic voluntary-aided schools, with a total population of 900,000.[72] In 1994 the pupil population of Catholic schools stood at 732,980 whilst non-Catholics accounted for 94,424.[73] Other sectors of the maintained system both county and voluntary, suffered disproportionately in comparison with the Catholic overall position. Consequently, problems arose between LEAs and diocesan school commissions, since the former attempted to manage the decline by restricting the movement of pupils, and this led to negotiations with the CEC.[74] With the growing problem of admissions, which had become increasingly linked to the issue of parental choice, the Labour government promised to introduce legislation in 1977 on admissions and school government. *The Universe*, the Catholic newspaper with the largest circulation, attacked the Education Bills of the Government as a direct assault on Catholic education, but the CEC said this was ill-informed and unfair.[75] Relations between the Government and the Council were still cordial, it would appear.

The role of the CEC was essentially to monitor legislation and offer advice to the bishops. In addition, it collected annual statistics on the age, numbers and type of schools and of the non-Catholic teachers and pupils. However, it never acted as a policy 'think tank'. According to Hornsby-Smith, such a proposal was specifically rejected, by the Education Commission of the bishops in 1971.[76] Dom Patrick Barry, the former headmaster of Ampleforth College and the first Catholic to become Chairman of the Headmasters' Conference, criticised the CEC in 1976 for not being equipped to deal efficiently with Catholic education policy.[77]

In 1975 the government set up the Committee of Enquiry into the Management and Government of Schools (the *Taylor Report: A New Partnership for Our Schools*, 1977). As a result of covert pressure by the CEC, the position of voluntary aided schools was clarified by the Secretary of State in a supplementary letter to the Chairman of the committee.[78] The Secretary of State stated that the committee was not intended to consider those aspects of the government and management of voluntary schools which arose essentially from their voluntary character. This was exactly what the Catholic authorities had asked for and it effectively ended any major review of the 'dual system'. The Labour Government in 1969 considered an Education Bill which the CEC requested should not interfere with the position of governors and trustees of voluntary schools.[79] Nevertheless, it was inevitable that the mounting pressure for changes in the way schools were managed would eventually impinge on voluntary schools by shaping their future direction and development. Indeed, the Inner London Education Authority, in evidence to the Taylor Committee, argued that the local authority should have powers to determine the general character of schools in both the county and voluntary sectors and that this should be especially be the case over admissions. It further claimed that since the voluntary bodies only contributed 15% to the establishment of the schools they should not thus enjoy a majority of foundation governors or managers. It asked that the local authority should have a greater say in voluntary-aided schools and its evidence ended with accusations that Catholic schools did not take their fair share of really difficult children.[80]

There was a limited Catholic contribution to the Great Debate that followed the seminal speech by James Callaghan in October 1976 at Ruskin College, Oxford. Increasingly, the voluntary sector, which also included Anglican, Methodist, Jewish and non-denominational schools, was being treated in a similar way to the LEA system, with little distinction being made for its semi-autonomous status. In a speech to a Catholic teachers association in March 1977, Mrs Shirley Williams, the first Catholic Secretary of State for Education and Science, accused Catholic schools of not preparing children for the real, largely secular world. This was the same criticism being made of all schools at the time. Mrs Williams went further and complained that Catholic schools provided children with a 'rigid set of values which collapsed when they met the outside world'.[81] This claim reflects overtones of the criticisms prevalent in *Slant* during the late 1960s. General criticisms about comprehensive education began to be linked with the concern for standards and the idea of a national curriculum. There was a recognisable consensus of opinion against the educational establishment, which crossed both social and political divisions. In brief, the functionaries of the education system, namely the teachers, were accused of subordinating the needs of children to their own interests and convenience. The roots of later intervention in the curriculum can be found in this period.

In regard to the curriculum in Catholic schools, the question can be raised of whether there had been any distinctive differences between them and the LEA school. Whilst a specificly Catholic curriculum was discussed in 1968 by the CEC, it was increasingly clear that the debate on the Catholic curriculum was becoming blurred. The CEC did institute a parallel study of humanities with the Schools Council, which proceeded against some opposition in the CEC concerning the divisive nature of such a project, but it eventually folded in 1972 without much in the way of any results for use in the Catholic classroom.[82] The issue of the Catholic curriculum is discussed in more detail in Chapter Six. However, the principal problem faced by the Catholic authorities in the 1970s was the economic recession and its implications for the schools. Bishop David Konstant, by this time Chairman of the CEC, complained about the 'swingeing cuts' in the following terms:

> It would be more equitable if we were to invite the government to settle our still considerable capital debts on school building, much of it incurred because as a body we have in the past co-operated enthusiastically and generously with government requirements.[83]

A number of articles began to appear, written by members of the Church, which drew attention to the decline in the birth rate and the still heavy financial commitments of the Catholic body as a whole. These articles questioned the assumption that the dual system should simply carry on without challenge or modification.

The supply of teachers is essential for Catholic schools and it is one of the functions of the CEC to co-ordinate the voluntary effort on this. In 1960 there were twelve Catholic training colleges for teachers and the numbers of students in them were co-ordinated by a Catholic Training Colleges Advisory Committee which had been formed in 1958 to shadow the National Advisory Committee on the Supply and Training of Teachers.[84] The aim of the Catholic equivalent was clearly to provide an adequate supply of teachers for Catholic schools and, to this end, the Catholic authorities were more eager to take up the Government allocation of college training places than were the Church of England.[85] In 1961 negotiations had already begun with the government to expand the Catholic provision in the colleges.[86] The CEC began to discuss the nature of teaching in Catholic schools and established a working party in 1971 to advise on the appointment of teachers.[87] One reason for this could have been the Catholic Teachers Federation's evidence to the House of Commons Select Committee on Teacher Training which showed concern about the anti-denominational proposals adopted by the National Union of Students and in particular expressed concern about the number of non-Catholics training in Catholic colleges.[88] In submission to the James Report the CEC was preoccupied with the Catholic community having a share of places in the colleges.[89] There was little thinking by the CEC on diversification for the colleges, as it was assumed that their main function would continue to be the training of teachers for Catholic schools.

The publication of the government's 1973 White Paper, *Education — A Framework for Expansion*, outlined major expansion but soon this was revised downwards. The CEC, recognising the threat to the colleges, established a Catholic Colleges' Planning Committee with the principals of all the Catholic colleges to negotiate with the government about the future of the colleges.[90] Circular 7/73 of March 1973 invited local authorities to consult with the voluntary colleges in their areas and to take account of their potential contribution both to the training of teachers and to their possible contribution to higher education more generally. This was interpreted by a number of colleges to signal the beginning of diversification, since they could fill some of their lost teaching places with students studying other courses. Catholic thinking had been that these colleges were monotechnic institutions, and any new role was not discussed at national level — for in effect there was no policy by the bishops on how the colleges should respond to a reduction in numbers. By 1975 there were fifteen Colleges of Education in the Catholic orbit, which represented 10% of the national system. Of these, five were scheduled for closure and four others were to merge. There was bitter opposition to these closures, but one college principal said that the Catholic college training system was part of the national system and not an enclave within it, and therefore Catholics should recognise that they were not being singled out for unfavourable treatment. Catholic colleges were to share in the general reduction of places, and he went on to claim that the Catholic colleges had an identity crisis. In addition, his article spoke of the substantial control exercised by national and local bodies outside Catholic influence.[91]

The reorganisation of the Catholic Colleges of Education in line with government policy caused further controversy in the late 1970s. There was great concern among the bishops over the reduction of initial Catholic teacher training, and they fought the proposals largely without success. In 1975 there had been 10,614 students in Catholic training colleges of whom 1,323 were non-Catholic. By 1981 there were 6,300 places left, and not all of the students on them were training to become teachers. However, government policy and attitudes towards the denominational colleges changed under Sir Keith Joseph's tenure at the Department of Education and Science. The Government began to question the proposition that the basic purpose of Catholic teacher-training provision was to secure an adequate supply of teachers for Catholic schools. Alone among the denominations the Catholic Church has been clear about the task of the colleges, namely to produce teachers for Catholic schools. It was also the case that the Church attempted to keep a straightforward personnel link between its colleges and schools. Nevertheless, many of the colleges contained significant numbers of non-Catholics, and many others were on other courses which did not lead to qualified-teacher status. The colleges had diversified in various ways and this had not been formally approved by the bishops, but rather carried out by the individual colleges themselves. It is also important to note that the DES abrogated the former principle of consultation and informed the bishops that:

> . . . in a changing world there could be no commitment to any particular share of the public sector initial teacher training intake for colleges supported by a particular denomination.[92]

The bishops had fought for a share based on Catholic numbers tightly related to the number of pupils in Catholic schools, but had to accept a reduced role which has left the Church with only three free-standing Colleges of Higher Education. In the schools themselves there was a growing trend, recognised earlier by Hornsby-Smith in 1978, towards a rise in the proportion of non-Catholic teachers and pupils, and a rapid decline in the number of Religious, especially Sisters, teaching in Catholic maintained and independent schools.

'Education for the world of work' became a favourite slogan of the Labour government in the late 1970s and politicians increasingly criticised schools for placing too much emphasis on the social development of children rather than on the economic needs of the country. The Conservative Party began, while in opposition, to formulate a policy on education which attempted to replace the post-war trends with a quite different order of priorities. The first among these priorities was the relationship between education and the economy. There was an anti-industrial ethos in schools, it was claimed, and the Conservatives pledged that they would give more emphasis to science and technology in the school curriculum. The Conservative Party began to promote actively the entrepreneurial ideal and a preference for selection within and between schools. In particular the belief that the content of the curriculum should be left to the teaching profession was dismissed. Parental rights in education were given greater focus and Chapter Five deals specifically with these issues. By the election of 1979 these ideas were being developed by the Centre for Policy Studies and in the early stages they were essentially a series of planned compromises. Many of the ideas had come from the Labour Party, which was heading in a similar direction. The first clash with the Catholic authorities came over the question of school transport, which the Labour government had been discussing with the CEC in 1979.[93]

Phase Three: Contraction and Conflict 1979–1990

Sections 55 and 39(5) of the Education Act 1944 make it the duty of each local education authority to provide free transport to the nearest school for all children of compulsory school age whose journey to school is greater than walking distance. Whilst local authorities did not have a statutory duty to provide free transport beyond the nearest school, many nevertheless provided discretionary transport for children attending Church schools. This practice was important to Catholics, since many of their schools attracted children from outside the normal catchment areas. The recently elected Conservative Government intended to abolish this provision through the Education Bill of 1980 which would have entailed the withdrawal of free transport. The CEC argued that the withdrawal of free transport would imperil enrolment to Catholic schools, in particular at those schools in rural areas, and it considered the Government's proposals represented an attack on the 'dual system' itself. The Secretary of State, according to the CEC, was completely 'impervious' to the Catholic claims and objections. Consequently, the bishops mounted a campaign against this provision in the Bill and wrote to all the Catholic MPs requesting support. A prominent Catholic Conservative MP, James Pawsey, voted against the government's proposal in the House of Commons. Section 23 of the Bill was finally defeated in the House of Lords by the Duke of Norfolk's amendment, by 216 votes to 112.[94] The government withdrew the clause and stated that it would not

attempt to reinstate it. At the time this defeat was widely interpreted as being forced on the government by an highly effective
pressure group — namely the Catholic Church. A reading of the
Duke of Norfolk's speech in Parliament clearly indicates that he
did not speak on behalf of the Catholic Church, but rather of the
rural interest — as did a number of other Catholic peers.[95] Soon
afterwards, the Church of England's Secretary of the Board of
Education complained that the Catholic body had used its power
to advance some 'self-interested, narrow, denominational interest'.[96] Nevertheless, it was the Catholic Church which had focused
attention on the issue in and outside Parliament.

In 1981 the publication of the Department of Education and
Science document *The School Curriculum* excluded religious education from its recommended core subjects. The CEC criticised the
Department of Education and Science for this omission and sought
its inclusion in future papers.[97] In addition, the bishops criticised
The School Curriculum since it implied no connection between the
aims of the school and the specific proposals for a 'core' curriculum.
Voluntary-aided schools under the 1944 Education Act had been
ascribed legal control of the curriculum, and so the bishops became
concerned at the interest and subsequent intervention of the
Department of Education and Science, which began issuing a
series of policy consultative documents on the curriculum. Circular
6/81 stated that the DES:

> . . . looks to governors to encourage their schools, within the
> resources available, to develop their curriculum in the light of what
> is said in 'The School Curriculum'.

The Education Act of 1986 confirmed the power of governors to
control the 'secular curriculum', but stated that they must have
regard to the LEA curriculum statement. The process of erosion
of aided schools' powers to determine their own curriculum had
begun and was bound to lead to conflict. It has been said that the
whole purpose and justification for the existence of Catholic
schools is that:

> . . . they continue to offer a genuine and needed form of education
> containing appropriate and significant differences from that offered
> in county schools.[98]

How this was done and, more importantly, how it could be done in
view of the process towards the centralisation of the curriculum
content for all maintained schools, is difficult to see. Between 1902

and 1944 the Catholic maintained school did not have direct control over the curriculum — the bishops had agreed to give this right up in return for aid. Indeed, they had offered on a number of occasions after 1944 to relinquish control of the curriculum in return for further aid.[99] In reality the Catholic position was weak since they did not propose any alternative to the Government proposals, nor did they specify how their general aims of the school translated into the practical reality of constructing a curriculum. Catholic values, they claimed, were inseparable from the curriculum, but no substantive details were ever provided of what this meant in practice.

The obvious lack of any detailed policy on the part of the Catholic Church can be seen in the committee report of the bishops, published in 1980 as *Signposts and Homecomings: the Educative Task of the Catholic Community*. The committee, which had been established in November 1977 under the Chairmanship of Bishop Konstant, had wide terms of reference. It was called upon to 'review the principles of Catholic education and to make recommendations'.[100] The report has some discussion of what is meant by a 'Catholic' as opposed to an LEA school, and there is some reflection upon the whole range of educational enterprises which the Church already supported, including the school system. However, a reading of the report gives the impression that there is a strong tendency to play down the differences between Catholic and LEA schools. The only concrete suggestion made was about the curriculum in recommendation 22 in a list of 32:

> That the diocesan and national commission for Justice and Peace, in consultation with Plater College, Oxford, suggest in what ways the school curriculum can reflect the teachings of the Church on justice and society.[101]

Vague and generalised comments are made throughout the report, which does not envisage a Catholic school system differing radically from the other maintained schools. No recommendations are made for the reorganisation of schools in the light of the fall in numbers. Walsh, commenting on the Report, said that whilst it provided numbers of teachers and pupils, and other valuable statistics, it did not provide any information on the amount of money the Catholic community pay to maintain the system, nor anything about the amount of debt, the amount and size of property each diocese held, and what income would be freed from the sale of redundant school buildings.[102] The report took three years to complete and yet produced few concrete proposals. It was soon largely forgotten.

Michael Hornsby-Smith, commenting shortly after the report was commissioned, claimed that:

> . . . in spite of its size and historical importance in the 'dual system' of state education in England and Wales, there is a conspicuous lack of information about the structure, organisation, legitimating ideologies, goals and achievements of the Catholic system.[103]

The publication of the report did not radically alter this state of affairs for no recommendations are made to guide policy decision-makers. The report referred to the *MacFarlane Report*, which suggested that those in the 16–19 age group would be better served outside the traditional sixth form in secondary schools.[104] The implications for Catholic teenagers was considerable, for it meant that they would have a choice between attending a college of further education for which no denominational provision was made, or attendance at a sixth-form college which would involve the Church in further reorganisation and expense. It is therefore remarkable that the bishops did not comment more fully on the *MacFarlane Report*, as it makes quite explicit that:

> . . . it is essential that governing bodies of voluntary schools should co-operate fully in plans to improve provision for 16–19 year olds.[105]

The *MacFarlane Report* was much concerned with the economic advantages of sixth-form colleges and emphasised vocational training and education for employment relevance. Catholic schools do not serve the full variety or reflect the diversity of educational provision available for the 16–18 year old in the State system. Consequently, the Church has found it impossible to make parallel provision to the local pattern. Nevertheless, by 1980, 85% of all Catholic schools were comprehensive compared with only 15% in 1968, the Church had followed government policies almost everywhere with a comprehensive model of schooling.[106]

The Education Act of 1980 (Section Six) was intended to enhance the scope of parental choice by allowing them 'to express a preference' of school, with which it was the duty of the local authority and governors to comply. Voluntary-aided schools could negotiate an agreement with the LEA in respect of admissions, which would effectively limit any preference expressed by parents. The CEC issued guidelines which stated that Catholic schools should offer their services first to Catholic families and that these children should have prior claim, which admissions policies should reflect. It also warned Catholic governors not to encourage applications of a kind which it would not be possible to accept, but did not specify the nature of such applications. The important consequence of this piece of legislation was that governors in voluntary-aided schools now had a legally defined responsibility to publish an admissions policy. The 1986 (No 2) Education Act (Section 33) imposed a duty on all voluntary-aided schools to pay regard to the LEA views, but the final decision over admissions still lay with the governors. Circular 8/86 (paragraph 18) commented on the 1986 Education Act and made it clear that a defensible basis for preferring one applicant over another must be part of a school's admission policy. Generally, schools were guided by diocesan school commissions on the wording and format of their admissions policy. In order to control the Catholic character of the school, Church guidance suggested a limit of 15% non-Catholic admissions for Catholic schools.[107] Most Catholic schools accepted these guidelines, but it was still for them, and them alone, with all the particularities of their own situation, to set out an admissions policy.

It is an important aspect of admission policies to realise that not all baptised Catholics attend Catholic schools, nor is it the case that Catholics who attend a Catholic primary school automatically proceed to a Catholic secondary school. Among the pupils in Catholic schools there are those who come from practising Catholic families, some from nominally Catholic homes and others who belong to other Christian denominations or adhere to other world faiths or no religion at all. There can be found a diversity of religious background and a pluralism of interest in and commitment to the Catholic faith within the Catholic school today which would have been unthinkable twenty years ago. Leslie Francis, in a study of Catholic schools in the Midlands claims that the needs of non-Catholic pupils are not reflected in the policies adopted by governors. He also found little change in the catechisation, liturgical and doctrinal assumptions in Catholic schools and proposed that these should change to reflect the changing intakes. A more legitimate policy, he advocates, is the closure of some Catholic schools.[108] However, there are many within the Catholic educational world who argue for more liberal and open admission policies. Often they advocate an alternative form of schooling which is not exclusively Catholic, nor Christian in nature.[109] The Catholic Church cannot make a conscious choice to operate schools not specialising in the

pastoral and catechetical care of Catholics without abandoning its
traditional philosophy of Christian education.

In May 1987 Kenneth Baker, the Secretary of State for Education, announced that if the Conservative Party was re-elected at
the forthcoming election, it planned to introduce an Education
Bill. Its intention would be to strengthen the rights of parents in
schools and further reduce the powers of LEAs. Consultative
documents were published over the summer of 1987 and a brief
period of time was given for responses. On its publication, the
effect of the Bill on Catholic schools was clearly seen by the
bishops, who, in November 1987, set up a Advisory Committee
under the Chairmanship of Bishop Konstant to press for amendments to the Bill.[110] In particular the attacks focused on the most
radical aspects of the Bill — the establishment of grant-maintained
schools. There appeared to be certain advantages for the 2,400
Catholic maintained schools in England and Wales since by 'opting
out' of local authority control a school would end the financial
burden of having to provide 15% of future capital expenditure to
ensure its voluntary-aided status. In addition, schools could feder-
ate themselves and Frank Field, Labour MP, urged the Churches
to do precisely this.[111] However, the CEC pointed out that it had
never been Church policy, at least since 1960, to seek 100% capital
grant for Catholic schools.[112] It is interesting to note that the
bishops did pursue a claim for extra financial assistance in 1988 in
the following terms:

> That the financial responsibilities assumed by the Catholic com-
> munity for the education of non-Catholics admitted to Catholic
> schools be considered and appropriate allowances made.[113]

More specifically the bishops objected to the fact that any liabilities in respect of the principal or interest on any loans were not
transferred to the grant-maintained school. The trustees, who
would remain the owners of the school premises, would still be
required to pay any debts taken out on behalf of the school whilst
it had been a voluntary-aided school. If the school proposed its own
discontinuance at some future date, the Secretary of State would
be able to secure compensation for any capital work for which he
had paid grant and there would be a charge on any sale of the
premises to meet redundancy costs or other debts. These debts
would fall on the trustees even though they might not have shared
in the original move to seek grant-maintained status. These serious
reservations about the financial implications of the Act are, how-

ever, only second to those regarding the position under the Act of the trustees themselves.

The bishops took severe exception to the clause that governing bodies had merely to consult the trustees about their own desire to seek grant-maintained status. The Secretary of State had simply to consider any objections made by the trustees and could even modify a trust deed if it appeared to him to be necessary. These provisions allowed parents and governors to remove a school from the LEA and become a semi-autonomous concern maintained fully by a grant from the Government, without the express agreement of the trustees. The bishops noted that 'opting out':

> ... favours the interests of a minority of parents and children at the expense of the majority. Such a general principle is difficult to reconcile with Catholic ideals.[114]

Cardinal Hume in a letter to *The Times* of 13th January 1988, stated that:

> The so-called process as now presented, offers a serious threat to the balance and very provision of Catholic voluntary education.

He proposed that the trustees should have a veto over any application by a Catholic school for grant-maintained status. In the campaign booklet, issued by the bishops, it was argued that the bishops themselves bear a special responsibility for the education of the Catholic community. This is a point they have consistently maintained, for they make clear that it is they who are ultimately responsible for decisions regarding policy. Their 1988 statement on schools said that 'the Bill in its present form could seriously impede the fulfilment of that responsibility'.[115] During the debates on the Bill, and subsequently, the bishops have insisted that Catholic schools cannot be viewed in isolation from each other. They claim that it is the diocesan bishop who must come to a decision, particularly in matters of controversy within the Catholic community, such as in cases of school reorganisation. The bishops claimed that all Catholic schools have an interest in the success of each other and that the Bill would make it impossible for them to co-ordinate overall planning. Transient groups of parents could take a school out of local authority control, thereby harming the interests of the wider Catholic community.[116] Catholics could find that their local Catholic school which had opted out was no longer open to them, except under the school's own admissions criteria. The government's response to this was that it is the responsibility

of the bishops to keep their own foundation governors in order.
Cardinal Hume remarked that the reliance on the bishops' power
to dismiss governors would lead to 'endless conflict and litigation'.[117] The bishops emphasised that Catholic schools which seek
grant maintained status 'without prior consultation and the con-
sent of the community expressed through the trustee' would be
harmful to the interests of the Church.[118]

Nevertheless, the trustees would continue to be responsible for
the appointment of the majority of governors to a potential Catholic grant maintained school:

> . . . for the purpose of securing, so far as practicable, that the
> established character of the school, is preserved and developed and,
> in particular, that the school is conducted in accordance with the
> provisions of any trust deed relating to it.[119]

This provision in the 1988 Act does not prevent parents or governors having different priorities from the diocesan authorities,
which inevitably places greater emphasis on the wording of the
trust deed. Diocesan trust deeds normally provide for:

> . . . property to be held on trust of advancing the Roman Catholic
> religion in the diocese by such means as the Ordinary [bishop] may
> think fit and proper.[120]

Planning for educational provision is an essential part of this
duty, which the bishop fulfils in partnership with the people. The
workings of the 'partnership' are not formally constituted, since
the bishop is regarded as the 'focus of unity' in his diocese. As Mgr
Vincent Nicholls, then Secretary to the Bishops' Conference of
England and Wales, puts it:

> As partners with the State in the dual system, Catholic authorities
> certainly accept that the Secretary of State must approve plans, or,
> if he so decides, veto them. But it is important that the proposals
> to be put to him be drawn up by the Catholic partner in a manner
> consistent with Catholic procedures, i.e. with and under the author-
> ity of the Bishop. In other words, with regard to Catholic schools,
> which are part of Church life, it is for the Church to propose and for
> the Secretary of State merely to accept or reject but not to arbitrate
> between dissenting voices within the Church.[121]

Mgr Nicholls emphasises that the functions of the bishops are not
simply administrative, but that they are responsible for Catholic
schools, which are rooted in communities with shared convictions
and values. However, in the controversy over the Bill and the Act,

some serious differences within the Catholic body emerged. It is clear that the bishops did not receive the same full support from the laity that they had enjoyed at the time of the 1944 Education Act. This last point illustrates how the Catholic community has changed since 1944. There has been an increased unwillingness among some lay Catholics to follow the educational policies of the bishops.

According to the bishops, the Education Reform Bill posed a major threat to Catholic schools especially since they represented over half the voluntary schools eligible for grant maintained status. During the campaign against the Bill the bishops wrote to all Catholic MPs, in an attempt to enlist their support. The reaction of some MPs, in particular members of the Government party, contrasts sharply with the position in 1967. The Education Act of that year increased the capital grants to Catholic schools and was remarkable for a prolonged debate on a Friday afternoon by the intervention of a large number of Catholic MPs who felt it necessary to add their testimonial to the benefits it would bring.[122] No such support was forthcoming from prominent Catholics in 1988. Among the 71 Catholic peers there was little support given to the bishops' campaign against the Bill. In the House of Commons, James Pawsey, a Catholic MP who had sided with the Church in 1980 over the transport clause in the 1980 Education Bill, refused to support the bishops. Many leading lay Conservative Catholics actually attacked the bishops in spite of the admission by the bishops that they were not, in principle, against the opting out provisions in the Bill. The Bill became an Act of Parliament in 1988 with little modification to procedures for the establishment of grant-maintained status. The lack of support for the official Church's position from influential Catholics demonstrates that the degree of consensus necessary for the bishops to claim political significance has declined.

With regard to the curriculum, Section One of the Education Reform Act of 1988 defined it in secular terms with definite instrumental goals as the ultimate objective. Preparation for working life is an avowed goal as is the total development of the child, which included spiritual and moral values. However, little substance was given to these 'spiritual' aims in the Act and the bishops continued to attack the government for the arbitrary idea of what subjects might be useful for earning a living. The bishops had strenuously opposed the Act and stated that Catholic schools had hitherto:

> . . . enjoyed the right to determine the complete school curriculum in the light of their understanding that the educational process serve and nurture the whole person. The proposed Bill takes away the right . . . In practice this means that the Secretary of State and his advisers have the last word on what shall be taught in Catholic schools even if this conflicts with the ideals and practice of Catholic education . . . Secular authorities with no professional competence in the matter . . . have ultimate control of the curriculum in Church schools.[123]

The passage of the Act through Parliament left the Church asking itself how it was to respond to an increasingly secular curriculum which is nationally determined outside its control and influence. Safeguards under Section 17 of the Act do allow for 'exception regulations' to be made on the curriculum and the Secretary of State has said that generally the 'exception' clause will be used in cases where aspects of the National Curriculum are unacceptable on religious grounds to Catholic schools.

In practice, Stuart Maclure asserts, governors of aided schools never exercised their powers over the curriculum, leaving the responsibility to the teaching staff.[124] Nevertheless, there are no longer any guarantees in statute with regard to the curriculum in aided schools. The bishops had proposed an amendment to place aided schools on the same basis as City Technology Colleges, which are exempt from the national curriculum and simply have to provide 'a broad curriculum with an emphasis on science and technology'. The bishops proposed that Catholic schools should have a broad curriculum but with 'an emphasis on the spiritual and moral development of pupils'. Failing this, the bishops argued for a 'Standing Curriculum Committee for Voluntary Schools' to make recommendations to the Secretary of State, which they claimed was needed as a safeguard.[125] All these proposals were rejected by the Government as was the demand of the bishops for representation on the influential curriculum bureaucracies set up by the Act. The bishops have simply been excluded from any formal representation on quangos established by the Government.

The initial fears over the position of religious education in the Education Reform Bill also caused the bishops to make objections. This was despite the assurances of both Section 25(2) of the 1944 Education Act, which made religious education compulsory, and the trust deeds of Catholic schools, which ensure the denominational content of religious education. Marginalisation of religious education in the school curriculum was the root of these objections, since the bishops argued that religious education was the foundation of the entire educational process and that:

> It should provide the context for, and substantially shape the school curriculum.[126]

In Catholic schools approximately 10% of time is usually given to religious education on the timetable, as opposed to only 2.5% in many LEA schools — four periods as opposed to one.[127] In the event, religious education was made part of the 'basic' curriculum. Nevertheless, any further development of the National Curriculum could have threatening implications for a Catholic school's curriculum due to the substantial position religious education holds within it.

The bishops have sustained two major setbacks as a result of the Education Reform Act of 1988. The curriculum structure in Catholic schools is decided by the Secretary of State, and the provisions for grant-maintained status has created a situation of ambiguity of authority which has led to internal conflict within the Catholic community. In both these matters the Church was treated in very much the same way as local authorities. In this context, a revealing comment was made by the deputy director of the Centre for Policy Studies, herself a Catholic, for (after claiming that Catholic schools were in fact State schools) she said, 'Many of the recent pronouncements of the bishops about educational issues have shown how far they have come to share the views, assumptions and aspirations of the LEAs.'[128] The Conservative Party at one stage used to claim that it was the only party which supported voluntary-aided schools — this increasingly looks doubtful. The Labour Party, as far back as 1982, committed itself to hold talks with the Churches to achieve greater 'harmonisation' on practices and policies,[129] so in effect continuing the already well advanced process of treating the voluntary sector identically to the rest of the maintained sector. As recently as March 1989 the Association of Metropolitan Education Authorities passed a resolution which found voluntary aided schools 'damaging' to the interests of education in some localities.[130] In addition, the Church has found considerable difficulty working with some Labour councils, including the 1985 'militant' council in Liverpool, which frustrated the diocesan authorities in operating their schools.[131] There still exists a real threat to the future of Catholic voluntary-aided schools.

As Catholic comprehensives tend to be smaller than their parallel LEA schools, this could result in a loss of competitiveness or even viability. An analysis of Catholic secondary schools in England and Wales in 1990 shows that 58% have fewer than 750 pupils and around 21% have fewer than 500 pupils.[132] In its only reference to denominational education, the government's White Paper, entitled *Better Schools* (March 1985) recognised this fact when it said:

> Such factors as geography, population sparsity, and the need for denominational choice within the dual system may sometimes necessitate unusually small schools.[133]

In July, 1990, Gwent County Council resolved to close St Alban's School in Pontypool, which had 580 pupils on the roll, on the grounds that it lacked viability as a comprehensive. The impetus for Gwent's proposal for the school's closure was government pressure for financial cuts in the local education budget, principally through removing excess places in the maintained system. This would seem to be only part of the reason, for it is surprising that the Labour group on the Council suspended two Labour councillors from the party for voting against this proposal, which it claimed was necessary because of a Conservative government's policies. Government thinking on viable numbers for secondary schools may be deduced from the fact that the very first school in England to be given grant maintained status was an 11–19 school exactly the same size as St Alban's.[134] Thus, the threatened closure of St Alban's seems to have been dependent on political reasons. If the proposals had been accepted by the Welsh Office, it would have been the first time that any county council in Britain had closed a Catholic school without the co-operation of the Church authorities; in the event it rejected Gwent's application to close the school.

A further example of how the government's declared policy of reducing surplus places within the schooling system as a whole can affect Catholic schools is provided by the diocese of Salford's reorganisation plans. Bishop Kelly of Salford sought to reorganise three primary schools, but was prevented from doing so by a ruling from the DES. The bishop's intention was to close the three schools and open one much larger. One of the reasons given by the DES was that there were already surplus places available at local non-Catholic schools and therefore the costs of reorganisation could not be met by the Department.[135] The clear implication here is that Catholic parents should consider sending their children to the local maintained school regardless of whether it is a voluntary-aided or an LEA school. It would seem that the principles which underlie voluntary-aided provision are being ignored by the Government in favour of viewing the maintained sector as a whole. Effectively this 'policy' as it progresses will limit the ability of parents to choose a denominational education for their children.

Ecumenism and Equality in Education Policy

In 1964 the CEC initiated talks with the other denominations on the proposed reorganisation plans for secondary education. Liaison with the Church of England had been a feature of the 1967 negotiations over the Education Act of that year.[136] In 1970 the Church of England and Free Churches invited the CEC to join their Central Joint Education Policy Committee.[137] The CEC accepted associate membership, instead of full participation. Catholic education policy was to remain separate from all others. During the late 1960s there were a number of calls for the Churches to proceed to 'ecumenical schools'. Among Catholics these calls began to increase during the 1970s, but to-date there are only two primary and eight secondary jointly managed schools, shared between the Catholic and Anglican Churches.[138] The arguments for them have varied considerably, but from the Catholic side a number of critics viewed separate Catholic schools as divisive and even a recipe for social division.[139] Vatican II did provide an incentive for further ecumenical discussions with other Churches, although the *Declaration on Christian Education* did not mention joint schools. Nichols has called for the 'dual system' to be worked out afresh in the light of the teachings of *Lumen Gentium* and *Gaudium et Spes*, both Second Vatican Council documents which address themselves to the question of the Church's relationship with the world. Nichols goes on to suggest that these documents should form the basis of policy decisions despite the fact that they are rather vague on concrete advice for educational matters.[140] Two main themes stem from these documents when seen in the light of Vatican II's *Declaration on Ecumenism*. There is the Council's concern to promote dialogue with other Churches, and its concern for the promotion of justice.

On ecumenism, Francis has conducted a number of surveys in which he concludes that Catholic educational policy should follow an ecumenical approach. He criticises the Church for not changing

its basic 'philosophical position' on Catholic schools even though
they admit ever increasing numbers of other faiths. Indeed he says:

> ... it is not sufficient for one denomination to attempt to perpetuate
> its historic educational policy and practice by recruiting pupils from
> other denominations.[141]

A number of Catholics have also criticised the policy of open
admissions and have spoken in particular against the admission of
non-Catholics to Catholic schools. Roy Wake, a Catholic HMI,
claimed that the admission of non-Catholics eroded the Catholic
ethos of schools.[142] However, since there are important differences
between the two major denominations in education, co-operation
and planning seem difficult. The Church of England has always
seen its role as the national Church and has largely merged its
concern for the nation's general education with its specific role in
denominational education. Anglican schools in the maintained
sector vary enormously in composition. The Catholic position has
been to educate Catholic children in Catholic schools with Catholic teachers. The Church of England in its report, *A Future in
Partnership*, published in 1983 rejected the idea of exclusive Church
schools. It advocated a distinctive Christian education, but one
which was open to all. Catholic policy has been to maintain a degree
of exclusivity, but Geoffrey Turner claims that Catholic education
needs to be more open in a world of many faiths, ethnic groupings,
and different values. He argues:

> We now appreciate that there can be a variety of ways of being
> Catholic.[143]

In 1987 the English Anglican / Roman Catholic Committee produced a discussion document, *Joint Schools*. The introduction by
the joint Chairmen makes clear that the contents of the document
are not in any way to be taken as the policy of either Church.
Unfortunately, however, the document contains a number of factual inaccuracies and erroneous assumptions. For example, it states
that joint schools are not a new phenomenon and offers this as an
encouragement to those who feel they are in uncharted waters.
The only evidence cited is the fact that the Jesuits ran a school in
London in 1688 which pupils from any denomination could attend
and their religious views would be respected.[144] Whilst this is true
there is no evidence whatsoever that the Jesuits developed inter-
denominational approaches for worship or religious instruction, or
any other specifically ecumenical educational technique. The

schools the Jesuits established were completely under their control and followed the policies of similar Jesuit schools in Europe which also admitted non-Catholics — although few of the pupils remained Protestants when they left. Indeed, in England it was a result of such schools that the Church of England organised its own free strictly Anglican schools. The two Jesuit schools in London lasted less than three years and were eventually burnt down by Protestant mobs. The discussion paper also speaks of 'minor modifications' to the Education Act of 1944: this completely ignores the major changes won by the denominations with the passing of the Education Act 1967. The response of the Catholic Church to this document has been minimal with no real movement towards joint schools visible except where there is an economic reason. It is significant that in the book written by the leaders of the Catholic and Anglican communities in Liverpool, called *Better Together*, there is little reference made to any co-operation on the education front.[145]

Along with ecumenism there has been a renewed concern for equality and justice, although many mistake this concern as deriving from the Second Vatican Council when in fact it has always been a major concern of the Catholic Church. Nevertheless, Catholic schools have been criticised for becoming, as some see it, bastions of white supremacy and having racist attitudes.[146] Whilst there is no evidence for these accusations, indeed some against them, there has been pressure to change both admissions and religious education policies in Catholic schools.[147] In regard to admissions, a number of Catholic schools have included within their criteria a statement which allows the admission of non-Catholics with special needs. However, criticism continues with some claiming that Catholic schools, despite recent changes, lag behind other schools in the country in regard to education for justice.[148] Theresa Sallnow speaks for a radical alternative and points out that Jesus himself chose the marginalised in society.[149] *The Tablet*, which began a new series of educational supplements from 1976 onwards, became the main journal for the expression of radical ideas and in this respect it has become the successor of the more radical *Slant* and *Herder Correspondence*. Most of *The Tablet's* articles on education have argued against exclusiveness in Catholic maintained schools, but few articles argued against independent schools. On the question of independent schools Lawrence Bright referred to them as extremely divisive for Catholics and said:

. . . official Catholicism is incapable of making any contribution to
the debate, because it is itself based upon a consensus, which holds
that there is no fundamental conflict to be faced.[150]

Since Catholic education policy has concentrated on building up a
parallel system of schools, Bright argues that building programmes
were simply a substitute for taking part in the real debate about the
future direction of education for Church members.

One of the fiercest critics of the independent sector within the
Church has been Alan McClelland, who said of them:

It is a scandal to witness the energy devoted by priests and Religious
to providing an exclusive education for the children of the rich, thus
blessing and perpetuating within the body of the Church itself the
social division of secular society which militates against the fullness of Christian living . . . A religious community holding dear a
Christian view of man ought not to promote, by means of its own
resources of men and ability and from its own volition, the education
of either the rich or the intelligent in a way which deprives the
poorer or less privileged section of society of its services. If it does
then it bears witness to using a double standard of its corporate
fulfilment of Christ's teaching and example.[151]

McClelland warns against the counter-witness of schools and paragraph 58 of the Vatican's 1977 document, *The Catholic School*, supports this argument, as it says that the Catholic school has a serious
obligation to resist any policies which might tend to maintain the
privileged status of a few people. This has become more of an issue
since the appointment of Catholic chaplains at Eton and Harrow
and other non-Catholic independent schools. The Church at the
same time has committed itself to a search for Justice as an integral
part of its mission. However, the line of argument by many radical
Catholics leads to the closure of all Catholic schools, not only
independent schools. Even surveys of student attitudes in Catholic
schools appear to indicate that further integration with the State
sector schools is called for.[152] In the area of religious education
critics have called for a bewildering variety of approaches and
schemes to increase the Church's mission for justice and peace.

For example, *The Tablet* in an article in 1981 called for the
curriculum in Catholic schools to be shaped in line with the gospel
demands of peace, justice and freedom. Freedom, especially in the
teaching of religious education has been a favourite topic among
critics of present and past religious education approaches.[153] The
conflict between the bishops and some liberal priests reached a
climax with the resignations of the staff at Corpus Christi College

in London in 1976. This was a college specialising in religious education and was established by the bishops to co-ordinate efforts in this area. The majority of its students were priests and religious, lay numbers being small, and the college as a whole encouraged a speculative type of theology. It became evident that the staff, in particular the senior staff, did not share the bishops' views nor did they share important aspects of Catholic teaching. As pressure was put on them by the bishops to change direction, they decided to resign as a result of what they called their impossible position. The bishops, Cardinal Heenan in particular, were accused of preventing the freedom to dissent within the Church.[154] A leading editorial in *The Tablet* for November 1980 commenting on religious education teaching said:

> They [pupils] want not the '*Ecclesia docens*' but a presentation of Christianity and the Church that evokes their co-responsibility and offers men's search for meaning and for God, and its relevance to all aspects of life, as something open to free discussion and choice.[155]

A head of religious education in a Catholic college of education, called for attendance at all religious services in Catholic schools to be made voluntary. This, he said, should also apply to assemblies which are legally binding on schools. Another Catholic education-alist said that religious education should be released from the task of formation in recognition of the increased variety of pupil com-mitment in today's pluralistic society. Others called for more time on other faiths to be provided during the religious education periods.[156] Controversy over religious education syllabuses contin-ues and there is even differences between the bishops. For exam-ple, the Archdiocese of Birmingham has refused to introduce the new religious education programme, *Weaving the Web*, into its schools and was criticised for not doing so in the Catholic press.[157] The Archdiocese objected to the size of the world religions' element in the syllabus and felt that it did not sufficiently foster and inform the faith. Other bishops have welcomed the new syllabus.

One area where there has been some movement in policy has been that of adult education. In a major article from the Westmin-ster Religious Education Centre, Rev. David Konstant, the future Chairman of the CEC, called for resources to be used in support of adult education.[158] In multi-cultural education each diocese has issued its own guidelines, but the Catholic Commission for Racial Justice claimed in 1982 that:

. . . most Catholic schools are not at present orientated towards multicultural education.[159]

An official Report of the Church, called *Learning from Diversity*, also published in 1982 came to the same conclusion. However, the Government's own report, published later in the same year as *Education for All*, commonly known as the *Swann Report*, concluded that religious education should be non-denominational and that educational approaches should be undogmatic. Separate schools were viewed as divisive and the report directly impinged upon the Catholic sector in attempting to counter the growing demands among the adherents of Islam in England for voluntary-aided schools.[160] This report would appear to have been reflected in the 1990 policy document of the Liberal Democrats, which seeks to end the creation of any further religiously-based schools within the State sector. The policy document says that religious schools might lead to the polarisation of society, particularly in multicultural urban areas.[161] It is clear that the idea of Islamic schools has been considered and ruled out by many in the education establishment. The effect on the Christian partners in the dual system would be to create a static situation which would inevitably begin to decline as a result of movements in the population. At the 1990 Labour Party Conference there was a motion debated for the abolition of all religious schools on the grounds that they were divisive of society.[162] Whilst it was defeated it remains an issue filled with a new sense of urgency and it is one which will not easily disappear from the political agenda.

The bishops established a consultative group at their Low Week meeting in 1991 to look at the question of Catholic schools and other Faiths. The final report, entitled 'Catholic Schools and Other Faiths', was submitted to the bishops' conference in November 1994. Among its recommendations and suggestions were a series of radical proposals which included: more open admissions policies; the possibility of partnership with other faiths in Catholic schools so that a quota system could operate based on the likely demand by different faith groups for admission to Catholic schools; the appointment of staff of other faiths to Catholic schools as role models for pupils of other faiths, the exclusion of catechesis and evangelisation from religious education programmes in Catholic schools which admit non-Catholics, the revision of trust deeds; mission statements, and the curriculum in Catholic schools to reflect multi-faith perspectives. Whilst these proposals did not form part of the official recommendations of the report, they nevertheless were implicitly included in the recommendations. The bishops have so far not approved the final report in its present form.[163]

Conclusion

For some observers, the building of Catholic schools has been a self-justifying quantitative goal with little attention being paid to other factors. There has been scant reflection on the outcomes from Catholic schools and little research on whether or not they improve the level of faith commitment and practice in adult life. Moreover, the structures by which the Catholic Church communicates and implements its policies within the dual system have broadly remained unaltered between 1945 and 1995. There has, it would appear, been an underlying assumption that these structures were basically adequate to deal with the problems which arose. Another underlying assumption has been that the stability of the Church's policy-making machinery corresponds to a similar stability in the schools which it serves. This was the case until the 1970s, since the main functions of the Catholic bodies, particularly of the CEC and the diocesan school commissions, were to service the expanding school system, notably in the areas of building, government and legal advice. This process was aided by rising school rolls which kept schools viable and an adequate supply of Catholic teachers mainly from the Catholic Colleges of Education. There was also a broad consensus on the content of religious education. Until the 1970s there was little to destabilise the system, since the few issues which did arise, including the initial plans for comprehensive schooling, were dealt with quickly by the bishops who were collectively responsible for Church education policy.

In the last decade or more, however, the position has changed radically. Catholic voluntary-aided schools have been profoundly affected by the reorganisation of schools and the closure of Colleges of Education. There has been a growing tendency by some LEAs and national educational organisations, including political parties, to regard denominational education as divisive. The increasing number of Government school reforms and the commitment to in-service education, teacher appraisal, local financial management of schools, and much more besides, represent an ever-growing area over which diocesan school commissions are largely unfamiliar. Indeed, they lack the support services to give an

appropriate Catholic response. Falling rolls and the methods to
deal with this, e.g. reorganisation, amalgamation and closure, are
eroding the base of the Catholic sector. Catholic parents appear
less constrained in conscience to send their children to Catholic
schools and consequently often make their choice on the grounds
of proximity and standards. In the absence of an articulated ecumenical policy, Catholic schools have admitted an increasing number
of non-Catholics for reasons of viability which will eventually bring
into question their *raison d'être*. Whilst there is greater emphasis
placed by the bishops upon the quality of Catholic schooling today,
they appear to have neglected the formulation of a distinctively
Catholic educational philosophy applicable to the situation in
England and Wales. There is a strong movement evident in national and local government to make few allowances for the existence of the dual system in their planning and policy decisions.
Voluntary-aided Catholic schools are facing a serious threat to their
continued existence. The fundamental question arises that if
government requirements seem to prejudice the deeper questions
underlying Catholic educational theory and practice, then Catholic
educators have to consider whether they can rightly co-operate. The
bishops are left in an dilemma, as it seems unlikely that they would
be able to mobilise Catholic voters in a campaign for distinctively
Catholic schools, at least partly outside the values expressed in the
Education Reform Act of 1988.

Notes

1. Kogan, M., *Educational Policy-Making*, George Allen and Unwin,
   London, 1975, p. 131.
2. Hornsby-Smth, M.P., *Roman Catholics in England and Wales*, CUP,
   1987, p. 27. See also Golver, D., *Roman Catholic Education and the State*,
   University of Sheffield, PhD, 1979, who argues that the greatest
   period of division in the Catholic Church was the nineteenth
   century and that the process of ghettoization was never complete
   and cites intermarriage and trade union membership as evidence.
   Pattison, R., *An Examination of the Political and Legislative background to
   the development of Catholic Elementary Education in the 20th Century*,
   University of Leeds, PhD, 1968, found that some Catholic parents
   sent their children to Board Schools because of the better material
   provision in them which provides further evidence against the
   'ghetto theory'.
3. Hornsby-Smith, M.P., *op. cit.*, p. 24. Also Hornsby-Smith, M.P., *The
   Changing Parish*, Routledge, London, pp. 2–3.
4. *Ibid.*, p. 216.

5. Winter, M., *Whatever Happened to Vatican II?*, Sheed and Ward, London, 1985, p. 19.
6. McSweeney, V., *Roman Catholicism*, Blackwells, Oxford, 1980, pp. 198–223.
7. *Ibid.*, p. 243.
8. *Ibid.*, p. 231.
9. Cunningham, R., 'Catholic Education Today', *The Dublin Review*, No. 591, Spring 1962, pp. 5–24.
10. Cunningham, R., 'The Big Teach Out', *The Tablet*, 5th March 1977, pp. 227–228.
11. *Education*, 'Church and State', 10th November 1961, pp. 798–804.
12. *Education*, 27th October 1961, p. 684.
13. Cunningham, R., 'Catholic Education Today', *op. cit.*
14. *Education.*, *op. cit.*
15. CEC, *Report 1962*, p. 16.
16. Cunningham, R., *op. cit.*
17. CEC, *Report 1963*, p. 13.
18. *Ibid.*
19. CEC, *Handbook 1964–1965*, p. 37.
20. CEC, *Report 1965*, p. 11.
21. Cunningham, R., 'Point of View', *Catholic Education Today*, Vol. 1, No. 2, May/June 1966, p. 3.
22. *TES*, 8th May 1964, p. 1250.
23. Blundell, M.J., 'Reorganisation of Catholic Schools', *Education*, 14th January 1966, pp. 61–64.
24. Rubinstein, D., *The Evolution of the Comprehensive School*, R.K.P., London, 1969, p. 88.
25. *Education*, 5th March 1965, p. 425.
26. *Education*, 1st January 1965, p. 46.
27. CEC, *Report 1965*, p. 11.
28. CEC, *Report 1964*, p. 19.
29. Blundell, M.J., *op. cit.*
30. Beck, G.A., *The Reorganisation of Secondary Education*, CEC, *Handbook 1964–1965*, p. 37.
31. Cunningham, R., 'The Catholic direct-grant Schools', CEC, *Handbook 1974*.
32. *The Tablet*, 21st October 1972, p. 1010.
33. *Education*, 5th March 1965, p. 425.
34. Blundell, M.J., *op. cit.*
35. *Ibid.*
36. Blundell, M.J., 'Reorganisation of Catholic Schools — Part 11', *Educaton*, 21st January, 1966, pp. 133–134
37. *Ibid.*
38. Murphy, J., *Church, State and School in Britain 1800–1970*, R.K.P., London, p. 114.
39. *TES*, 15th December 1967, p. 1374.

40. Beales, A.C.F., 'The Schools Debate', *Catholic Education Today*, Vol. 1, No. 1, March/April 1967, pp. 11–13.
41. Tucker, B. (ed.),*Catholic Education in a Secular Society*, Sheed and Ward, London, 1968, p. 1.
42. Tucker, B. (ed.), *op. cit.*, pp. 2–3.
43. Nowell, R., 'How Necessary Are Our Schools?', *Herder Correspondence*, Vol. 5, No. 10, October 1968, pp. 295–299.
44. Spencer, A.E.C.W., 'Tasks of Catholic Educational Research', *Catholic Education Today*, Vol. 1., No. 4, JulyAugust 1967, pp. 12–15.
45. Cunningham, R., 'Catholic Schools: Expansion and Achievement', *Catholic Education Today*, September/October, Vol. 1, No. 5, 1967, pp. 16–18.
46. Jebb, P. (ed.), *Religious Education — Drift or Decision*, Darton, Longman and Todd, London, 1968, pp. 137–164.
47. Tucker, B (ed.), *op. cit.*, p. 71.
48. *Ibid.*, p. 13.
49. Cloud, D., *The Catholic School and its Function*, The Old Palace, Oxford Catholic Chaplaincy, Paper No. 6, 1962.
50. Jebb, P. (ed.), *op. cit.* ., pp. 165–221.
51. Cameron, J.M., *Images of Authority*, Compass Books, London, 1966, p. 111.
52. Eagleton, T., 'The Bending of a Twig', *Slant*, Vol. 1, No. 4, Spring 1965, pp. 4–9.
53. Hennessey, M., 'Catholic Educational Policy', *Slant*, Vol. 5, No. 6, March 1970, pp. 27–29.
54. Jebb, P. (ed.), *op. cit.*, p. 216.
55. *Catholic Herald*, 22nd July 1966.
56. CEC, *Handbook 1973*, p. 5.
57. Blundell, M.J., *op. cit.*
58. Cunningham, R., 'Catholic Education — 25 Years Review', CEC *Handbook, 1975*.
59. *Ibid.*
60. *Ibid.*
61. CEC, *Report 1975*, p. 10.
62. CEC, *Report 1975*, p. 11. In a survey of 47 county education authorities in 1964 it was found that 28 county education authorities gave assistance to Catholics at independent schools as a direct result of the lack of Catholic grammar school provision in 40 of the LEAs. See *TES*, 28th February 1964, p. 504.
63. CEC, *Report 1973*, p. 22.
64. Cunningham, R., *op. cit.*
65. *The Tablet*, 12th July 1975, leading editorial, pp. 641–642.
66. CEC, *Report 1974*, p. 12.
67. CEC, *Report 1972*, p. 22 and p. 25.
68. Wake, R., 'Catholic Education, *The Month*, April 1975, pp. 106–109.
69. Francis, L., 'Are Our Schools Good for Non-Catholics?', *The Tablet*, 15th February 1986, pp. 170–172.

70. CEC, *Report 1976*, p. 9.
71. CEC, *Report 1976*, p. 10.
72. Hornsby-Smith, M.P., *Catholic Education — The Unobtrusive Partner*, Sheed and Ward, London, 1978, p. 3.
73. Catholic Education Service, *Report 1993*
74. CEC, *Report 1977*, p. 10.
75. CEC, *Report 1978*, p. 11
76. Hornsby-Smith, M.P., 'Educational Advice', *The Tablet*, 28th October 1975, pp. 1027–1028.
77. *The Tablet*, 28th February 1976, p. 213.
78. Sallis, J., *School Managers and Governors*, Ward Lock Educational, London, 1977.
79. CEC, *Report 1969*, pp. 16–17.
80. *The Tablet*, 29th May 1976, p. 525.
81. *The Tablet*, 5th March 1977, leading editorial, pp. 217–219.
82. CEC, *Report 1968*, p. 13.
83. Konstant, D., 'Swingeing Cuts', *The Tablet*, 17th November 1979, p. 1123.
84. CEC, *Handbook 1960–1961*, p. 9.
85. *Education*, 10th November 1961, pp. 798–804.
86. CEC, *Report 1961*.
87. CEC, *Report 1971*, p. 14.
88. CEC, *Report 1970*, p. 18.
89. CEC, *Report 1972*.
90. Bell, D., 'Have Catholic Colleges a Future?', *The Clergy Review*, April 1973, pp. 251–257.
91. Quinlan, S., 'The Catholic Colleges', *The Tablet*, 27th September 1975, pp. 924–925.
92. CEC, *Reports 1983*, p. 11 and *1985*, p. 12.
93. CEC, *Report 1979*, p. 9.
94. *Ibid*.
95. *Hansard*, 13th March 1980, House of Lords, Vol. 406, pp. 1206–1277.
96. Moyser, G., *Church and Politics Today*, T. and T. Clark, Edinburgh, 1985, p. 250.
97. CEC, *Report 1980*, p. 11.
98. Roehampton Group, 'Maintaining the Catholicity of Catholic Schools', *The Month*, April 1988, pp. 135–137.
99. Hout, D., *Denominational Schools as a Problem in England and Wales 1940–1959*, DPhil, University of Oxford, 1961.
100. *Signposts and Homecomings — The Educative Task of the Catholic Community*. A Report to the Bishops of England and Wales, St Paul Publications, 1981, p. 1.
101. *Ibid*., p. 154.
102. *The Tablet*, 1st August 1987, p. 810.
103. Hornsby-Smith, M.P., *Catholic Education — The Unobtrusive Partner* Sheed and Ward, London, 1978, p. 133.

104. *Signposts, op. cit.,* p. 31.
105. Hackett, P., 'MacFarlane and Voluntary Schools', *The Month*, April 1981, pp. 121–123.
106. Cumming, J. & Burns, P. (eds.), *The Church Now*, Gill and Macmillan, London, 1980, p. 60.
107. Roehampton Group, 'Admissions Policy in Catholic Schools', *The Month*, May 1985, pp. 157–159.
108. Francis, L., *op. cit.*
109. Cf. 'Catholic Schools and Other Faiths', A Consultation for the Bishops' Conference of England and Wales, Final Draft Report, 1994.
110. *Briefing*, Catholic Information Services, December 1987, Vol. 17, No. 22.
111. Field, F., *Opting Out — An Opportunity for Church Schools Church in Danger*, London, 1989.
112. CEC, *Catholic Schools and the 1988 Education Reform Act*, 1988, p. 35.
113. *Briefing*, Catholic Information Services, 29th April 1988, Vol. 18, No. 9.
114. *Briefing*, Catholic Information Services, 13th May 1988, Vol. 18, No. 10.
115. Catholic Bishops' Conference of England and Wales — *The Education Reform Bill — A Commentary for Catholics*, 1988, pp. 10–11.
116. *Ibid.*
117. *Briefing*, Catholic Information Services, 13th May 1988, Vol. 18, No 10.
118. Hume, B., *op. cit.*, p. 117.
119. Leonard, M., *The 1988 Education Reform Act* Blackwells, Oxford, 1988, p. 140.
120. Hume, B., *op. cit.*, p. 116.
121. CEC, *Catholic Schools and the Education Reform Act 1988*, p. 37.
122. Kogan, M., *op. cit.*, p. 133.
123. Catholic Bishops' Conference of England and Wales — *Education Reform Bill — A Commentary for Catholics*, 1988, p. 11.
124. Maclure, S., *Education Reformed*, Hodder and Stoughton, London, 1988, p. 8.
125. Catholic Bishops' Conference of England and Wales — *Education Reform Bill — A Commentary for Catholics*, 1988, p. 7.
126. *Ibid.*, p. 5.
127. CEC, *Catholic Schools and the Education Reform Act 1988*, 1988, p. 6.
128. Lawlor, S., *Opting Out*, Centre for Policy Studies, London, 1988, p. 13.
129. *Education*, 'Voluntary Schools', Digest, 1984.
130. M.L.E.A., Resolutions of the Education Committee at the 99th Meeting of Metropolitan LEAs, March 1989.
131. Eckersley, H.P., 'Catholic School — A Pause for a Thought', *Clergy Review*, Vol. LXII, No. 2, February, 1987, pp. 74–76.
132. CEC, Extracted from the Council's Published Statistics 1989–90.
133. *Better Schools*, Government White Paper, March 1985.

134. Archdiocese of Cardiff, *Secondary Schools in Gwent*, 1990. See also *Catholic Herald*, 20th August 1990, and *The Universe*, 16th July 1990.
135. *The Universe*, 23rd September 1990.
136. CEC, *Report 1964*.
137. CEC, *Report 1970*, p. 12.
138. Chadwick, J.P. and Gladwell, M., *Joint Schools: a Discussion Document on Ecumenical Education*, The English Anglican / Roman Catholic Committee, 1987.
139. Judd, J., 'Schools with Open Doors', *The Tablet*, 14th February 1987, p. 166.
140. Nichols, K. 'The Dual System', *The Clergy Review*, No 5, May 1973, pp. 331–341.
141. Francis, L., 'Roman Catholic Schools', *Journal of Educational Studies*, Vol. 12, No. 2, pp. 119–127.
142. Wake, R., *op. cit.*
143. Turner, G., 'Out of the Ghetto', *The Tablet*, 28th May 1988, p. 622.
144. *Joint Schools., op. cit.*
145. Sheppard, D. and Warlock, D., *Better Together: Christian Partnership in a Hurt City*, Penguin, London, 1988.
146. *The Guardian*, 29th August 1981.
147. O'Keeffe, B., *Faith, Culture and the Dual System*, Falmer, London, 1986.
148. *The Tablet*, 19th February 1983, pp. 160–165.
149. Sallnow, T., 'Truly Catholic Schools', *The Tablet*, 14th February 1987.
150. Bright, L., and Clements, S. (eds.), *The Committed Church*, Darton, Longman and Todd, London, 1966, p. 268.
151. Cumming, J. & Burns, P. (eds.), *op. cit.*, pp. 112–113.
152. Egan, J., *Opting Out: Catholic Schools Today*, Fowler Wright, Leominster, 1988.
153. Jackson, D.A., 'A Catholic Curriculum', *The Tablet*, 30th May 1981, pp. 528–530.
154. *The Tablet*, 8th January 1972, pp. 20–22, and 15th January 1972, p. 45. For a detailed account see McClelland's article in Hastings, A. (ed.), *Modern Catholicism*, London, 1991, pp. 372–373.
155. *The Tablet*, 'Schools Without Religion', 22nd November 1980, p. 1140.
156. *The Tablet*, 5th August 1978, pp. 749–754, 23rd August 1986, p. 874. *TES*, 24th March 1967, pp. 991–1006.
157. *The Tablet*, 28th May 1988, pp. 619–620.
158. Konstant, D., 'Strategy for Catholic Education', *The Tablet*, 31st January 1976, p. 107.
159. Catholic Commission for Racial Justice, *Notes and Reports* April 1982, No. 11, p. 3.
160. Arbuckle, G.A., 'Racism, Multicultural Education and the Church — Implications of the Swann Report', *Clergy Review*, Vol. LXX, No. 12, December 1985, pp. 431–440.
161. Liberal Party Policy Document 1990; also reported in *TES*, 24 August 1990.

162. Labour Party Conference 1990 — Minutes and Agenda.
163. 'Catholic Schools and Other Faiths', A Consultation for the Bishops'
      Conference of England and Wales, Final Draft Report, 1994.

5

Lay Participation in
Education Structures

Introduction

When the Second Vatican Council was convened, about 75% of
those teaching in Catholic schools around the world were priests
or religious. Today, this great clerico-religious enterprise has un-
dergone a radical transformation with over 80% of teachers now lay
men and women.[1] However, many of the educational control structures which formulate policy for these schools are still clerically
dominated and under strong episcopal leadership. Whilst the
Church has called for shared responsibility together with parental
and lay involvement in Church life, it remains a strongly hierarchical organisation. It is still the case that it is the diocesan bishop,
and he alone, who may set up agencies through which the laity can
express their opinions. In 1931 Pope Pius XI, in his letter *Non
Abbiamo Bisogno*, encouraged lay action within the Church. His
successor, Pope Pius XII, in a speech in 1946 called for the laity to
be in the 'front line of the Church's life'.[2] The *Decree on the Apostolate
of the Laity*, of Vatican II in 1965 went further and advocated revision
of the institutions and structures within the Church so that the
laity could exercise their 'rightful' role in the mission of the
Church. The *Decree on the Ministry and Life of Priests*, of the same year
encouraged the clergy to recognise the experience and competence
of the laity and to entrust to them responsibilities in the service of
the Church.[3] Moreover, since the new Code of Canon Law was
formally promulgated in 1983, it has strengthened this more positive image of the laity, especially in Canons 224 to 231. There
appeared to be a developing concept of Church organisation which
stressed participation and subsidiarity. In regard to education,
Canons 793 to 806 detail the rights and responsibilities of parents

vis-a-vis the education of their children by insisting on the primary role of parents.

The post-conciliar statements from the Congregation of Catholic Education have reflected this movement for greater lay participation. In 1977, in its publication, *The Catholic School*, the Congregation urged that in consequence of the principle of participation and co-responsibility, all should be associated with the decision-making concerning Catholic schools.[4] The 1982 statement on *Lay Catholics in Schools* spoke of the need for the laity to have a genuine share of responsibility in the Church's educational mission. The most recent document produced by the Congregation, *The Religious Dimension of Catholic Education*, published in 1988, states that the Church is prepared to have lay people in charge of Catholic schools. At the same time it reminds lay people that only the bishop can recognise the school as Catholic, but it emphasises that all, whether lay or cleric, must participate and co-operate in the common mission of Catholic education. This document offers 'enthusiastic encouragement' to Religious Orders to establish new schools whilst simply recognising the fact that lay people may themselves establish schools.[5] Nevertheless, lay involvement has been clearly stressed from official sources. Other Church documents such as the *General Catechetical Directory*, and *Catechesis in Our Time* have also spoken of the need for lay participation in the enterprises of the Church. The principle of lay participation has been long accepted in the structures of the Church, but its practice varies widely from one country to another.

The Second Vatican Council sought to order the Church's affairs in a way which was more in harmony with its nature. This view was later advocated by modern educational management theorists who found that if an organisational system is to attain maximum effectiveness and efficiency it should reflect the system's basic philosophy.[6] The Council encouraged the Church generally to shift to more open and participative organisational structures. In a review of the Church's organisational features Miller observes that:

> The organisational structures of the Church are the channels of communication by which those who are the Church make visible the image of the Church which they hold.[7]

Consequently, it is essential that some idea of the definition and nature of the Church is given through exploring some of the basic models of the Church which have arisen in history and continue to be held by its members.

The institutional model, which dominated the structures of the Church prior to the Second Vatican Council, is marked by a number of characteristics which are detailed by Avery Dulles.[8] In this model the Church is seen as a society with an emphasis on its own visibility. Stress is placed on the structures of government and this makes for order, clarity and respect. It provides a strong corporate identity for members and is concerned with preserving the heritage of the Church. The Church in this model has a constitution, a set of rules, a governing body and a set of members who accept the institution and rules as binding on them. Emphasis is given to the rights and powers of office holders, in particular their use of sanctions on members. The bishop is endowed with a 'ruling' pastoral authority and there is little democracy or representation allowed in the system, which perpetuates itself by co-option alone. The model exacts a high degree of institutional loyalty from members to accept the declared goals of the Church, so that they know who they are, what they believe and what their mission is. It has stable organisational features and views the clergy as the source of all power and initiative within the Church. Stability is all important and the hierarchical structure which is based on power maintains this stability. Finally, the model conceives authority in the Church rather closely on the pattern of jurisdiction in the secular State, thereby amplifying the place of law and penalties. There are many direct instances of this model at work in the educational structures of the Catholic Church in England and Wales today which will be discussed later. Dulles rejects the total institutional model and claims that the style of organisation most appropriate to the Church is the participative style. He argues that authoritarianism, which he associates with the institutional model, undermines the trust relationship on which the Church is founded. However, the models which Dulles uses are neither new nor is it the first time they have been used for an understanding of the educational structures of the Church. In 1966, Miller wrote an article on 'The Administration of Christian Education', which was an early attempt to use certain scriptural images for an understanding of the Church's organisational structures.[9] In particular he used the images of 'Body of Christ' and 'People of God' in his analysis.

Miller used the metaphor of 'Body of Christ' to produce an organic view, as opposed to a sociological view of the Church. He sees the Church as a family in which all members have a certain affinity and act as one. As a result each member loses himself in the being of Christ, but at the same time is formed by the whole structure. This view of the Church produces specialised leaders for designated educational tasks. There is a degree of clarity and certainty of thought in this model, for the Church is seen as analogous to the human body and so is equipped with various specialist organs. The model is also more democratic than the institutional one. The second metaphor used by Miller is the 'People of God'. This view sees the Church as groups of people responding in various ways to the will of God. Each group is or becomes autonomous and make its own decisions. Status within the group is not obtained by one's contribution, but by the strength of one's commitment to the cause. The structures are flexible because God calls some people at particular times. Dulles also describes both these models, but places emphasis on their common features which he sees as the mutual service of members to each other. There is, according to Dulles, subordination of the members' particular good to that of the whole Body or People of God.[10]

Dulles offers four other models which are worth summarising at this stage. First, he describes the 'Church as Sacrament', where the structural aspects are essential, but never sufficient to constitute the Church itself. This model leaves ample room for the workings of divine grace, but appears to have little application to the educational structures of the Church. Second, he outlines the 'Herald' model of the Church which appears directly applicable to the Church's educational mission. This model implies a mission to proclaim, the Church receives a message with the commission to pass it on. The 'Word' is primary in this model and faith is seen as a response to the Gospel. Third, the 'Church as Servant' has been a popular model for the Church which is not seen here as primarily gaining new members, but rather being of help to all, wherever they are. It seeks to give the Church new relevance, modernity and a sense of mission. It is secular in tone and gives priority to promoting justice and peace. Finally, the 'Church as Community' has also been a popular model, with the Church seen as the fellowship of persons in communication with each other and with God. This model has a horizontal and a vertical dimension. From this brief survey it would seem that each model brings out certain important and necessary points for an understanding of what it means to be the 'Church'. The nature of the Catholic school is dependent on the nature of beliefs about the Church and the

Church is fundamentally the model for the community that the school should be. Any one model used exclusively would provide an incomplete picture and yet, with regard to the educational structures of the Church, officials have a strong tendency to prefer the institutional model. This places officials, normally clerical, in positions which are almost invulnerable to criticism and pressure from below. These clerics prescribe the limit of tolerable dissent and represent the community in an official way with those in authority. Conflict arises, but is quickly ended, for the institutional model can be repressive and encourage a form of juridicism which exaggerates the role of human authority. Dulles argues that the monopolistic tendencies of this model are unacceptable today and that the structures of the Church must be seen as subordinate to its communal life and mission.[11]

All members of the Catholic Church are called by virtue of their baptismal commitment to participate in the education of community members. There is a learning function in the very decision of commitment to be within any community. Catholics belong to a whole series of communities ranging from the most local and personal to the national and international and in all of them they play different roles. In regard to Catholic schools, the term 'community' is used constantly to convey the notion that there should be a consensus of aims and values and mutually supportive relationships. The implied unity within community here is inherently consensual since the source of oneness is entirely a matter of conviction. However, there is considerable confusion surrounding the word 'community' and its use in a variety of contexts, not least in the terminology of education. The formal leaders within the Catholic community are easy to identify as the bishops, but the 'Catholic community' is a looser and less specific entity in which power is not so centralised. In England and Wales the Church's education provision gradually became clerically controlled, a process which was fully complete by the Restoration of the English and Welsh hierarchy in 1850. The reasons for the growth of this strong institutional Church lie in the make-up of the English Catholic community at the time, especially the 'immigrant experience', which helped to focus community interests. Adherence to Catholicism has a consequential dimension which includes those religious prescriptions which specify what people ought to do and the attitudes they ought to hold. This consequential dimension would appear not to be as strong today and there are growing signs of excessive individualism among Catholics.

Michael Hornsby-Smith's *Survey of Roman Catholic Opinion* in 1978[12] has not been repeated, but he has continued to write widely on the sociological aspects of Catholicism as a whole. The principal conclusions from his most recent attempt to summarise the findings from the various empirical studies on English Catholicism are illuminating. He does not deal explicitly with any secularisation theories, but points to the conclusion that in the post-war years there has been a dissolution of the boundaries which previously kept English Catholicism as a distinctive sub-culture. This appears to be his major theory along with his observations that there has been a process of socio-economic embourgeoisement during this period among Catholics and that the Catholic Church can be regarded as a safe 'domesticated denomination'.[13] In justification for his 'dissolution of the English Catholic subculture' theory he quotes Peter Coman's work from the 1970s, who lists the main elements of the religious changes which have characterised this 'dissolution':

> The gradual assimilation through education and mixed marriage, the dissent over traditional teaching in birth regulation, the questioning of the limits of papal authority, the gradual substitution of English for Latin in the liturgy, the tentative movements towards ecumenism, the softening of traditional disapproval of mixed marriages and the abolition of Friday abstinence ...[14]

It is clear that Hornsby-Smith's theory is in fact a restatement of Coman's, who was the first to speak of the weakening of the traditional Roman Catholic sense of boundary and demarcation in relation to the wider community and the weakening of the general Catholic identity. Hornsby-Smith's aim has been to demonstrate the heterogeneity of English Catholicism in terms of belief and practice. This continues to be hindered by a dearth of empirical studies, but there is enough information to make the modest claim that the Catholic community is showing increased signs of individualism and strain which has led in a few cases to fragmentation within the Church.

With regard to education it has been the consistent policy of the bishops to foster a State-Church partnership in the provision of schools. All important questions of policy have been determined by the bishops as they deliberate on the issues of the moment and develop a strategy for the Church as a whole. They have been the sole agents in entering into agreements with the State which have committed Catholic education policies. All this takes place within a Church whose composition and characteristics are in a process of change, at least socially. The period since Vatican II in England and Wales needs careful examination to trace how lay involvement in the Church has developed.

Lay Participation in Educational Policy

The relationship between Catholic education and the diocesan bishop has become problematic in England and Wales. Since the 1960s, a growing and an increasingly central issue within Catholic education policy has been the concept and exercise of episcopal authority, in particular, the extent to which it should allow a mature role for the laity. There appears to be an apparent contradiction between the fundamental importance of the parental role in the Catholic education belief system and its neglect in the structures of the Church. In defending parental rights in education the Church is often seeking to defend its own rights. At the Second Vatican Council, the rights of parents in the education of their children was debated and affirmed. Bishop Birch of Ossory, Ireland, spoke of the highest importance attached to parental involvement in schools, but said that often the role of parents lacked any real power. Bishop Beck on behalf of the English bishops advocated that the Church should defend the rights of parents in education. Prior to the recent demand in Britain for Muslim and Christian fundamentalist schools, he said that all had the right to equal treatment before the State to establish and support religious schools. This was strongly echoed by Bishop Konstant at the North of England Education Conference in 1990. However, other bishops, at the Second Vatican Council, such as Bishop Donohue of Stockton in California, warned against replacing a monopoly of the State with one of the family or parents.[15] Nevertheless, the whole question of parental control in schools has been a relatively new one for the Catholic community in England and Wales, since parish priests were a dominant influence on schools and often considered parent associations unnecessary on the grounds that Catholic schools were a parochial affair.[16] According to Anthony Spencer, this was particularly true of Catholic primary schools: in a study of them in the late 1960s he found that they were less likely to have parent teacher associations than LEA schools.[17] As schools are essentially a lay concern, the nature of lay participation in the formulation of

Catholic education policy in the educational structures of the
Church is an important area for consideration.

By way of contrast, in the 1962–1963 CEC *Handbook*'s editorial
note, the Rev. Maurice Couve de Murville's article, on the Dutch
Catholic education system, is commended in the following terms:

> His account of parental participation should be of special interest
> at a time when Catholics in this country must be concerned to
> strengthen the community of endeavour between home and school
> which has always been one of the most important characteristics of
> Catholic education.[18]

In England and Wales, demands for greater lay representation on
diocesan education commissions were made by the Catholic
Teachers' Federation in 1963 and a resolution was passed at its
annual conference in December 1964 which sought lay involvement at all levels within the Church's decision-making processes.[19]
The following year the CEC agreed that contact with parents at
all levels was insufficient and Noel Hughes, addressing the CEC
conference of the same year, insisted that Catholic schools should
be controlled by the laity.[20] However, it was not until 1968 that the
CEC began talks with the National Council for the Lay Apostolate
on the possibility of further lay representation on its own Council.
The talks soon foundered on the question of who would be truly
'representative' of lay interests and no decisions were made.[21]
Unofficial groups of parents claiming to represent lay interests in
their children's schooling were often opposed by the Church's
diocesan authorities. In one case of January 1969 a group of Catholic parents formed an association to influence policy decisions
about their children's schooling, but it was successfully opposed
by the diocesan bishop, the Bishop of Hexham and Newcastle.[22]

However, after Vatican II, lay participation in the work of the
institutional Church was re-emphasised and new structures of
consultation and advice were established at all levels in England
and Wales. At parish level there had always been many charitable
organisations with opportunities for lay initiative and leadership,
but this had not extended to educational policy which was still
firmly controlled by the diocesan clergy. Nevertheless, in response
to the Second Vatican Council, the bishops established a Laity
Commission and an Education Commission, two of a number of
advisory bodies set up to advise them on a wide range of matters.
These commissions were directly responsible to the bishops and
reported to them through their Presidents who were also bishops.

They were in effect sub-committees of the National Conference of Bishops.[23] They were formed to 'assist' the bishops and had no legislative or executive power. Membership of these commissions was theoretically open to any member of the Church, lay or clerical, but the choice of candidates was made by the bishops on the grounds of either outstanding personal achievement or as 'representatives' of diocesan or Catholic societies. Hornsby-Smith in a study of the social composition of the Church's national committees found that the Laity Commission consisted of a majority of people who had a high level of formal education and were overwhelmingly middle class.[24] They differed significantly from the existing socio-economic characteristics of English Catholics. The religious attitudes of the majority of the lay members on the commission he termed 'progressive', since they were enthusiastic about the 'perceived' changes of Vatican II. They were more favourable towards change in the Church than the average parishioner. The Education Commission had no legislative or executive power, and Rashid Mufti concluded that this commission had minimal influence on policy formulation; he referred to 'the cycle of authoritarian and bureaucratic control by the bishops'.[25]

The Education Commission itself comprised the CEC, the Department for Catholic Higher Education, the Department for Catechesis and the Catholic Youth Service Council. It had a Standing Committee whose function was:

> . . . to coordinate the work of Catholic education and to promote discussion with the various specialised groups and associations involved.[26]

There was no lay representative on this committee: it was composed exclusively of five bishops. The bishops also rejected any idea of a 'think tank' for the Education Commission. The CEC was overwhelmingly clerical in composition, especially its executive committee, as were the diocesan school commissions. In April 1971 the CEC established a joint group with the Laity Commission to discuss ways in which the laity could 'share' in the work of the Council.[27] A paper was prepared on the implications of Vatican II for parental participation in schools and read to the Council and a further meeting was held in September to discuss the issue. However, once again no action or decisions were taken or made at subsequent meetings.[28] Hornsby-Smith in the same year began a study of parents and their involvement in schools, which was sponsored by the Social Science Research Council. He found that

members of the Laity Commission were frustrated at the largely
abortive attempts to arrange 'fruitful discussion' with the CEC on
the question of parental involvement and participation in the
education of their children and the appointment of school governors.[29] Early in 1972 the Laity Commission presented a draft
discussion paper to the CEC, but again no decisions were taken
and the composition of the Council remained unchanged.[30] No
further discussions on lay involvement by the Council have taken
place since that year, other than the publication of a leaflet in 1977,
at the request of the National Conference of Priests, on *Parents and
Education*. The leaflet focused on teacher-parent associations and
did not consider any possibilities for changes to the composition
of the Council itself.[31]

Conflict and tension between parents and diocesan authorities
have arisen more frequently in recent years and some of it has been
bitter. Beales details three cases from the early 1970s which serve
to illustrate the point. In Stockport, the LEA requested that two
Catholic voluntary-aided schools should amalgamate, but the local
Catholic community was totally divided on the issue. The diocesan
school commission approved the LEA plan by the casting vote of
the Chairman, a narrow decision which created local controversy.
In Liverpool, the diocesan reorganisation plans were, it was
claimed by parents, produced without consultation. In Crosby, in
April 1972, a plan for comprehensive schools had to be postponed
because a Religious Order, the Christian Brothers, refused to
co-operate with the diocese. This opposition arose after the diocese, LEA and the Secretary of State for Education had approved
the plan. The parents responded by forming an association in
favour of comprehensive education which was independent of the
diocesan schools commission. The parents claimed they were
aiding communication with the diocese, but it led to much animos-
ity and division within the local Catholic community.[32] However,
by far the most controversial case in the 1970s was the comprehensive reorganisation plan for the City of Birmingham which caused
some bitter exchanges in the Catholic press. The Birmingham
diocesan schools commission was accused by many within the City,
both Catholic and non-Catholic, of denying parents an opportunity
to comment on the proposals. In particular, the Commission was
accused of presenting its own reorganisation plan as a *fait accompli*,
in alliance with the ruling Labour Party on the Council. In Francis
Hartley's study of this controversy, it appears clear that consult-

ation was minimal. In their defence the diocesan authorities claimed that it was the policy of the Church to fit its school provision with the LEAs scheme of educational provision.[33] Effectively, this meant that Catholics would be denied the right to consultation in reorganisation plans, since they would not have been consulted about the future of LEA schools.

A particularly bitter and complicated controversy, also in the Archdiocese of Birmingham, raged between 1992 and 1995 around St Philip's Sixth-Form College and the desire of its trustees, the Oratorian Fathers, to close the college as they perceived it to have lost its 'Catholic nature'. Parents, many of them non-Catholic, organised a campaign in alliance with staff, local politicians and elements of the Catholic clerical establishment against the governors and trustees. The violence of the attacks, often personal in nature, against the governors and Fathers would have been inconceivable even twenty years ago and is very revealing of the shift in attitudes towards the clergy. In January 1995 the college's proportion of Catholic students was under 18% and the trustees had begun the legal process of terminating the lease on the college buildings. The college was eventually absorbed by a secular college and lost its Catholic title in August 1995. In this bitter dispute the local bishop did not publicly intervene or present his office as a focus of unity for the Catholic community until the closing stages. In this one dispute there is much to be learned by all those involved in Catholic education.

These disputes reflect the changing educational priorities and attitudes of the Catholic community. Occasionally, in almost all local authorities there arose conflict with parents, especially over the choice of school. Indeed, prior to comprehensive reorganisation the combined number of parental appeals to the Secretary of State on the choice of school approached 100 per annum. After reorganisation in the late 1970s the number climbed to about 1,000 a year despite the fact that there was a very low success rate.[34] Parental choice became a major concern in educational policy and a national issue in the 1970s. The Conservative Party produced a *Parents' Charter* in August 1974, which was incorporated into the Conservative election manifesto of October 1974.[35] The rationale for parental involvement in schooling was developed by the Conservative Party, and they began to exploit the mounting concerns of parents in an attempt to draw support away from the Labour Government. They promised that, if elected, they would give greater control to parents over their children's education and this caused the government to respond to the challenge. One action of the Wilson government, as described, was to establish the Taylor Committee in 1977.

Included among the members of the Taylor Committee was the representative of the CEC, the Rev. Peter Reilly, who was the secretary of the Birmingham diocesan schools commission which had been the focus of the 1970s dispute in Birmingham about reorganisation and the lack of consultation with parents. He argued that participation by parents in Catholic schools was secured in other ways, since the Church was a community and had a family concern for all its members.[36] No details of these 'other ways' were spelled out and the Archdiocesan directory simply stated that 'the natural complement of the Catholic family is the Catholic school'.[37] However, Joan Sallis, a parent member of the committee commented soon after the publication of the *Taylor Report: A New Partnership for Our Schools* in 1977:

> I think it quite unrealistic to expect parents whose children attend voluntary schools — which after all are part of the State system and now largely financed from rates and taxes — to observe a great extension in public participation in county school affairs, without asking some awkward questions about their own school. Many Churches have tried hard within the framework of the dual system to meet parents' aspirations, but any parent member, even if he were elected, would still be a foundation governor, and, as such, answerable to the foundation, not the parent body.[38]

The Laity Commission did not, it appears, comment on the *Taylor Report* formally, but in 1978, whilst endorsing the Catholic school as the best choice in the then 'present context', reminded the bishops that the context was not static and that alternative options could be considered by parents.[39] In a personal statement the lay Secretary of the CEC said he favoured the appointment of parent and teacher governors.[40] The Labour Government issued a consultative paper in October 1977 entitled *Admission of Children to the School of their Parental Choice* which anticipated legislation. The eventual Education Bill fell when Parliament was dissolved in April 1979. The Conservatives returned to office committed to legislation that would shift the balance towards parents and away from local education authorities. As Stuart Maclure said, the processes which were then to be devised by the government to reduce the influence of LEAs directly impinged on the Churches.[41]

Lay participation in the structures of the Church was a topic of the National Pastoral Congress in 1980. This Congress was called by the bishops to assess the various efforts made nationally to implement the call of Vatican II for renewal. It was an attempt to plan some pastoral strategy for the future. The Congress was overwhelmingly lay in composition and it emphasised that the laity had the ability to take on duties which priests ought to shed.[42] Clerics, it was said, often acted as if they where the sole custodians of the Church. The bishops' response to the Congress was to issue *The Easter People*. Published in August 1980, it was long on theological reflection on the sharing Church and recommended the 'open model' of the Church, but there were no specific recommendations for action on education. *Signposts and Homecomings*, which was published in 1981, did propose the reorganisation of the Education Commission and especially the CEC. However, it made no distinction between lay or clerical members and simply said that a new Commission should consist of members chosen to represent different areas of the country and different educational experience and expertise.[43] This vague proposal was never acted upon and the review of structures by the bishops in 1983 recognised that there was a long way to go in securing representation of the Catholic community on committees of the Church. Indeed, the Extraordinary Synod of Bishops called by Pope John Paul II in 1985 in Rome was also lengthy on theological reflection of the sharing Church, as was the 1987 Synod on the Vocation of the Laity. Both spoke about collaborative ministries from both lay and clerical states in the Church. However, no concrete proposals were made and it has been left entirely to the local episcopate to suggest, or not to suggest, change in the structures of the Church.

In the wider society, the right of people to share in the control of education has long been established. However, in the Church this has not been a tradition and any shift in the locus of power away from the clergy remains a formidable task involving many fundamental changes in the organisational life of the Church. In the original negotiations with the Government concerning the establishment of financial aid to Catholic schools, the crucial point was the question of lay involvement. The bishops' response to the *Taylor Report* was to secure, as far as possible, the clerical structures of appointment to school governing bodies. As parent power has increased, the Church has attempted in negotiations with the government to filter out or inhibit regulations which bring the

Catholic voluntary-aided schools into line with LEA maintained
schools. There are no defined democratic procedures in the Catholic Church for the appointment of the majority of governors to
schools nor for the establishment of diocesan commissions nor national education bodies. Participation it seems is restricted to
'active' support for the bishops' policies. Decision-making is neither open nor accountable. The main method of representation is
co-option under the control of the bishop. This model in education
is clearly institutional. Its aim is to secure a firmer basis for the role
which the hierarchical Church wishes to play in assuring that
Catholic schools comply with the mission of the Church. Bruno
Manno has suggested that the laity's motto in education should be
'From paying, praying and obeying to leading, governing and ad-
ministering'.[44]

Parents and the 1988 Education Reform Act

The Education Act of 1980 extended the role of parents' influence
on schools by their appointment to school governing bodies.
Voluntary-aided schools were required in law to make arrangements for the election of parents to governing bodies and these
parents were completely independent of the trustees. Governors
appointed by the trustees have a duty of 'oversight' of the Catholic
character of the school which, it is said, often goes beyond their
legal responsibilities and is sometimes referred to as a 'duty in
conscience'.[45] The Education Reform Act of 1988 intentionally
strengthened the position of parents and weakened that of the
Church authorities. The bishops responded to the parental clauses
in the Bill by saying that parents were transient groups and that
they were not the only legitimate shareholders in the enterprise of
preparing future Catholic children — the wider Catholic community was equally significant in this regard. It was argued that the
local Catholic community, which included parents, had a continuing and legitimate interest in the local Catholic school. This was
the line taken by the CEC in negotiation with the government who
largely ignored these claims. The argument presented by the
Catholic side appears to have included another dimension. This
was that if the Catholic school existed only to satisfy the requests
of parents, it would be an enterprise at the mercy of its clients
obliged to provide the product they desired. Moreover, the product
might no longer correspond to the aims of the school's original
mission. Such a school would cease to be Catholic. At about the

same time as the publication of the Education Reform Bill in 1987, Cardinal Baum, Prefect of the Congregation for Catholic Education in Rome, wrote to Cardinal Hume on the subject of school governors, commenting:

> Individual Catholics who are 'governors' of Catholic schools in the 'dual system' must not only know and fulfil their statutory obligations but must also know their ecclesial rights and obligations. In other words they are to respond to the State's and the Church's legitimate expectations of them in such a way as to fulfil their responsibilities both as citizens and as Catholics. The management of one Catholic school should be conducted with due regard for the needs of other Catholic schools and for the interests of Catholic education in general as determined by the bishop of the diocese.[46]

The extent to which governors can defer to outside authorities has been questioned by the Court of Appeal in the case of *Jones v Lee and Another* of 1979. One of the judges concluded:

> . . . although there must be a right to take advice, there must also be some limit to the scope of the advice which is sought and taken, so as not to pre-empt the ultimate decision of a quasi-judicial body such as the managers or make their decision a foregone conclusion.[47]

However, the letter from Cardinal Baum had a more immediate and direct concern, since in the month before its issue the trustees of the Archdiocese of Westminster had dismissed two foundation governors of the Cardinal Vaughan Memorial School in London. These two, both parents and foundation governors, Mr Mars and Mrs Flynn, had opposed the policy of reorganisation presented by the diocesan authorities which would have entailed the loss of the school's sixth form. Subsequently, these two governors were replaced with others supportive of the diocesan policy. Additionally, four other foundation governors were replaced by 'agreement'. The diocesan authorities were following the local authority pattern of reorganisation and presented proposals affecting the distribution of school pupils in the diocese which included the establishment of a sixth form college.[48]

The Cardinal Vaughan Memorial Boys' School was one of eight voluntary-aided Catholic secondary schools in the Central London Episcopal Area of the Archdiocese of Westminster. In June 1986 the school's trustees, the Westminster Roman Catholic Diocese Trustee, a company limited by guarantee with Cardinal Basil Hume, Archbishop of Westminster, as President of the company's board of directors, formulated a proposal whereby two of these

schools were to be closed and the sixth-forms removed from a
further six schools to form the basis of a new sixth-form college.
The proposal had the support of the Inner London Education
Authority, but had been rejected by the governing body of the
Cardinal Vaughan school by a narrow majority on three separate
occasions.[49] These diocesan proposals were rejected by an overwhelming majority of the school's parents and unanimously by the
head teacher and his staff. Cardinal Hume, as president of the
trustees of the school, wrote in June 1987 to the two foundation
governors who had voted against the diocesan plan, urging them to
support diocesan policy. This long and detailed letter reminded
foundation governors of the principles by which Cardinal Hume
thought they should carry out their responsibilities. He wrote:

> It is the first responsibility of foundation governors to represent the
> trustees in the governing body and the educational policy which has
> been determined by the trustees. They are thus limited in the
> exercise of their office by the requirement of the trustees that they
> should work within the overall educational policy laid down by the
> same trustees. It is not within the competence of foundation
> governors to determine or affect educational policy within the
> diocese.[50]

Mr Mars and Mrs Flynn replied to this letter by informing Cardinal
Hume that they could not in conscience approve the diocesan
plans. Both governors were subsequently removed from office by
the trustees.

The aggrieved governors, fully supported by their parents' association, took the unusual step for Catholics in dispute with their
bishop, of applying for judicial review to quash the decision to
dismiss them. Their claim was that the trustees had usurped the
function of the governors, placed on them by the civil law, and had
imposed a plan upon a governing body which had consistently
rejected it. On 16th December 1987 the two governors lost their
case. The Judge did not accept that the trustees were bound to
leave them in office and concluded that:

> . . . the legal responsibility for determining the character of the
> school, including its age range, rested squarely upon the governing
> body and not upon the trustees . . . the trustee was entitled to have
> a policy of its own provided always that such policy was in conformity
> with the provisions of the trust deed and were entitled to exercise
> their statutory powers in order to secure implementation of their
> policy, and it was therefore legitimate, in the last resort, for the
> trustees to exercise the power contained in section 8(5) of the

Education (No 2) Act 1986 to remove any foundation governors from office whose consciences precluded them from discharging their role as governors and were thwarting the trustees' own policy . . .[51]

The case was significant because it appeared to confirm the powers of the trustees to dismiss foundation governors as contained in Section 8(5) of the Education (No 2) Act of 1986 which states:

> Any foundation governors of a voluntary school . . . may be removed from office by the person or persons who appointed them.

However, subsequent developments have disappointed the hopes placed in this legal decision by the bishops.

In a separate case, with analogous circumstances, which proceeded to the House of Lords in 1989 involving the dismissal of foundation governors by the Inner London Education Authority acting as trustees of a voluntary-controlled school, one of the judges, Lord Bridge, made reference to the Cardinal Vaughan case in the following terms:

> In the light of the views I have expressed, I find it difficult to see how the reasoning of Simon Brown J in R v Trustees of the Roman Catholic Diocese of Westminster ex p Mars (1987) 86 *LGR* 507, can be supported.[52]

The highest court in England and Wales had cast doubt on the outcome of the Cardinal Vaughan case. It was therefore clear that a lower court could not ignore the implications of this statement. During the House of Lords judgement it was announced that leave to appeal against the decision in the Cardinal Vaughan case had already been granted, despite the fact that the time limit in which to make an appeal had expired. It is interesting that Mr Mars and Mrs Flynn did not proceed with this appeal and that another took the appeal forward on behalf of the Cardinal Vaughan School's parent association. The appeal was heard on 20th July 1989 and whilst the judges accepted that the trustees had an overlapping role with governors in formulating educational policy, the actual control of the schools management and any changes to the character of the school was held to be a matter 'exclusively for the governors.'[53] It was not seen as a matter over which the trustees had control. The earlier decision which held that the removal of Mars and Flynn from the governing body was not unreasonable was concurrently over-turned.

It is now plain that the trustees cannot prevent a determined governing body or group of parents from taking its own line and frustrating diocesan plans. It is also explicit that in law the ultimate power to determine the character of a voluntary school lies with the governors. The apparent power of trustees to remove governors remains unclear, especially in the context of differences of policy. Cardinal Hume later commented that two lessons had been learnt from the initial controversy. First, that it was essential from the earliest stage to involve parents in the process of reorganisation and to enlist their active support for the policy of the diocese. In particular, he drew attention to the parents who needed protection since they were not able to articulate their needs. Second, that foundation governors must ensure that the decisions of the trustees are implemented in full.[54] In many respects these two lessons are simply a restatement of previous diocesan policy towards parents and governors. It is interesting to note that the Cardinal Vaughan case was not the first occasion in which the trustees of the Archdiocese of Westminster had been required to defend diocesan school reorganisation plans in the courts, as there had been a similar case in 1983.[55] The diocesan plans for school reorganisation drawn up between 1982 and 1983 had, in any event, been rejected by the Secretary of State for Education in August 1985. During the course of the preparations of these diocesan proposals, the legal adviser to the trustees of the Archdiocese of Westminster advised them in a series of letters that foundation governors are not appointed to carry out the wishes of trustees. He said they were not 'puppets on a string' but 'free men and women good and true'.[56] This advice appears not to have been fully accepted by the trustees. After the above court cases, Cardinal Hume, in a speech to lay head teachers, emphasised in an unspecific way that:

> Our aims are identical, our collaboration essential, but our roles are different.[57]

It is evident from the Cardinal Vaughan case that diocesan trustees have a wider concern with the provision of education in their areas, while the governors' primary concern is with the interests of their own particular school. The representatives of the collective interest, the diocesan trustees, sought to circumvent the established statutory procedures (Section 62 of the Education Reform Act of 1988 provides the statutory mechanism for trustees to object to opting-out proposals) by exerting pressures on selected governors whom they had appointed and who were unsympathetic to the collective cause.

At the same time as the Cardinal Vaughan case, another of the eight Catholic secondary schools in central London had refused to participate in the diocesan reorganisation plans. The trustees of the London Oratory school were not the diocesan bishops and senior clergy, but the Oratory Fathers. A minority of voluntary-aided schools are still owned and controlled by Religious Orders and consequently, in law, there was no need to agree to any reorganisation planned by the diocesan education authorities. However, in Canon Law it is the bishop who is charged with the responsibility for all schools which bear the title 'Catholic'. Catholic schools maintained by Religious Orders are not exempt from the diocesan bishop's right of oversight and visitation. The 1917 Code of Canon Law had given Religious Orders exemption from visitation, but this was revoked in 1983.[58] Canon 806 specifically authorises the diocesan bishop to regulate the educational policies of Catholic schools, including those operated by Religious Orders, since it declares that they are subject to these policies. However, the language used implies general guidelines rather than specific regulations and in the debates about the Oratory School in the Catholic press there were, surprisingly, no references made to Canon Law. Both the Cardinal Vaughan and the Oratory schools eventually opted out of local authority control and by so doing threw into some confusion the diocesan plan for a sixth-form college in the area, but the sixth-form college proceeded as planned. Cardinal Hume attempted unsuccessfully to block the application of the Cardinal Vaughan School for grant-maintained status by refusing to nominate foundation governors, who were necessary to proceed with the plan to opt out. As a result the Secretary of State for Education threatened to use his overriding powers in Section 99 of the 1944 Education Act to appoint the initial foundation governors on behalf of the trustee company. The parents also threatened to take Cardinal Hume back to the courts and after the Cardinal threatened to place himself in contempt of the courts, he finally withdrew active opposition to the plans of the school's parents and teachers.[59]

These cases have indicated how weak the present legal powers of the bishops are when they act as trustees of a group of schools. The law treats each voluntary-aided school as a separate and independent charitable foundation and not as a unit of a combined diocesan educational charity. In addition, the cases also indicate how the ordinary episcopal authority of bishops is received by parents with different priorities. Catholic schools, when owned and overseen by a diocese, Religious Order or in some cases even by a group of lay people, tend to have a very loose control structure so that the school typically can act freely within a general diocesan or religious framework. Lay school governors have increasingly become crucial elements in the formulation of the general policies which schools adopt. In 1983 Maurice Kogan led a study of school governors, not specifically Catholic, and found them unsure of their powers, their purpose and their identity.[60] He later described them as 'sleeping beauties still waiting for the kiss of politics'.[61] There is no reason to believe that Catholic school governors did not exhibit similar characteristics to the ones which Kogan found in the general population.

With the passing of the Education Reform Act in 1988, it would appear that this 'kiss of politics' has been given and has thrown Catholic school governors into a state of flux especially with regard to their relationship to the trustees and their delegated agencies, the diocesan school commissions. The bishop's theoretical authority over Catholic education within his diocese is clearly expressed in Canon Law. Nevertheless, he requires subordinates to assist him in the formulation of policy decisions and these have, since the late 1930s, evolved as the diocesan school commissions which have been endowed in each diocese with delegated authority. However, the nature and extent of this delegated authority is not clear for neither in Canon Law nor in diocesan practices does one find any definition of the authority of diocesan school commissions. Since these commissions act on behalf of the local Catholic community in directing a whole range of educational issues, the potential for conflict is evident. Within the Catholic community there are divergent and increasingly conflicting views held about where the real power should lie in terms of educational policy decisions at the local level. The diocesan bishops's position and relationship to the Catholic community on educational matters has become increasingly problematic.

In attempting to analyse and understand the relationship between diocesan authorities and the laity, it is useful to employ Frederick Wirt's development model of conflict.[62] This is especially worthwhile in the specific case of the Cardinal Vaughan School controversy. Whilst the model has been developed for the secular domain of public policy it has been modified here to apply it to the policy and religious questions raised in Catholic education. Wirt's model of conflict entails five stages; 'Quiescence', 'Issue Emergence', 'Turbulence', 'Resolution', and 'Closure'. In the first, 'Quiescence', the clergy dominate and the laity are supportive of their domination. This would have been the typical model operating in the Cardinal Vaughan School up until the 1970s, with parents and governors largely accepting diocesan plans without question. The second stage involves 'Issue Emergence', which Wirt describes as individual complaints resulting from the clergy's definition of service. Early diocesan comprehensive reorganisation plans did cause complaints about possible effects on academic standards, but the school remained single-sex entry, becoming a comprehensive of sorts. However, further diocesan reorganisation which included the proposed removal of the sixth-form caused widespread complaints and the issue was now clearly the opposition of parents and staff to the loss of their sixth-form. The third stage, 'Turbulence' in which all the complaints from parents escalate to become an unstructured set of interactions between themselves and the diocesan authorities resulted in the Cardinal Vaughan court case. Parents and governors openly opposed the diocesan proposals and questioned the quality of service provided by the diocesan authorities. The fourth stage, 'Resolution', has been reached. The school has used the escape route provided by the Government and become a grant-maintained school and therefore has resolved the issue for itself. According to Wirt's model there needs to be a final stage of 'Closure' which re-defines the function of the diocesan authorities in accordance with the demands of the school's new status. This stage has not yet arrived and will be an interesting development as some form of accommodation seems inevitable, which will affect established relationships between the diocese and parents. At present the Archbishop of Westminster has begun to re-define the relationship between himself and the foundation governors whom he appoints. It remains the case, however, that at any time in the Catholic school system there are many potential policy issues that could lead to conflict.

The Church's official emphasis on collegiality and participation has encouraged many within the Catholic community to view the Church's educational structures in a more democratic light. Consequently, Francois Houtart's analysis of 'contestation' within the Church is particularly relevant to the increasing amount of litigation cases initiated by members of the Church against the Church leadership. Houtart proposed that the first object of 'contestation' within the Church was legitimacy — a refusal to recognise the competence of the religious authority's intervention in a specific domain.[63] This was clearly the case with the Cardinal Vaughan parents and has been one of the arguments used in other cases of conflict with diocesan school commissions. On the basis of Houtart's analysis, three specific responses or reactions by the Church leadership to 'contestation' can be described. First, the ecclesiastical leadership may refuse to accept 'contestation' and seek to suppress or exclude individuals or groups who promote the 'contestation'. By dismissing two governors from the Cardinal Vaughan school this is exactly what the trustees sought to do. Second, the Church's leadership could give 'contestants' a certain legitimacy in order to limit their demands or third, they could accept the contestation. The last two options have been used by the Church leadership in other cases of conflict with parents.

In a case of conflict between governors and diocesan authorities which received national publicity in December 1987, six foundation governors were dismissed. The six governors of the Trinity School in Leamington Spa were removed from office by the trustees of the Archdiocese of Birmingham two days after the favourable Vaughan judgement for Cardinal Hume. The issue concerned the appointment of a new head teacher, since the then incumbent was retiring. The dismissed governors claimed it was an attempt by the diocese to alter the ethos of the school and impose a stricter, more 'traditional' Catholic system. There were no compulsory or regular religious education lessons in the school and this caused much anxiety within the Archdiocese. The head teacher justified the school's policy by reference to his own personal interpretation of the documents of Vatican II. However, these omissions contravened both the 1944 Education Act and the Trust Deeds of the school, two important points which were lost in the ensuing publicity about 'parent power'.[64] In addition the school had a majority of non-Catholics on the roll, due to the operation of an open admissions policy. The parents or contestants organised support for the dismissed governors by raising funds and presented a petition to the Archbishop. The Archbishop, as one of the trustees, was faced with almost total opposition from the school community and with a threat of legal action, the trustees decided to rescind the dismissals and accept the contestation. The case brings into sharp focus the practical limitations of the power of the trustees over governors when the parents are fully supportive of their governing body and teaching staff.

In December 1990 four governors at a Catholic primary school, in Richmond, south-west London, attempted to appoint a divorced and remarried man as head teacher. The Archdiocese of Southwark, in which diocese the school is located, dismissed four of the foundation governors and appointed others who would implement their policy which excluded the appointment of divorced and remarried people to senior Catholic positions. Parent leaders accused the diocesan education authorities of being out-of-date, of being undemocratic and of sacrificing the well-being of the school for principle.[65] Significantly, they also said that the Church's dismissals raised serious questions about the power of the Church when the government encouraged parents to assume more responsibility for their schools. Once again, half the parents of the school were non-Catholic and could not therefore have been expected to share the Catholic Church's moral position. Many of the parents supported the dismissed governors and one of these governors, Peter Kemmis-Betty, was reported as saying:

> The Archdiocese says the governors failed to uphold the Diocesan Trust Deed. Not a single governor can produce the deed because we've never seen it. Depending on what the deed says we may ask for a judicial review in the High Court.[66]

Leave was subsequently granted by the High Court for judicial review of the case, but the contestants eventually decided to make an undisclosed out-of-court settlement. This further example confirms the readiness of Catholic governors to resort to legal action, with the support of parents, against their diocesan bishop in order to uphold their own educational priorities. These educational priorities are clearly stated values derived from sources other than the Catholic Church.

An outspoken Catholic critic of the bishops has been Sheila Lawlor, who as deputy director of the Conservative Centre for Policy Studies launched numerous attacks on the bishops' education policy. In an article in *The Tablet*, 20th February 1988 she argued that diocesan authorities were fearful of parental power and added:

> . . . the hierarchy reject the prospect of parents exercising a voice, unless that voice happens to echo its own . . . The danger to Church schools lies not in 'opting-out' but in a refusal of diocesan planners to respect the wishes of those for whom they plan.[67]

In another place she wrote:

> There is no justification for denying parents of pupils in these
> schools the rights which parents of pupils in other State schools
> enjoy.[68]

She subsequently stated that the problem was one of organisation
and that the laity were best placed to decide this matter. She was
not alone in her criticisms and thus the bishops found little support
in Parliament in dealing with the issue of parental rights. James
Pawsey, a Catholic MP, commenting on the Leamington Spa affair,
accused the Church of denying parents a democratic say in their
children's education.[69] The bishops responded by claiming that
there had been much false information published in the press and
Cardinal Hume wrote to the Cardinal Prefect of the Congregation
of Catholic Education in Rome once again, to clarify the Church's
teaching on the respective roles and relationship between parents
and the diocesan bishop in the matter of Catholic schooling. He
asked in particular for a comment on paragraph six of the Vatican
II *Declaration on Christian Education* which was much quoted in the
Cardinal Vaughan School case. Paragraph six states that:

> . . . parents, who have a primary and inalienable duty and right in
> regard to the education of their children, should enjoy the fullest
> liberty in the choice of their school.[70]

This paragraph is also incorporated into the Code of Canon Law
and this requires some preliminary explanation.

In Canon Law, the parents are seen as the first educators
because they mediate between the Church and their offspring.
Canon 226(2) strongly reflects paragraph three of the Second
Vatican Council's *Declaration on Christian Education* which makes
clear that parents have the serious obligation and the right to
educate their children in accordance with the teaching of the
Church. Canon 793 affirms that parents have the duty to select the
most appropriate means and schools for the Catholic education of
their children. This duty implies the obligation to see to the
formation of their children in the Catholic faith in the best way
open to them. It also involves the right to make the determination,
among schools available, of those which are most suitable for their
children. Previously, bishops simply expected parents to send their
children to the local Catholic school and in addition emphasised
their 'obligation' to support these schools. However, the Church in
England and Wales is clearly not able to provide alternative means

by itself and therefore Canon 793(2) is really directed at the State
rather than Church authorities. This part of the Canon claims that
the State should provide parents with a choice of schools so that
Catholic education will be possible. The more basic responsibility
of the local Church is to see that effective Catholic education is
made genuinely available to the parents, taking into consideration
their economic and social conditions. Canon 794 states that the
responsibility for arranging things so that all the Catholic faithful
might have the benefit of a Catholic education is laid upon the
'pastors of souls' i.e. the bishops and clergy. The bishops are seen
as the stimulators and co-ordinators of the effort, but it is obvious
from a practical view that the real responsibility for making Catholic education available clearly rests with everyone in the local
Catholic community. Canon 798 modifies the prohibition of the
old Canon 1374 which forbade attendance at non-Catholic schools.
The new Canon can still be interpreted narrowly, since it states
that Catholics must send their children to schools wherein Catholic education is provided, when such schools are available to them.
Cardinal Baum's response to the 'parental rights' issue in his reply
to Cardinal Hume was to interpret the documents of Vatican II in
support of the diocesan plans. He said:

> We have noted a frequent misapplication of the above (para. six)
> text. It is clear . . . that the purpose of that text is to defend the
> rights and full liberty of parents to choose a Catholic school for their
> children . . . It is quite inappropriate . . . to quote paragraph six in
> resistance to the diocesan plans as though Catholic schooling were
> being denied, whereas, in fact, the diocesan plan has emerged after
> extensive consultation to secure an equitable system for as many
> Catholic children as possible. It would appear that at present too
> little attention is being paid by some groups of parents to the heavy
> responsibility and duties of the diocesan bishop in educational
> matters as the focus of unity, and teacher of the People of God in
> their particular Church (England and Wales).[71]

The Cardinal went on to explain that the bishop is charged with
co-ordinating all works of the apostolate and that these should
operate under his direction. He ended with a call to unity and more
particularly for parents to respond to the bishop. Whilst his comments were widely repeated in the Catholic press, little response
was made to them. The Vatican had clearly attempted to support
a bishop in some difficulty with lay members of his community.

The Church's dispute with both government and some of its
own members can be located in the differing interpretations of

parental rights. The government's stress on parental involvement and choice gives predominance to 'the market' and emphasises individual rights over the rights of the community as a whole. By contrast, the Church's distinctive mission places greater emphasis on the rights of the whole Catholic community in determining the future of Catholic schools. The Church does not recognise that the rights of parents and pupils already placed in Catholic schools can override the rights of the whole Catholic community. This is the source of the basic conflict between the leadership of the Church and some of its members.

Disputes have continued since the publication of Cardinal Baum's letter. The St Francis Xavier School in Liverpool organised a ballot of parents to opt out of local authority control in 1989. The ballot was successful and the school was accorded grant-maintained status against the wishes of the diocesan bishop. In April 1991, St Augustine's school in Trowbridge became the fourth Catholic school in England to be awarded grant-maintained status against the advice given to parents during the ballot by the trustees. By January 1992 there had been successful ballots in three other Catholic secondary schools: Bishop Vaughan School in Swansea, La Retraite High School in Clapham, south-west London, and St John Fisher School at Purley in Surrey.[72] St Joseph's School, Widnes had a ballot organised by a group of parents opposed to diocesan reorganisation plans. The diocese opposed the parental objections and a campaign was organised by local priests urging parents to vote against 'opting-out'. A similar exercise was held at Catholic schools in Stoke-on-Trent and Warrington.[73] The final result was a 'no' vote for grant-maintained status in all three schools. The bishops re-viewed their position on grant-maintained schools at a special meeting in June 1991 and continued to express their opposition to the procedures for obtaining grant-maintained status, unless a school faced an actively hostile LEA. They said that they would not recommend Catholic schools to opt out until the financial, practical and moral implications for the school in question and for the education system as a whole had been clarified. The bishops also stated that:

> We are concerned that the emergence of a more pronounced market as a divisive force in education means that the partnership between Church and State has begun to change both locally and nationally.[74]

Despite these strong reservations about opting-out, the number of Catholic schools which have sucessfully sought grant-maintained status and established their own association to promote their views, with or without the support of their bishop, reached 140 in 1995.

The Renewal of Catholic Educational Structures

Catholic educational structures in England and Wales continue to be incomplete since they do not provide any central machinery for drawing together the many national and local Catholic bodies involved with schools. The official and quasi-official structures governing Catholic education are many and overlapping and do not easily lend themselves to long-term decision-making. The Rev. Dominic Milroy argues that many decisions on Catholic education at all levels tend to be 'fragmentary, disparate and inconclusive' as a result of past structures, which he claims are now inadequate.[75]

There are several Catholic teacher bodies, none of which enjoys any defined official status. The Catholic Teachers' Federation, one of the oldest, is lay run and draws its membership from primary and secondary schools. It organises its own annual conferences and regional meetings, providing publications and other material for its members in Catholic schools. Representatives of this association are found on most diocesan education commissions. The Conference of Catholic Secondary Schools and Colleges, although originally more representative of the independent sector, is also mainly lay run with increasing membership from the maintained sector of schools. Its object is the advancement of Catholic education through the provision of facilities for the interchange of ideas and information; the study of educational problems and the provision of representation for its members on appropriate Catholic national and local bodies. The Association of Principals of Catholic Sixth-Form Colleges and the Association of Catholic Grant-Maintained Schools are relatively recent organisations serving the interests of these expanding areas. The effective membership of these bodies is small, there being only 16 Catholic sixth-form colleges and under 150 grant-maintained schools, and they have no set pattern of links with each other. However, the membership of most national committees established by the bishops usually reflects these bodies, which are involved in servicing Catholic education. Nevertheless, clerical or religious bodies tend to have greater representation on such national committees. The Association of Religious in Education is consistently over-represented.

The Association of Diocesan School Commissioners, despite a growing number of lay appointments, is still dominated by the clergy, as is the National Board of Religious Advisers and Inspectors. Both inspectors and commissioners are diocesan based, but meet at national level a number of times a year. Since each represents an autonomous diocese they are answerable to their diocesan bishop and not to any national collective. At diocesan level there are also a number of loosely organised Catholic associations of parents formed to take an interest in education in the diocese as a whole. There is once again no set pattern of contacts between these bodies. Governing bodies in schools are predominantly lay in composition, but the method of their appointment as foundation governors varies between each diocese. Some bishops request a written promise of support for the trustees' policies before appointment can take place. Other bodies at national level have included the CEC and the Principals of Catholic Colleges of Higher Education. Each body varies in expertise, influence and the structures and methods they employ to promote their message. As policy is decided by the bishops alone, these national and local bodies whose collective experience is great are not considered 'representative', since they cannot develop an overview of the Catholic education system. Fragmentation and single interest groups within Catholic education have rendered these bodies weak and there have been increasing calls for some structural changes.

One such call was made by the Conference of Catholic Secondary Schools in April 1987. The Conference sent a letter to Cardinal Hume on what it described as 'issues of great importance requiring an early reply and decision'.[76] Two of these issues addressed the question of how Catholic education was to be organised and managed in the future. The Conference sought the establishment of a national 'think-tank' which would be concerned with the programmes, organisation and management of a number of groups and committees currently working on various aspects of the Catholic education service. It also sought representation on diocesan school commissions and other national education bodies. The main issue appeared to be that the Conference members felt that their professional expertise was not being fully utilised by the Catholic Church and indicated that they wished have a right to membership of Catholic education bodies established by the Church and not be dependent on co-option by the bishops. The Conference also sought a clearly identified structure headed by a bishop with sole responsibility for Catholic schools.

Under such pressure, the bishops established a committee in the same year to review national and local structures and this committee reported in November 1988.[77] The Committee constituted by the bishops was composed of a majority of clerics with two lay people appointed by the Church authorities and representing no lay organisation within the Church. This seemed surprising, since the recent practice had been to have 'representatives' from the lay and religious associations in Catholic education on national committees appointed by the bishops. However, its recommendations did not extend the laity's influence on policy formulation, since the committee envisaged a new body dominated by the bishops as before. The report made the recommendation that the Church's policies needed to be made more precise. Lay participation, the report suggested, should be part of the structures, although any lay members should be appointed by the bishops.[78]

The CEC was consequently abolished in April 1991 and a new Catholic Education Service (CES) was created with a lay Director and two assistant directors.[79] It was noticeable as early as 1986 that some of the functions normally expected of the CEC, such as commenting on in-service provision, appraisal of teachers, producing the campaign literature during the passage of the 1987 Education Reform Bill, and even surveys of schools, were being carried out by officials of the Bishops' Conference. It could be said that the CEC was already losing substantial areas of influence. Its replacement functions as an 'agency' of the Bishops' Conference and offers a service of information and advice on all aspects of education to diocesan school commissions and to the personnel of Catholic schools, sixth-form colleges, and Colleges of Higher Education. Another explicit aim of the 'agency' is for it to be responsive to policy-decisions taken by the Bishops' Conference. The chair of the CES is taken by a bishop who also acts as a major spokesman in England and Wales on Catholic educational matters. It is planned to create two further bodies, a co-ordinating council and an annual conference. The annual conference is designed to bring together all the 'recognised' groups involved in the field of Catholic education. Significantly, the bishops say that 'among the candidates for such recognition would appear to be the following' and then lists the main groups discussed earlier in this chapter.[80] This indicates clearly that none of these bodies has ever been formally recognised by the bishops. The National Conference on Catholic Education in 1995, only the second of its kind, had five keynote

speeches delivered by three bishops, one bureaucrat in the bishops' secretariat, and one head of a government education quango.
This can hardly be seen as drawing together interested groups in
Catholic education, especially when the Catholic Teachers' Federation held its own annual conference at the same time in another
city. The conference appears to function as a forum for policy-makers
to present their views.

The co-ordinating council is designed to have nineteen members, including a 'weighted' representation from three designated
'forums'. The membership of these three 'forums' are, first, the
diocesan school commissioners; second, representatives of the
Catholic teacher groups; and third, the diocesan inspectors and
members of the national religious education project.[81] The co-
ordinating council was to meet twice annually to ensure that the
management of the CES discusses appropriate matters at national
level. There was no mention of research in Catholic education or
support services, other than secretarial assistance for the new CES.
More fundamentally, parents seem to have been completely excluded from the official structures, as are other national Catholic
bodies. A co-ordinating committee was established and a fourth
'forum', further and higher education, was added. Therefore, these
new structures remain incomplete since they do not bring together
all the Catholic bodies with an interest in Catholic education. This
seems surprising, especially since the bishops have constantly
stressed the central role of parents and the wider Catholic community in maintaining Catholic schools.

Summary

The Church is by nature hierarchical. This was clearly confirmed
recently by the Extraordinary Synod of 1985 and the Synod on the
Vocation of the Laity in 1987 in Rome. Canon Law unequivocally
confers on the diocesan bishop the primary responsibility for all
Catholic schools including those directed by Religious Orders.
Catholic schools in England and Wales provide the bishops with a
practical means of exercising their teaching authority. In addition,
to his primary exercise of the teaching office through preaching and
catechetical instruction, the bishop also exercises this function
through providing schools in the diocese. Canon Law provides for
this involvement by the bishop in schools in both supervisory and
directive forms. The diocesan bishop is not encouraged to decide
all educational matters alone, since co-responsibility, collegiality,

and participation have all been advocated before and since Vatican II. Nevertheless, as Nichols warns:

> Principles of subsidiarity and local initiative, unless cross-grained by principles of solidarity and union, serve as centrifugal forces allowing the denigration of the Church into a congeries of congregational bodies whose experiences of faith are no more than analogues one for another.[82]

Active lay involvement is essential for the survival of Catholic schools and the principle of subsidiarity encourages decision-making at the lowest possible level. It is also the local Catholic community which gives the Catholic school the practical model for living the faith. None of the models of the Church described in this chapter has been found to be complete in itself. Nevertheless, the structures and forms of Church life are clearly dependent on the mission of the Church and need to be designed to facilitate participation. They must assist rather than hinder the laity's capacity to co-operate with the Church's mission. The polarised views that all the people of God are fundamentally equal in status or that there are only some in the Church who possess authority and the power to exercise it, appear to be unsatisfactory models. For whilst the Church remains firmly hierarchical, which entails authority and obedience, it does not entail superiority and subjection for their own sake. After consultation and participation from the laity, it is the diocesan bishop who declares what Catholic education is to mean in practice. The only definition of what constitutes a Catholic school is that it must be one recognised as such by the diocesan bishop.

Nevertheless, there are clearly differing educational priorities within the Catholic community. Cunningham commented that grant-maintained status had been criticised by the bishops primarily because of the procedures, and observed:

> The status had the curiosity that the Act [1988 Education Reform Act] laid down only a procedure for its acquisition, not any criteria.[83]

He identified the main concern, namely:

> ... that individual schools might be seeking to opt out, not so much of aided status as of unpalatable but necessary reorganisation schemes involving a number of Catholic schools.[84]

Bishop Konstant said that opting out would seriously damage the relationship between school and local community and that it would 'encourage a selfish elitism'. By contrast a Catholic head teacher

in Bishop Konstant's own diocese disputed his conclusions on
'opting-out' and said that the bishop was not to be taken as
speaking on behalf of all Catholic schools. The head teacher argued
that grant-maintained status represented a far greater opportunity
for funding capital development in Catholic schools which, he
claimed, lagged behind LEA schools with sub-standard accommodation. Rejecting the charge of 'elitism' the head teacher pointed
out that aided schools were already different from LEA schools and
that little would change if they 'opted-out'. Another Catholic head
teacher in Stoke-on-Trent employed similar reasons in support of
an opting-out ballot at his school which was narrowly rejected by
the parents.[85] This, and the other examples in this chapter, demonstrate the clear differences on educational policy within the
Catholic community.

The description of the new educational structures by the Bishops' Conference seem to confirm McSweeney's observation that:

> . . . allocation of power and responsibility in the Church is still
> accomplished in the traditional way with little more than rhetorical
> concessions to participative government.[86]

The idea, expounded at Vatican II, that governance involves the
governed through some form of shared responsibility, is almost
wholly absent in the new structures. The bishops have always had
it within their power to extend the presence of lay members at
every level in the Church, but have consistently chosen not to do
so. Instead, they have merely reacted to government policy for
greater parental participation by attempting first to oppose it, and
secondly, to nullify its effects in Catholic schools. The new structures make clear that the bishops will decide policy whilst the CES
is their executive agency and the annual conference is purely
consultative. National and local groups involved with Catholic
education within the Church will continue to meet independently
from each other and discuss similar issues. It is difficult to see how
their deliberations will have much impact on an annual conference.

In response to central government, the national Catholic bodies
and structures have always lacked efficient and well-resourced
support systems. This is also true of local diocesan school commissions, which have none of the professional organisation matching
that of the LEAs, with which they deal. What assistance they
receive often comes from willing and retired lay professionals on a
voluntary basis. The Catholic Church's educational structures
cannot match the expertise and the output of local and national

government agencies. The Church's policies cannot be instigative, but remain largely reactive. Whilst the new structures give the impression of a unified approach, it is far from certain that this will be the result. In addition, the CES is essentially a data-gathering and service organisation which does not exercise any determining authority over Catholic schools. Bishops remain free to speak independently of their own National Conference despite one of their number being designated the national spokesman on education. Groups such as the Catholic Teachers' Federation are also free to evolve their own policies and issues and to campaign for them. In such a situation it will become apparent to the government that the Catholic voice in education is neither united nor coherent. In those managerial areas which could be performed by professional lay people, clerical control is almost total.

Conclusion

One of the central claims of the Church in education is that the whole Catholic community has a legitimate interest in the future direction of Catholic schooling. Whilst the Church recognises that parental rights are fundamental in the choice of school, it also acknowledges that these rights must be balanced against those of the community. Catholic schools are not to function in isolation from one another or from the Catholic community in general. Consequently, some aspects of government education policy and legislation, especially the 'opting-out' provisions in the Education Reform Act of 1988, would appear to be incompatible with Church teaching. By 'opting-out' a Catholic school may be acting independently of the wider Catholic community whose interests in the school would be denied. Cardinal Hume urges the Catholic community to support its diocesan bishops who should make the final decision in areas of controversy, but this has been ignored by some parents, governors and teachers in Catholic schools. At both national and local level, Catholics with a direct interest in schooling have successfully challenged the decisions of the bishops and in some cases totally rejected them. This development raises new and fundamental questions about the role of the diocese as the decision-making mechanism in the institutional life of the Church. The present structures to facilitate the Catholic community's participation in educational policy-making remain dependent on co-option by clerics. There is a conflict between diocesan bishops and their schools commissions on the one hand, and many of the structures operating in schools within the diocese. In future, schools may not, in some cases, be inclined to support and develop Catholic education if it is perceived by head teachers, governors and parents as inflexible and constraining.

Notes

1. Hunt, T.C., (ed.), *Religious Schools in America: A Selected Bibliography*, Garland Publishing, New York, 1986, p. 109.
2. Donohue, J.W., 'A Vatican Salute to Lay Teachers', *America*, October 1982, pp. 251–252.
3. Abbot, W.M. (ed.), *The Documents of Vatican II*, Geoffrey Chapman, London, 1966.
4. *The Catholic School*, Congregation for Catholic Education, Rome, 1977.
5. *The Religious Dimension of Catholic Education*, Congregation for Catholic Education, Rome, 1988.
6. Likert, R., *The Human Organisation*, McGraw-Hill, New York, 1967, and especially *Profile of the School*, 1978.
7. Taylor, M.J.(ed.), *An Introduction to Christian Education*, Abingdon Press, Nashville, 1966, p. 105.
8. Dulles, A., *Models of the Church*, Gill and Macmillan, Dublin, 1976.
9. Miller, H., 'The Administration of Christian Education', in Taylor, M.(ed.), *op. cit.*, pp. 105–116.
10. Dulles, A., *op. cit.*
11. *Ibid.*
12. Hornsby-Smith, M.P. and Lee, M., *Survey of Roman Catholic Opinion 1978*, University of Sussex, 1978.
13. Hornsby-Smith, M.P., *Roman Catholics in England and Wales*, Cambridge University Press, 1987, p. 204.
14. *Ibid.*, p. 210.
15. Hurley, M.J., *Declaration on Christian Education — A Commentary* Paulist Press, New Jersey, 1966, pp. 70–75.
16. Hornsby-Smith, M.P., *op. cit.*, p. 5, see also Michel, G.J., 'Parent Participation in Catholic Schools', *Catholic Education Today*, Vol. 11, No. 1, January/March 1977, p. 10.
17. Spencer, A.E.C.W. 'PTAs in Catholic Schools', *Catholic Education Today*, Vol. 3, No. 2, March/April 1969, pp. 17–23.
18. CEC, *Handbook 1962–1963*, editorial note.
19. CEC, *Report 1963*, p. 19., see also *Education*, 1st January 1965, p. 46.
20. CEC, *Report 1965*, p. 21 and *Catholic Herald*, 7th May 1965.
21. CEC, *Report 1968*, p. 14.
22. Spencer, A.E.C.W., *op. cit.*
23. Cf. notes 79, 80, and 81.
24. Hornsby-Smith, M.P., *Roman Catholics in England and Wales*, CUP, 1987, p. 134.
25. Cumming, J. & Burns, P., (ed.), *op. cit.*, p. 105.

26. Hornsby-Smith, M.P., 'Educational Advice', *The Tablet*, 25th October 1975, pp. 1027–1028.
27. CEC *Report 1971*, p. 14.
28. CEC *Report 1971*, p. 23.
29. Hornsby-Smith, M., *Catholic Education — The Unobtrusive Partner*, Sheed and Ward, London, 1978, pp. 126–127. The CEC version of these negotiations can be found in the CEC *Reports* 1969, p. 23; 1971, pp. 14–23; and 1972, p. 12.
30. CEC *Report 1972*, p. 12.
31. CEC *Report 1977*, p. 12.
32. Beales, A.C.F., 'Parental Rights in Education', *Catholic Education Today*, Vol. 7, No. 2, March/April 1973, pp. 4–6.
33. *The Tablet* editions for October and November 1972 especially 21st October 1972, p. 1010 and 14th October p. 985. See also Hartley, F., *The Diocesan School Commission and the Reorganisation of Catholic Secondary Education in Birmingham 1972–1976*, MEd, University of Birmingham, 1983.
34. Adler, M. et al, *op. cit.*, p. 32.
35. Adler, M. et al, *op. cit.*, pp. 29–30.
36. Sallis, J., *op. cit.*, p. 109.
37. Archdiocese of Birmingham, *Directory* 1963.
38. Sallis, J., *op. cit.*, p. 109.
39. Laity Commission, *Empty Schools*, Catholic Bishops' Conference of England and Wales, 1978.
40. *The Tablet*, 5th November 1977, pp. 1059–1060.
41. Maclure, S., *op. cit.*, p. xv.
42. Liverpool 1980 Official Report of the National Pastoral Congress, St Paul Publications, Slough, 1981, p. 157.
43. Signposts, *op. cit.*, p. 151.
44. Manno, B.V., 'Lay Involvement in Catholic Schools', *America*, October 27th 1984, pp. 246–247.
45. Archdiocese of Birmingham — *Your School — Guidelines for Governors*, 1987.
46. Hume, B., *op. cit.*, p. 116.
47. Jones *v.* Lee and Another, *L.G.R.*, 78(1) 1979, p. 213 ff.
48. *The Guardian*, 17th December 1987, *The Independent*, 3rd February 1989. See especialy *Education and the Law*, Vol. 1, Nos. 1, 2, and 3 of 1989.
49. R *v.* Trustee of Roman Catholic Diocese of Westminster, *ex p.* Mars (1987) 86 *LGR* 507. The governing body of the Cardinal Vaughan School had rejected the diocesan plans on 4th November 1986 by 11 votes to 2, on the 9th of June 1987 by 9 votes to 8, and on the 6th July 1987 by 9 votes to 7.
50. *Ibid*.
51. *Ibid*.
52. Brunyate and Another *v* Inner London Education Authority (1989), 2 *All ER* 417.

53. R *v* Westminster Roman Catholic Diocese Trustee *ex p* Andrews reported in *The Independent*, 27th July 1989, p. 9.
54. *The Tablet*, 9th September 1987, p. 1013.
55. Woolfe. J in R *v.* Inner London Education Authority *ex p.* Byrne and Sharpe (unreported) referred to in the case in note (48).
56. R *v.* Trustee of Roman Catholic Diocese of Westminster, *ex p.* Mars (1987) 86 *LGR* 507.
57. *Briefing* Catholic Information Services, 30th September 1988, Vol. 18, No.19.
58. Cordiden, J.A. et al., *The Code of Canon Law : A Text and Commentary*, Geoffrey Chapman, London, 1985.
59. *The Independent* 21st July 1989, see also *Briefing*, 4th August 1989, Vol. 19, No.17. See 'Baker May Sidestep Archbishop's Defiance', *TES*, 26th May 1989, 'Hume Determined Not to Give Way', *TES*, 28th July 1989, 'Cardinal Accepts Vaughan Case is Unwinnable', *TES*, 11th August 1989.
60. Kogan, M., *School Governing Bodies Project 1980–83*, Educational Studies Unit: Brunel University, November 1983.
61. *TES* 2nd March 1984.
62. Wirt, F., 'Professionalism and Political Conflict — A Developmental Model', *Journal of Policy Studies*, Vol. 1, Pt. 1, February 1981, pp. 61–93.
63. Houtart, F., 'Conflicts of Authority in the Roman Catholic Church', *Social Compass*, Vol. 16, No. 3, 1969, pp. 309–325.
64. *TES* 15th January 1988.
65. *The Independent*, 17th December 1990.
66. *The Universe*, 13th January 1991, p. 2.
67. *The Tablet*, 20th February 1988, pp. 200–207.
68. Lawlor, S., *op. cit.*, p. 13.
69. *The Independent*, 2nd December 1988.
70. Abbot, W.M. (ed.), *The Documents of Vatican II*, Geoffrey Chapman, London, 1966, *Declaration on Christian Education*.
71. *The Tablet*, 29th July 1989, p. 881.
72. *The Universe*, 5th May 1991, 30th June 1991, and *Catholic Herald*, 19th July 1991, 6th December 1991.
73. *The Universe* 17th September 1989, 30th June 1991, and *Catholic Herald*, 6th December 1991.
74. *Catholic Herald*, 21st June 1991.
75. Milroy, D., Letter to Cardinal Hume on behalf of the Conference of Secondary Schools, dated January 1987.
76. 90th Annual Conference of Catholic Secondary Schools, April 11th–13th, 1987, Published Proceedings, pp. 33–34.
77. Catholic Bishops' Conference of England and Wales — *Servicing Roman Catholic Schools*, reprinted in *Briefing*, 16th December 1988, Vol. 18, No. 25.
78. *Ibid*.
79. In the Bishops' Conference of England and Wales Statement on the Catholic Education Service of August 1990 there were to be three

assistant directors. However, the Catholic Education Service's own statement (August 1991) of introduction to its services lists only two assistants with one consultant — the former secretary of the CEC. Indeed, the only change to the new agency is the replacement of the former secretary.

80. Catholic Bishops' Conference of England and Wales — *Servicing Roman Catholic Schools*, 1988, reprinted in *Briefing*, 16th December 1988, Vol. 18, No. 25.
81. Catholic Education Service — Statement of Services, August 1991
82. Nichols, A., 'Review Article', *Priests and People*, Vol. 5, No. 5, May 1991, p. 203 ff.
83. Cunningham, R.F., 'The Education Reform Act 1988', *Law and Justice*, No. 104/105, 1990, pp. 39–46.
84. *Ibid*.
85. *TES*, January 11, 1991, and February 8th 1991, p. 11.
86. McSweeney, V., *Roman Catholicism*, Blackwells, Oxford, 1980, p. 240.

6

Issues in Catholic Educational
Policy since 1965

Introduction

The period since the Second Vatican Council has seen significant changes within the Catholic Community and in national educational policy. Four central concerns for Catholic schools have arisen and been exemplified by an extended process of legislation leading to the Education Reform Acts of 1988, 1992 and 1993. First, the control and nature of the curriculum; second, the training and appointment of teachers; third, the admission of pupils and finally, the control and management of Catholic schools. The central object of the Church's direct participation and provision in education, at least at the level of principle, has been to ensure the existence of a Catholic education (curriculum content) for Catholic children (admissions) taught by Catholic teachers (appointments) in Catholic schools (control). Therefore, the major policy areas for the Church are: curriculum, admissions, staffing and the overall control of the Catholic school. However, though largely determined by the bishops, formulation of official Catholic education policy is subject to three compelling influences which predominate in the framing of those policies. They are: assertions of principle by the Second Vatican Council and subsequent statements from Rome; the influence of national educational legislation and local government regulations; and the social and ecclesial changes within the Catholic community. All three have led to new influences on policy formulation and implementation.

The Curriculum

The governors and head teachers in every voluntary maintained school in England and Wales are under a duty to exercise their

functions according to Sections 1 and 2 of the Education Reform
Act of 1988 with a view to securing that their school curriculum is
balanced and broadly based. The curriculum must also promote
the spiritual, moral, social, mental and physical development of
children and prepare the them for the opportunities, responsibilities, and experiences of adult life. Sections Two and Three of the
same Act designate the core and foundation subjects which must
be taught. The dominant values in these educational provisions of
the Act are largely secular, defined by Denis Lawton as 'moral
pluralism'.[1] In England and Wales the education system acknowledges that there are many ends and that, whilst these ends may
conflict with each other, none is necessarily paramount. Prior to the
Education Reform Act of 1988 there was a lack of consensus about
the purpose and content of school education and it would have
seemed reasonable to expect that different value systems or ide-
ologies would generate different objectives and curricula. For example, since Catholicism is a value system which believes that the
world is ultimately meaningful and that fundamental values are not
arbitrary, a significant and distinctive contribution to the purpose
and content of the curriculum would appear inevitable. As a consequence adherence to Catholicism should make a difference to
the focus and content of the curriculum in Catholic schools. Some,
like Patrick Walsh, have argued that Catholic schools must draw on
Christian sources and resources if they are to remain Christian,
which implies an appropriate 'Catholic curriculum'. He asserts that
education is 'good in a Christian way' when the content is based
on the Church's heritage and tradition.[2] Unfortunately, no substance or concrete application to the content of the Catholic school
curriculum is given to these statements other than a few references
to the Christian aims of some school subjects, such as science
which he believes must provide children with a respect and understanding for God's creation.

   In order to assess the Catholic responses to the curriculum
proposals initiated by Government or quasi-official State agencies
since 1965, it is necessary to provide a brief historical background
to the Church's policies on the curriculum. Catholic elementary
schools in the nineteenth century did not provide religion on the
school curriculum as a parallel subject to reading or writing. The
secular and religious were seen as inseparable. Some subjects, such
as religion and liturgy, directed the student immediately to God
whilst the greater number (history, art, science) directed them

mediately to God. It is one of the reasons why Catholic inspectors often found themselves in conflict with the Privy Council's committee on education.[3] It is also why there was conflict over the Privy Council's grant for the purchase of books from their 'approved list'. The problem was made more complex by the use in many Catholic schools of Irish textbooks which were not on the Government's list.[4] Controversy continued over the appropriateness of secular school textbooks well into the twentieth century. The Catholic Teachers' Federation, for example, established a sub-committee in the early 1920s to look at anti-Catholic bias in textbooks. The committee approached publishers to seek the removal of offending passages and was largely successful in this aim.[5] After the Second World War the Catholic Social Guild produced a number of school textbooks for Catholic schools, especially in the humanities. The Catholic Education Council (CEC) in its house journal, *Catholic Education: An Educational Review,* promoted the continued development of a Catholic view of the curriculum and dedicated a full edition in 1956 to the Catholic school curriculum, mainly in the arts. In another issue in 1956, the Review's editorial warned against over-specialisation and utilitarian tendencies in the Catholic school curriculum, but it failed to provide any definition of how it understood the Catholic school curriculum.[6] The balance between secular and religious education continued to be a source of tension for Catholic schools in the 1960s.

Throughout the 1960s there was continuing discussion about the Catholic dimension of the secular curriculum within the Catholic educational periodicals. However, there was growing criticism of the very idea of a 'Catholic curriculum' from some within the Church. For example, Terry Eagleton openly attacked the Church for its policy on the curriculum which he viewed as damaging. He argued that there was no such thing as Catholic history, or Catholic science and it was damaging for the Church to attempt to seek to create them.[7] There is no evidence that this was what the Church sought, yet Eagleton continued his criticisms especially about the place of religion in the Catholic schools' curriculum. He could not see how religion and secular subjects could be combined or integrated without damage to subjects such as history.

At this time the DES began to take an interest in the school curriculum by establishing the Schools Council, a national body set up in 1965 under teacher control and independent of central Government. One of the Council's early activities involved the production of many educational projects which it offered to schools. There was nothing prescriptive about the Council's activities, but it did have a substantial influence on curriculum development in maintained schools. Some of the projects it offered schools dealt with controversial areas and this was especially true of the Schools Council Humanities Project (SCHP) begun in 1967 with its original duration of three years, subsequently extended to 1972, under the direction of Lawrence Stenhouse. The SCHP contained materials on topics such as poverty, war, family and marriage and was aimed at low achieving 14–16 year olds. The teaching principles behind the humanities packages emphasised open discussion among pupils with the teacher acting as a neutral chairman. It had 'discussion' rather than 'instruction' at its core and advocated progressive methods in the classroom. In addition, the content stressed the acquisition of moral values through the study of literary and historical texts — it was more properly a moral education programme. With its criterion of neutrality and its clear moral implications, the project attracted considerable hostility. Stenhouse, and others who carried out evaluations of the diffusion of the project, did not indicate if any of this hostility came from the Catholic Church who were represented on the governing body of the Schools Council by the CEC.[8]

In one evaluation of a Catholic school's use of the project it was recorded that the head teacher was enthusiastic about its introduction into the school and that the staff had decided not to consider examining the pupils on the project. The only indication of Catholic responses in the subsequent evaluations was the fact that the Catholic Truth Society bought all the project materials except the one with the title *Relations between the Sexes*. There is a curious comment recorded about a nun who by using false labels and under cover of darkness, to evade customs, imported the project into Ireland.[9] The most important response by the Church to the Schools Council Humanities Project was to establish its own Catholic Schools Humanities Projects under the directorship of Tony Higgins in 1968. This was charged with developing suitable Catholic materials for Catholic schools as a 'distinctive Catholic effort' on the themes which the SCHP had already outlined.[10] The rationale behind this initiative was that the Catholic Church had its own particular view of the humanities and of the notion of neutrality. Neutrality for the Schools Council required a sense of balance between different viewpoints, but for the Church this sense of balance was considered to be different for Catholics. Although some materials were produced, the Catholic project lacked financial support and suffered from a lack of agreement on what the particular Catholic vision of the humanities should be. There was division on the CEC which sponsored the parallel Catholic project. Some argued that it was divisive and unnecessary as the SCHP was acceptable to most Catholic schools. Others argued that the Church must have a distinctive contribution to make in areas where morals are being discussed and that the SCHP's selection of materials was coloured by a secular mentality or as Higgins later explained:

A concern for objective truth, as taught by authoritative Church from whom the Catholic teacher has a mission was the most funda-mental and specifically Catholic of the reasons why many Catholics were opposed to the (Schools Council) Humanities Project.[11]

The Catholic project was abandoned in 1972 and no practical attempt to provide an alternative Catholic vision of the secular curriculum was made by the Church until 1990.

Central Control of the Catholic School Curriculum

Section 23 of the 1944 Education Act, which dealt with 'control of the secular curriculum', gave governors of Catholic voluntary-aided schools control over the secular curriculum in their schools, unless their articles of government otherwise provided. Sections 1 to 4 of the 1988 Education Reform Act removed this control and returned it to the DES. The 1944 Education Act's overall provisions con-cerning the secular curriculum emphasised local discretion and there was a total absence of prescription. The processes which led to this outcome are well documented, but require some elaboration.

It is important to begin with the observation that Government intervention in the curriculum debate of the mid 1970s was di-rected at LEA schools. There are few references to voluntary-aided schools in any of the documents. Nevertheless, it was clear that Government interest in the curriculum would impinge eventually on the voluntary-aided sector. Legal control of the secular curricu-lum in maintained schools lay with the LEA. In voluntary-aided schools, legal control of the curriculum was vested in the governing body. During the committee stage of the 1944 Education Bill, discussion had centred on this distinction and some feared that the character of a school would be radically changed by religious bias pervading certain areas of the secular curriculum.[12] Following the Act the statutory distinction between the control of the curriculum in voluntary-aided and LEA schools is often blurred by Government reports and circulars. In effect, the Government did not take the distinction seriously.

Following the Ruskin College speech by James Callaghan in 1976, a Government Green Paper was published in July 1977, *Education in Schools: A Consultative Document*, which made references to a 'core curriculum' and reaffirmed the Secretary of State's responsibility for the curriculum. This was followed by Circular 14/77, which asked LEAs for information about curricula, thus indicating the need for a national view on the curriculum. The DES became more interventionist as subsequent documents indicate. There was an attempt to define a national curriculum with the appearance of the DES's *A Framework for the School Curriculum* in 1980, which met with hostility from the teaching profession. This document was a centralist discussion document which appeared in modified version in 1981 as *The School Curriculum*. None of these documents directly addressed the legal position of voluntary-aided schools, but the Secretary of State stated that he was 'confident' that the governors of voluntary-aided schools 'will wish to play their full part'.[13] The Catholic responses to these documents was on the whole muted. The CEC submitted critical comments on the 1980 paper, in particular about the omission of religious education which was later included in the 1981 DES version.[14] The CEC also made the point that in its approach the 1980 document implied there was no relationship between the aims and rationale of the school and a possible 'core curriculum'. This second point by the CEC was not elaborated upon and no concrete example of its intentions was provided.[15] Subsequently, the DES in its revision of the 1980 paper made no reference to the point whatsoever. The Catholic position was simple — that a school curriculum should serve the aims for which the school was established. The curriculum in a Catholic school was required to be different because of the school's distinctive aims and any proposed 'core curriculum' would need to consider this distinction. Official Church statements about Catholic schools indicated that their aim was no less than the creation of a Christian milieu through which the philosophy of the curriculum and the ethos of the school are harmonised. As the Congregation for Catholic Education argues:

Catholic schools need to have a set of educational goals which are 'distinctive' in the sense that the school has a specific objective in mind and all the goals are related to this objective.[16]

In 1985 the Government issued an important White Paper entitled *Better Schools*, which had only a single reference to denominational schools within the dual system, and this was concerned with the size of schools and not the curriculum.[17] The White Paper sought to set out a programme for the establishment of a clearer consensus over the objectives and content of the curriculum and for the reform of examinations and assessment. The 1986 Education Act dealt specifically, in Section 19, with the curriculum in voluntary-aided primary and secondary schools. It recognised that their articles of government were to provide:

> ... for the governing body to have regard to the policy of the local education authority as to the curriculum for the authority's schools.[18]

Whilst the CEC produced a document on the implications of the Education (No 2) Act 1986 for Catholic schools, in regard to the curriculum, it simply detailed the changes made without any critical commentary.[19] Section 19 of the Act certainly sought to bring the voluntary-aided sector closer to the model of the LEA school. It was a threat to the powers of governors which was made more explicit in the following year with the publication of the Education Reform Bill 1987. The Bill sought to define the curriculum in secular terms with clear instrumental goals forming part of the ultimate objectives. It also proposed the removal of control over the secular curriculum by Catholic voluntary-aided governors. Preparation for working life was an avowed aim as was the total development of the child which included spiritual and moral values. Little in the way of substance was given to these 'spiritual' and 'moral' aims in Section 1 of the Act. Therefore, substantial erosion of the right of governors of voluntary-aided schools to determine the curriculum best suited to the character of their school was achieved with the passage of the Education Reform Act of 1988.

Pressure had been building up gradually to remove the control of voluntary-aided governors over the curriculum in national reports such as the *McFarlane Report* and the *Swann Report*. The latter was fundamentally opposed to any separate educational provision for religious groups and recommended a 'common educational experience' for all.[20] The Catholic Church launched a campaign

against the provisions in the Education Reform Bill. The bishops
fought hard and stated that Catholic schools had hitherto 'enjoyed
the right to determine the complete school curriculum in the light
of their understanding'.[21] However, the Church's campaign suffered from a major weakness from the start. The theoretical principles which govern design, implementation, development and
evaluation in terms of contributing towards the aims of Catholic
education were almost wholly absent from the debate. The question of whether or not there could be a Catholic school curriculum
based on its own distinctive aims was raised, but there appeared
to be some confusion about this question. Robinson in a study of
the curriculum in Catholic schools in the early 1980s found little
evidence to suggest that Catholic schools were conscious of any
specifically Catholic considerations in designing their curriculum.[22]
In Robert Burgess's study of 'Bishop McGregor' School in London,
he claims that Christian principles were transmitted through secular subjects and he lists them as home economics, child care, sex
education, and science.[23] Roy Wake, who cites a fellow HMI's
comment on visiting a Catholic school, says:

> Apart from the crucifix on the wall, in what way does the place differ
> from a maintained school?[24]

Or as a parish priest put it:

> It is the Catholicity of our schools which is especially in question.
> We all admit that they should be something more than 'state schools
> with statues'; but the vexed question is the nature of that 'some-
> thing more' — for unless the difference is really significant, is there
> any value in keeping them?[25]

The move from a system that emphasised school autonomy to one
that produced a centrally prescribed curriculum was made easier
as a result of this confusion about what the nature of the Catholic
school should be. Central Government was now to be responsible
for designing the curriculum in Catholic schools regardless of what
these schools thought they were supposed to achieve through their
own school aims. In a sense the aims of the Catholic school were
to be determined by non-Catholics. The Catholic community's
response to this, especially parents, was similar to that of the
general population. Whilst the bishops took the lead and distributed leaflets in each parish to present the Catholic case, the laity
and clergy appear to have been uninterested.[26] This was despite
the bishops' warnings against the slide towards secularism through

exclusive emphasis on monetary gain, productivity, training for skills and market values, which they claimed did not accord with Catholic teaching or values.[27] Most schools are marked by a high degree of formal control emphasising selection, competition and vocationalism and these are linked to future career opportunities and potential social status. This approach to education conflicts with the Catholic view of knowledge described in Chapter Three. It is a secular approach which views education in terms of curriculum structure and course content and which tends to treat knowledge as a product for consumption. Apart from viewing knowledge as a value irrespective of its usefulness, the Church teaches that education is not to be given for the purpose of gaining power or as a means for material prosperity and success, but rather to serve others. These Catholic considerations appear to have been secondary among many Catholic parents and this has left the Church asking itself how it is to respond to an increasingly secular approach to the curriculum which is determined outside its control.

Some 'safeguards' under Section 17 of the Education Reform Act 1988, which allow 'exception clauses' or 'specified modifications' to be made to the National Curriculum, were added, partly through Catholic pressure. Consequently, the 'technology of contraception' aspect of the national science curriculum will not apply in Catholic schools. However, it is the Minister who will arbitrate on such exception decisions, even if his decision conflicts with Catholic teaching. Thus, there are no longer any guarantees in statute with regard to the curriculum in Catholic schools. In 1988 the bishops had proposed an amendment to place aided schools on the same basis as City Technology Colleges, which are exempt from the National Curriculum.[28] Their proposal was rejected by the Government and the bishops subsequently called for Catholic representation on the influential National Curriculum and School Examinations Assessment Councils which were set up by Section Fourteen of the 1988 Education Reform Act. Members of these Councils are appointed by the Secretary of State and Section Fourteen of the Act outlines the dominant position of the Secretary of State by the requirement that each Council in exercising its functions shall 'comply with any directives given, and . . . act in accordance with any plans approved, by the Secretary of State'.

Fears that non-statutory curriculum areas will be further restricted by the National Curriculum and the budgetary demands on governors by the Local Management of Schools remain. In practice though, governors have only had nominal oversight of the curriculum with such factors as examination syllabuses, teaching materials, local inspectors, the availability of teachers and the subject choices of pupils influencing most of the decisions. The Rev. Peter Hackett had made this point in 1983 when he said:

> . . . how small is the initiative that the Catholic governor has in promoting Catholic education, and how unformulated and disorganised the help that the Catholic Body can offer in this matter. The independence in law of each voluntary-aided school is proving a great practical weakness.[29]

Since 1983 major new curricular developments, such as the Technical Vocational and Educational Initiative, have continued to emerge and affect Catholic as well as LEA schools. However, it would be misleading to suggest that the secular curriculum is unrelated to the policies of most Catholic school governors. Their model of the school is or should be one in which the Catholic faith is all-embracing. As one bishop recently put it:

> We do not accept that we can include religious education in any curriculum and be content that our duties are fulfilled. Nor can we be satisfied with a situation where a teacher is competent in a particular discipline but does not share in an agreed vision of the whole task.[30]

Pope John Paul II has referred to religious education as the 'core of the core curriculum' in a Catholic school.[31] It has been said that the ethos of the Catholic school is 'synonymous with and inseparable from its curriculum'.[32] Also, that the Catholic school's curriculum has a spiritual dimension which Cardinal Hume elaborates upon when he says:

> Religious Education has to be part of the core curriculum for a Catholic School, because it is committed to the aims, values and teachings of the Catholic Faith that influences the whole of the curriculum, shapes the daily pattern of school life and is the reason for the separate existence and identity of Catholic schools.[33]

It can be seen that Cardinal Hume follows the line of argument used by the Pope about the 'core of the core curriculum'. Indeed, in the 1990 Bishops' Conference papers on the curriculum there is much use of the Congregation for Catholic Education's statements.[34] It is repeated that the curriculum, in all its aspects, must reflect the fact that Christ is the foundation of the whole educational enterprise in a Catholic school. The document, using the same words from Rome, goes on to say that:

> Although it may be convenient to speak of the 'religious' curriculum and the 'secular' curriculum in the Catholic School, as though these were separate and distinct, in reality the curriculum as a whole, and every part of it, is religious, since there is nothing which does not ultimately relate to God.[35]

The working out of the application of these statements is left to individual schools with the warning that Catholic schools must not allow:

> ...our curriculum to be influenced detrimentally by pressures from groups within or without the Church.[36]

Since there are no Catholic examination boards, no specifically Catholic inspectors of the secular curriculum, no Catholic publishing houses of school textbooks, no national Catholic curriculum projects, no national Catholic curriculum advisory committee to parallel that of the State, it is difficult to see how the Catholic Church can have any more influence than that of a loose pressure group. Hackett's revealing comment on the Catholic curriculum is worth mentioning here:

> The task, however, of grounding idealism in a proper integrity and in some thorough realism is not simple.[37]

It could be argued that the Catholic Church in England and Wales has neither the resources nor the competent personnel to transform its idealism on the curriculum into a practical reality for its schools. Most Catholic schools seem content to search no further than the structures and curricula developed by others.

The Education Committee of the Bishops' Conference has attempted a preliminary study of the National Curriculum in the light of the Church's understanding of education. It has sought to provide a series of subject commentaries in the hope that these will provide teachers in Catholic schools with the means of being more aware of the contribution they should make to the vision of life distinctive of the Catholic school. For example, the draft science commentary begins:

> The values of the school are conveyed through the whole curriculum. While the relationship of the teacher and pupil will convey many of the qualities expected in a Catholic school community, each area of the curriculum opens doors of human discovery and achievement,

and has something specific to convey in developing a Christian understanding of human life and knowledge.[38]

The criticisms made earlier of Patrick Walsh's idea of a Christian understanding of science can be applied here also. Indeed, the draft commentary is in some ways a repeat of Walsh's ideas. Other draft commentaries speak of how the National Curriculum can offer positive opportunities to enhance the values and ethos of the Catholic school, but do not specify how.[39] This is a complete reversal of the bishops stand against the original Education Reform Bill which first proposed the National Curriculum. In the draft commentary on *Economic and Industrial Understanding*, it is advocated that teachers should have an understanding of creation, incarnation, redemption and the Church's social teachings in their teaching of economics and business studies. It suggests that the fundamental principles in Vatican II's declaration *Gaudium et Spes* and Pope John Paul II's encyclical, *Laborem Exercens* should be used as the foundation for all economic teaching in Catholic schools.[40] Whilst these drafts have never been published, they indicate the thinking of at least some in the Catholic Church's educational structures. The commentaries are written by Catholics involved in education, but are entirely the product of voluntary effort without much financial support. They would have a number of policy consequences if ever formally produced for Catholic schools, including the introduction of extensive in-service training. Since the project itself is so poorly resourced it is doubtful if anything further will come of it.

The bishops have not followed up their earlier claim that the National Curriculum is an infringement of the Catholic schools' traditional right to determine their curricula. Instead, they have spoken of their growing concern that religious education in all schools may be marginalised. In a joint Pastoral Letter of January 1991 the bishops 'insist' (their word) that religious education be given at least ten per cent of the teaching time in Catholic secondary schools.[41] The bishops did not explain how the percentage was determined, but it is interesting that the Culham Institute's survey of religious education in schools in 1989 found that Catholic schools gave an average of ten percent to religious education in their timetables.[42] This figure was widely quoted in the Catholic press at the time and the CEC used it in its subsequent published commentary on the 1988 Education Reform Act. Whilst the bishops feared that religious education would be marginalised, no accurate information about schools exists to judge whether or not their fears were well grounded. They themselves have not initiated any such research. In addition, the National Curriculum has progressively become less rigid and there are now only four compulsory subjects beyond the age of fourteen — Mathematics, English, Science and, of course, Religious Education.[43]

The main justification for the National Curriculum in the Education Reform Act of 1988 was that it would allow consumers (a term used of the parents by the Conservative Government) to know their rights and to have uniform criteria by which they could judge. There were also pressures from business and the public for stronger technical and vocational education in which the Government had shown a lead with the Manpower Services Commission. Demands were also made for a national system, both in subjects and in standards, with regard to the school curriculum. Therefore consumerism, control by the DES, and attempts to raise standards were the main pressures which culminated in the passing of the Education Reform Act 1988. The Government's advocacy of the National Curriculum was associated with the belief that a nationally determined curriculum would result in higher academic standards in schools. The Government felt that there was a need for greater uniformity in standards of assessment in a mobile population.

By way of conclusion to this section, the bishops have generally attempted to follow the authoritative line from Rome on matters of the curriculum — at least at a theoretical level. However, since Rome not only approved the 'Scottish Solution' in 1918, but has subsequently held it up as a model arrangement for bishops in other countries,[44] it cannot be said with any confidence that control of the secular curriculum is a principle which has always been given universal validity in the Catholic Church. It would appear to have been used more properly as an intermediate principle which is relevant and operational in particular contexts. The 'Scottish Solution' entailed the secular curriculum being controlled by the LEA, an arrangement that the English bishops claimed was unacceptable to them in 1988. In 1931 the CEC supported the 'Scottish Solution' for Catholics in England and Wales.[45] It should be said that at that time Catholic governors did not control the curriculum in England and Wales. After full statutory control of the curriculum was returned to Catholic governors in 1944, Bishop Beck thought it was more important *who* taught rather than *what* was taught.[46] The Government's financial crisis of 1957 led the CEC once again to put forward the 'Scottish Solution' to the Government which would have entailed the loss of Catholic control over the secular curriculum.[47] The bishops compromised on curricular matters and used the control of the curriculum as a bargaining tool in negotiations with the Government. Nevertheless, since Vatican II the emphasis has been on the integration of religious truth with the rest of life — a synthesis of faith and culture. In other words, Catholic school aims and principles should be reflected in, and translated into, the implementation of the curriculum. This would imply a degree of control over what is taught. Anglicans share this ideal which is echoed in the Church of England's official statement on the National Curriculum:

> . . . in choosing what is appropriate content we reveal and express a set of values. It would be unfortunate if schools followed the requirements of the National Curriculum in a way that allowed the content of that curriculum to support, or even create, a set of values with which the Christian could not be in sympathy.[48]

Alan McClelland makes a more fundamental point for Catholic schools when he says:

> The weakness of the Catholic school, however, has often been its inability to establish a confident internal polity that eschews that element of divisiveness inherent in the attempt to develop practices operating in secular schools: aggressive competition, the premium placed upon worldly success, the use of selfish rewards . . . the need for outward conformity in social attitudes.[49]

Evidence that many Catholic schools may be adopting current secular models for their curriculum is provided by the 1990 School Survey conducted by the Bishops' Conference. This survey found that only 41% of Catholic schools had a mission statement whilst 82% had a Curriculum Policy Statement.[50] Yet it is from the mission statement that the Catholic school's curriculum should be derived. It was also found that many Catholic schools had used none of their allocated inset days for discussion of their Catholic ethos and identity. There would appear to be a great deal of confusion and apathy surrounding the search for a Catholic inspired school curriculum from within the Catholic community.

Admissions and Staffing: an Introduction

A school's distinctive identity and ethos is largely defined by the values, convictions and beliefs that prevail amongst its members.

To maintain these standards, policy-makers must incorporate them into their policies and actions, which give a sense of direction and purpose to the school community. Catholic educationalists emphasise the shared nature of these values within Catholic schools and it is for this reason that they claim that admissions have to be controlled in order to safeguard identity. This same principle is applied to staff appointments and therefore both admissions and staffing policies are of outstanding importance because together they make a clear statement about the nature and character of the school. Whilst many Catholic schools have, since their foundation, admitted non-Catholics and appointed non-Catholic staff, some have been careful to try and ensure that the schools ethos, based upon Catholic values and beliefs, is not diluted. They have been able to ensure the school's ethos in the past by exercising their rights to admit and appoint, rights which are now, for a number of reasons, far from clear or effective.

Teacher Training and Appointments

On the issue of staffing, Cardinal Hume described teachers working in Catholic schools as being 'at the heart of all good education — and absolutely crucial to the process'.[51] The Cardinal's address largely repeated the Second Vatican Council's view of Catholic teachers:

> Let teachers realise that to the greatest possible extent they determine whether the Catholic school can bring its undertakings to fruition . . . Above all let them exercise their function as partners of the parents.[52]

The teacher is seen here as sharing with the parents in the role of herald of the Gospel to children. It is quite clear that the Church's expected role of the Catholic teacher goes beyond the ordinary professional role of most teachers. Cardinal Hume in the same address made the further point that 'no teacher should be appointed who is unable to support the Catholic school's aims and identity'.[53] Appropriate staff are required who will freely embody and express Church policy on Catholic schools and education. It is therefore not surprising to see the training and appointment of teachers being a central and continuing policy concern of the bishops. It resulted in the establishment of a parallel Catholic system of teacher training in the nineteenth century which, although very much diminished, has remained as one of the Church's educational commitments in the 1990s. The certification of Catholic teachers for Catholic schools was a major responsibility of the bishops through their diocesan religious inspectors who met annually at national level. These inspectors took charge of the religious examinations for prospective pupil-teachers before they could be admitted to a Catholic training college. They produced rules for the annual examinations and no Catholic seeking to enter a Catholic training college with the intention of teaching in a Catholic elementary school could be accepted without their approval, regardless of subject.[54]

The Catholic authorities had difficulty in maintaining their supply and strict control over potential teachers for Catholic schools. Increasing threats were made to their ability to provide sufficient Catholic training provision as can be seen from the religious inspectors' report for 1891, which passed a motion that:

> . . . viewed with great fear the establishment of Day Training Colleges, and beg[ged] for strong legislation to prevent the attendance of Catholic students at them, and the employment of Catholics hired therein.[55]

Their unrealistic claim was that pressure should be brought to bear on the Government to discriminate, through Parliamentary legislation, against Catholics who chose freely to attend or teach in a day training college. Catholics often attended non-Catholic colleges and taught in non-Catholic schools and this was always a concern of the bishops. Indeed, they even considered sanctions against such teachers. By 1908, with a Government hostile to Catholic schools, the problem grew more intense and the diocesan inspectors appealed to the bishops about the:

> . . . evils arising from attendance of Candidates for the Teaching Profession at non-Catholic centres and Secondary Schools in nearly every portion of England.[56]

The inspectors did recognise that with the absence of Catholic day training colleges and secondary schools in some areas, Catholics had been forced by necessity to attend non-Catholic institutions.[57] The Catholic authorities simply did not have the resources to compete with the State in terms of teacher training provision.

A relaxation of the inspectors' control over who could be admitted to Catholic training colleges had been made in 1933, when the diocesan inspectors agreed that the Catholic secondary school's Catholic Religious Certificate could replace the pupil-teacher examination and thereby qualify candidates for entry into the training college.[58] In 1959 there were calls from among the inspectors to lower the standard of the religious examination because of the shortage of teachers.[59] By 1968 there was discussion about the possible abolition of the examination. Instead it was agreed that each diocese should run its own examination in its 'own way'.[60] Effectively the religious examination prior to entry on a course at a Catholic teacher training college was abandoned. The colleges now made their own selection of candidates with their own criteria. In a study of Christian teacher training colleges in England in 1984, Gay concluded that alone among the denominations, the Catholic Church had been clear about the task of its training colleges, which was to train teachers for Catholic schools.[61] Consequently, Catholics have maintained a straightforward manpower link between colleges and schools. However, the Department of Education and Science abrogated the former practice of consultation between the bishops and the department over teacher training.[62] Many Catholic colleges were closed or reorganised as a result of Government action and whilst the bishops fought hard against these closures they were forced to accept a much reduced role which has left only three Catholic colleges free standing with a further three either federated or amalgamated into larger institutions.

Government action since the 1970s has adversely affected the provision of Catholic teachers from Catholic colleges, but it cannot be claimed that this is the only reason for the dramatic reduction of new entrants to Catholic schools trained at Catholic colleges. Certainly, the Department of Education and Science has sole control over whether institutions can be recognised for the purposes of teacher training. It also controls the numbers who may be admitted to each institution, the exact balance between secondary and primary, the numbers for each subject, the duration of the courses on offer, and has begun to determine the balance of content between practical teaching and educational theory, as specified in the *Education (Schools and Further and Higher Education) Regulations* of 1989. It has even specified how much time should be spent on science and other aspects of the National Curriculum in the college education courses. The real independence of Catholic colleges is somewhat negligible considering that extensive Government regulations have also been combined with college affiliations and federations.

There has also been criticism of the colleges from within the Catholic community. Some bemoan their secular outlook on

education and it has been claimed that their courses merely dupli-
cate those of other institutions. From a reading of their prospec-
tuses it is difficult to see how they are distinctive as Christian
institutions. Moreover, external examiners have found little evidence of Catholic values in the education scripts and essays of
college students.[63] The extent to which the Catholic colleges serve
the Catholic community is clearly shown by the recent survey of
the Bishops' Conference. It was found that in the year 1989 to 1990
only 20% of new entrants to the teaching profession in Catholic
schools came from these colleges, and not all of this 20% were
Catholic teachers.[64] On closer examination it is clear that there is
a decrease in the numbers from Catholic colleges applying to
Catholic schools. The colleges as a whole have a majority of
non-Catholics on roll and have also largely diversified their courses
into fields other than teacher training. This has important implications for the future supply and training of teachers for the
Catholic sector especially as the 80% at present who come from
non-Catholic institutions is set to rise. New ways of inducting such
newly qualified teachers into Catholic schools have not as yet been
devised. More detailed research conducted by the Catholic Education Service in 1994 confirms the findings in the 1990 survey.[65]
It was found that in 1992, of the 394 secondary trained teachers
leaving the Catholic colleges, only 93 began their teaching career
in a Catholic school and not all of these new teachers were Catholics. Head teachers noted that many Catholic applicants did not
understand the mission of Catholic education and often failed to
articulate a case for applying to a Catholic school. The colleges
themselves recorded a low proportion of Catholic applicants
against a dramatic increase in total applicants. In addition, the
colleges were often unable to identify Catholic applicants from
their application forms, and in one college the identification of
Catholic students was not a priority in the admission of students.
Attention has been almost exclusively focused on the remaining
Catholic colleges in an attempt by the bishops to help them survive
the Government reorganisation of higher education in the belief
that the colleges still serve Catholic schools, when all the evidence
points so glaringly in the other direction. The 'Catholic' colleges
do not principally serve the Catholic school system.

At the level of principle, the bishops have attempted to endorse
the Second Vatican Council's *Declaration on Christian Education*,
especially its section on the role of teachers. They have re-empha-

sised the importance of the apostolate of teachers in the total saving mission of the Church and placed on them the prime responsibility for creating the ethos of Catholic schools.[66] Consequently, the bishops, in their 1974 *Memorandum on the Appointment of Teachers*, issued specific advice to governors of all Catholic schools.[67] The memorandum urged governors to enquire carefully into all aspects of applicants for posts in their schools and made clear to them that professed atheists and agnostics were unacceptable. The paper also advised governors not to appoint non-Catholics to senior pastoral positions, nor to headships or deputy headships. This memorandum was revised and re-issued in 1990.[68] The second version did not differ much from the original, but significantly it abandoned the advice to enquire into the background of candidates and also dropped the specific mention of professed atheists and agnostics. It is known that a number of Catholic schools have senior and pastoral positions, as high as deputy head teacher, filled with non-Catholics, contrary to the advice contained in this memorandum. One reason is obviously the acute shortage of suitable Catholic teachers as described in the Bishops' Conference survey of 1990, but another reason must be the increasing willingness of governors to appoint non-Catholics to senior positions in Catholic schools. The supply of Catholic teachers for the future is a major priority of the bishops and recent statistics indicate the problem is growing. Between 1978 and 1993 the number of teachers in maintained Catholic schools who are not Roman Catholic increased from 22% to 29% — in the secondary sector rising from 34% to 40.2% and in the primary from 9% to 12.5%.[69] The number of teaching religious in maintained schools has declined yearly, and in 1995 stood at less than 550 — a huge decline since 1980.[70] The trend for both lay and religious teachers in maintained Catholic schools is downwards, the latter more dramatically than the former. In Catholic independent schools the number of teaching religious in 1989 stood at 1,444 — again this shows a steady decline.[71]

There are three inter-related staffing areas in which the bishops have attempted to directly apply their principles to policy implementation with varying degrees of success. These areas are: teacher contracts, teacher disciplinary proceedings and teacher appraisal.

Catholic Teaching Contracts

Teachers in voluntary-aided schools have employment contracts with the governing body who have the power to appoint, suspend

and dismiss staff under Section 45(3) of the Education Reform Act
1988. Consequently, contracts of service that are specifically designed for teachers in Catholic voluntary-aided schools are not
new.[72] The CEC produced model contracts in the 1950s for use by
Catholic governors and in 1981 they revised these by adding clause
4 (III) (a) to the effect that the teacher agrees:

> . . . to have regard to the Roman Catholic character of the school
> and not to do anything in any way detrimental or prejudicial to the
> interests of the same.[73]

The clause was originally drafted by R.J. Harvey QC, a leading
expert on employment law. The new clause generated some opposition from the teacher unions, but despite this the CEC has
consistently encouraged its use. Every teacher employed within a
Catholic maintained school is normally expected to sign this contract. With the passing of the Teachers Pay and Conditions Order
in 1986 the CEC proposed new contracts which, combined with
the new statutory teacher job descriptions, became major issues of
conflict with the National Association of Schoolmasters.[74] The
CEC had advised governors to refer to the duties of the teacher in
respect of the school's religious character and provided the following wording for standard incorporation into all job descriptions in
Catholic schools:

> The teacher should endeavour to maintain and develop the Catholic
> character of the school, in accordance with the direction of the
> governors and, subject thereto, the directions given by the
> headteacher.[75]

This clause appeared all-inclusive and met with some opposition
among Catholics. The clause was later abandoned by the CEC.
Clearly, it was an attempt to enforce by legal means the obligation
of all teachers in a Catholic school to actively develop its ethos
under the direction of the head teacher. Case law would suggest
that this was already an implied term in the contract of a teacher
in a Catholic school. The question of why the CEC felt it necessary
to recommend such a clause when it was not legally required arises
here. It could be that it was an attempt to guarantee the initial free
choice of the teacher to act in certain specifically Catholic ways.
Despite the withdrawal of this wording in teacher contracts, clause
4 (III) (a) remains an integral part of the contracts used in Catholic
schools and its wording makes explicit the obligations of teachers

to act in certain specifically Catholic ways. The bishops soon after the publication of the clause said:

> Any educational legislation should show clearly the trust the government has in the teaching profession. Without mutual trust, no amount of legislation can achieve genuine improvement. Trust, not law, is in the end the guarantee of progress.[76]

The new CEC Contract is widely used in Catholic schools, but it still mainly relies on the trust the governors have in their teachers.

Disciplinary Proceedings in Catholic Schools

Disciplinary action against teachers who are no longer able to maintain and develop the Catholic character of the school according to clause 4 (III) (a) of the CEC contract is not common. It is well established that certain public acts or activities of teachers employed in Catholic schools, which might be viewed as a facet of an individual's private life in any other type of school, can be judged by governors as incompatible with the role of a teacher.[77] Hence, acts or activities which would not incur the wrath of an employer in another school or profession could have major repercussions for the teacher in a Catholic school. Moreover, the standards of moral behaviour expected from the Catholic teacher are even more pronounced. There is potentially a wide range of behaviour which could be viewed as breaking a teacher's contract with a Catholic school's governing body. The intermix of religion and employment conditions in Catholic schools and the affect this has on the teaching staff is illustrated by the decision of the Court in *Jones v Lee* in 1979.

A well-regarded and apparently effective head teacher of a Catholic voluntary-aided primary school divorced and remarried an assistant teacher who had worked at his school and who was also a divorcee. The school managers suspended him and contacted the local Bishop of Clifton who appointed a tribunal of three to inquire into the matter. Whilst finding no fault in the head teacher's professional position, the tribunal stated:

> We the members of the tribunal were of the unanimous opinion that Mr Jones should be dismissed from his post . . . we feel that the position of a head teacher in a Roman Catholic school makes a person a leader in the religious community and it is unthinkable that such a person could be permitted to retain that position while blatantly refusing to conform to the teachings of the Roman Catholic faith.[78]

The managers of the school resolved to apply this finding and the head teacher was dismissed. The tribunal was simply repeating the policy of the Catholic Church regarding the standards of conduct expected from Catholic teachers. These standards invariably refer to moral behaviour and the nature and scope of the behaviour which is viewed as incompatible with the life of a Catholic in Church teaching is wide-ranging as only a cursory glance at the Catechism of the Catholic Church would confirm.

The head teacher took his case to the Court of Appeal which held that he had not been dismissed in accordance with his contract of employment, since he had not been granted the right of being heard before the managers dismissed him. The Master of the Rolls, Lord Denning and Lord Justice Roskill expressed the view that the managers had been wrong to delegate their authority to the ecclesiastical tribunal as it was for them to make the decision. Although the court held that a decision to dismiss him was invalid because of procedural irregularities, the governors still removed him from office. The case raised questions of who really employs the head teacher in voluntary-aided schools.

There are a number of other unresolved questions which arise in the implementation of clause 4 (III) (a). First, what are the obligations of the non-Catholic teacher employed in a Catholic school? While the non-Catholic teacher will have signed the CEC contract, can it be expected that they have formally accepted to live the Church's moral code? If not, then it would appear to endorse 'uneven treatment' if governors only discipline Catholics who publicly breach the moral tenets of the Church. A case before an industrial tribunal in 1994 illustrates the contradictions inherent in the application of clause 4 (III) (a).[79] An unmarried Bedford religious-education teacher became pregnant by the school chaplain. The governors dismissed her and she took her case to an industrial tribunal, claiming among other things that two other unmarried members of staff at the same school had become pregnant and that no action had been taken against them. The governors responded that neither of these teachers was a Catholic. It does seem that only Catholic teachers are subject to the full implementation of clause 4 (III) (a). The implications seem clear also for the school community, as surely the pupils would notice moral precept and practice were at variance, and would draw undesirable conclusions from such observations.[80] The industrial tribunal, whilst agreeing that there had been procedural irregularities in her dismissal, nevertheless ruled that she was in breach of clause 4 (III) (a).

Second, what are the obligations of non-practising Catholic teachers? Do they place themselves in the same category as the non-Catholic teacher when action under clause 4 (III) (a) is being considered by governors? If a teacher holds a position in the school which was given subject to them being a practising Catholic at the time of the appointment, then it would appear that they had breached their contract by their decision to cease practising their religion. A Catholic teacher in Cardiff in 1994 married a Muslim in a registry office and therefore entered into a canonically invalid marriage. The governors felt that there was a *prima facie* case for dismissing her because of breaching clause 4 (III) (a) in her contract.[81] The teacher took her case to an industrial tribunal as she felt that her marriage did not affect her ability as a teacher in a Catholic school. A growing number of cases appear to confirm the willingness of teachers dismissed under clause 4 (III) (a) to challenge the decision of governors. Since the CES's own research reveals that 'Catholic' applicants often do not understand what the nature of Catholic education is,[82] it would seem that disciplinary disputes involving conflict between the Church's teachings and the personal lives of staff are set to increase.

Third, what are the obligations of governors in enforcing clause 4 (III) (a)? The underlying approach adopted by governors in discharging their responsibility must be one of genuine consideration for staff as individuals. However, does it also mean that as employers governors can dispense from applying clause 4 (III) (a)? The answer appears to depend on the governing body, since what may be perceived as a disciplinary matter for one governor may be seen as a private matter for the teacher by another governor. If a case does not reach the public eye then governors, it seems, rarely proceed with disciplinary matters. The problem is more acute when a governing body publicly accepts behaviour or actions contrary to the Church's teaching by promoting staff who have refused to conform to the Church's teaching on divorce and remarriage. A governing body in 1990 in the Archdiocese of Southwark, as described in Chapter Five, sought to appoint a divorced and remarried man to the headship of their school. The Archbishop as a trustee perceived that some governors were pursuing policy values derived from sources other than the Church. The case was secretly settled between the governors and the Archbishop of the diocese.

The employment relationship between governors and teachers is complex and regulated by a variety of norms; legal, social and religious. The use of specifically Catholic terms in contracts are justified so long as such provisions are not so broad and vague as to create ambiguity and uncertainty for teachers. Catholic contracts need to be specific and spell out clearly and distinctly what constitutes the Roman Catholic character of the school and what conduct would be considered detrimental to that character. Misconduct is a broad rubric covering a multitude of transgressions, and these specifically Catholic aspects must be clearly stated. It should also be borne in mind that there appears to be a marked reluctance on the part of many Catholic teachers to seek employment in Catholic schools, as the overall number of Catholics employed in Catholic schools decreases each year. One reason may be that they find the moral standards expected from such schools too exacting.

Teacher Appraisal in Catholic Schools

The response of the bishops to the teacher appraisal arrangements in Section 49 of the Education (No. 2) Act 1986 have generally been favourable. The bishops have echoed the profession's demands that appraisal should be well resourced and positive in nature.[83] Indeed, as part of their preparations for the introduction of national legislation on the professional appraisal of teachers in schools, many bishops inaugurated working parties to consider the implications of such legislation for the Catholic schools in their area. These diocesan working parties contributed to a national body which was set up in 1987 to parallel the Government's National Steering Group on Appraisal. Its title is the Co-ordinating Committee for In-service, Evaluation and Appraisal in Catholic Schools and it is, unusually, widely representative of the Catholic teaching profession, but still operates under the auspices of the bishops. The principal conclusion of this committee has been to emphasise that, above all, teacher appraisal must assist the spiritual growth of both the staff and pupils.[84] It states that appraisal should have due regard for the Christian value of the individual and assist his personal contribution to the Catholic ethos of the school. Much is said of fostering Christian attitudes towards staff, but little in the way of guidance is given on the concrete application of specifically Christian appraisal methods. It is clear that any appraisal depends on the aims of the school and its results will largely determine in-service training. The difficulty arises when tensions emerge between the professional and the denominational expectations of the school aims. This is especially the case when attempting to delineate Catholic professional appraisal techniques based upon concepts of the distinctive nature of Catholic schools.

Since Catholic schools have diverse aims, the assumption, often made by Cardinal Hume, that every Catholic school has a 'single Christian vision, an integrated concept of what makes a fully authentic and mature human being' cannot be sustained.[85] Peter Birks, who was a member of the Portsmouth diocesan working party on appraisal in Catholic schools, has written that this 'single vision' idea contributes little to attempts at defining professional appraisal procedures for use in Catholic schools as they are *actually* staffed.[86] He lists a number of factors which bear upon the interpretation of 'the distinctive nature' of Catholic education and therefore must be considered in designing teacher appraisal strategies for Catholic schools. Some of the factors he lists are: that 25% of all teachers working in Catholic schools are not members of the Catholic Church; pressures from parents who want better job prospects for their children and who may want the school to place less emphasis upon denominational requirements if they appear to militate against academic success; parents who may wish to see more emphasis on the denominational agenda; the large numbers of non-Catholic children in Catholic schools, and that one cannot assume that all Catholics have the same beliefs or practice of the faith. Birks's answer to these issues is to abandon the idea of a 'single Christian vision' for he says:

> The aims of Catholic education should not derive from the merely narrow and potentially divisive notions of denominational imitation.[87]

and he warns teachers working within Catholic schools to be prepared to:

> ... resist the occasional baleful influence of the local Church where dogma can sometimes seem to replace support and criticism supplant healing.[88]

His whole approach to teacher appraisal is based on the perceived needs of the children within the school, rather than on any preconceived religious aims. The views he expresses are not part of official Church policy on appraisal, but they do raise some issues which have not been addressed by the bishops. Whilst the bishops are eager to use appraisal to encourage greater spiritual growth in

Catholic schools, there are fundamental questions left unanswered about the relationship between Catholic principles and policy on appraisal and how they might or should be implemented.

Admissions to Catholic Voluntary-aided Schools

The issue of admissions control is often seen as particularly vital in the Catholic sector. For it is a sector which has traditionally schooled its own community. Many Catholic independent schools, mainly convent schools, continue to admit large numbers of fee-paying non-Catholics, often the majority. In 1993 there were 59,990 pupils in Catholic independent schools of whom almost half were non-Catholics.[89] This has not been the normal practice within Catholic maintained schools. At the peak of admissions in 1974 there were a total of 944,536 children in all maintained Catholic schools of whom only 14,000 were non-Catholic — less than 2% of the total.[90] The CEC noted in 1975 that there was a wide diversity of policies on admissions operating in Catholic schools throughout the country.[91] This comment did not refer to the admission of non-Catholics, but to the practice of admitting only 'practising' Catholics in areas where there were insufficient Catholic places. The question was raised of whether the Church could have the same expectations from schools where only 30% of the pupils came from 'practising' homes, as opposed to schools where 100% did so.[92] By 1994 the situation and the type of questions raised had changed dramatically with the population in Catholic maintained schools standing at 732,980 of which non-Catholics accounted for 94,424 of these — 13% of the total and rising.[93] How accurate are these figures? Some would argue that the number of non-Catholic pupils is larger than official statistics would suggest, since there have been cases were schools have made returns to the CES which have consistently inflated the number of Catholic pupils. With falling rolls during this period, Catholic schools had admitted more non-Catholics so that the schools may survive and remain viable. The rate of non-Catholic pupil increase is equivalent to the Catholic Church opening two large comprehensive schools each year. There is no suggestion that Catholic schools became, officially at least, more pluralist or ecumenical during this period. They were certainly criticised by Leslie Francis for taking children who would under normal circumstances have gone to the local LEA school.[94] Even in the few cases where joint schools were established between the Church of England and the Catholic Church there is evidence that this was for reasons of viability rather than for the furtherance of ecumenism. As Bernadette O'Keeffe puts it:

> In areas where the demand for places in a Church school exceeds the supply of available places, the admissions criteria are used with precision. Where demand falls short of supply, admissions policies become flexible and open to a more varied pupil intake.[95]

The questions now being raised by the Catholic authorities were related, not only to the balance of 'practising' and 'non-practising' Catholics in schools, but also to the large numbers of non-Catholics being admitted. The Catholic practice on admissions had clearly moved on to the admission of non-Catholics before it had resolved for itself the expectations it had of its schools with increasing numbers of non-practising Catholics. Some Catholic schools faced the stark choice of closure or admitting non-Catholics in order to remain economically viable. If they opted for the latter then they were able to maintain their own strength at the expense of the LEA school sector. Catholic schools from the mid-1970s were no longer homogeneous communities where it could be assumed that the school atmosphere and teaching reflected the religious commitment of the home.

The principle of parental preference, in Section 76 of the 1944 Education Act, states that parents in general have the right to choose the form of public education for their children. In practice, this 'right' was always severely limited by the fact that additional public expense could not be incurred in its application. Voluntary-aided schools could and did set their own admissions criteria. Catholic voluntary-aided schools in particular were not open to the wider public. Section 8 of the Education Act of 1980 required governors for the first time to publish the policy they had established for admissions.[96] Governors, by publishing criteria for admissions, were making a significant statement about their schools. To ensure a degree of uniformity, diocesan school commissions provided draft wordings and the general format of admissions policies for the Catholic schools in their areas. Section 6 of the 1980 Education Act allowed parents to 'express a preference' with which it was the duty of governors to comply. However, Catholic schools could make an agreement with their local education authority in respect of admissions which could effectively limit any such preference by parents. The CEC issued guidelines soon after the Act came into force which stated that Catholic schools should offer their services first to Catholic families and that these children should have a prior claim which admissions policies should reflect. It also warned Catholic schools not to encourage applications of a kind which would not be possible to accept but did not specify the nature of such applications.[97]

The 1986 Education Act (No 2) Section 33 further imposed a duty on all voluntary-aided schools to have regard for the views of LEAs, but the final judgement on admissions remained with the governors. Thus the ability of governors in Catholic maintained schools to establish their own admissions policy was largely maintained. Whilst the Education Reform Bill of 1987 caused some initial fears about the ability of governors to protect the Catholic identity of the school through control of admissions, Section 30 of the resulting Act of 1988 offers the possibility of protecting the position of voluntary-aided schools in this matter. It is conditional since there are no statutory guarantees which allow governors to refuse to comply with 'parental preference'. Governors still have to agree an annual admissions statement with their local education authority and if there is a dispute the matter can be referred by either party to the Secretary of State for his legally binding decision. From this perspective it is clear that the 1980, 1986 and 1988 Education Acts have eroded the sole discretion once allowed to governors in voluntary-aided schools to operate their own admission criteria. Governors appointed by the trustees have reduced legal powers to define the character of their school through the control of admissions. It must also be recognised that there are differences among Catholic governors regarding the value of this 'character'. This has led to varied admissions policies from one Catholic school to another and this practice has been summed up by a group of Catholic educationalists who stated that:

> The governors' aims must embody a clear perception of the balance envisaged between Catholic and non-Catholic pupils, and the reason for that balance. This may be considered negatively to protect Catholic interests while trying to maintain viability or positively as a stated desire to be of wider service to the community.[98]

These points illustrate some of the conflicting values and perceptions of many Catholic governors.

Most diocesan school commissions have advised school governors to limit the number of non-Catholics to between 10% and 15% of the total.[99] In addition, model admissions criteria were framed by the diocesan schools commissions which gave priority to Catholic children over others. In many respects these model criteria have reminded foundation governors of their responsibilities to the trustees. Current practice with regard to the control of admissions can most easily be illustrated with reference to the provision of schools in the Archdiocese of Birmingham. In 1992 there were a total of 271 schools, both voluntary and independent, with 79,234 pupils of whom 21,513 were non-Catholics. Clearly, many of these schools had exceeded the diocese's own 15% guidelines, for whilst some schools had over 50% non-Catholics on their roll, other schools had much lower proportions. The Archdiocese of Liverpool has the largest percentage of Catholic pupils in its maintained schools with 96.4%, whilst the Diocese of Plymouth has the lowest with 65.5%.[100] Among the pupils who attend Catholic schools there can be found many who come from families who are committed to the Catholic faith and many others who come from nominally Catholic homes. Others come from families who belong to other Christian denominations or adhere to other world religions or more commonly subscribe to no religion at all. There is to be found in each Catholic school a diversity of religious background and a pluralism of interest in and commitment to the Catholic faith. It follows that there may well be little coherence between the home, parish and school with regard to the majority of pupils in Catholic schools today. Catholic schools are no longer single faith structures. It would appear that, at least officially, these schools have taken little account of their changing intakes.

Leslie Francis in his study of Catholic schools in the Archdiocese of Birmingham claimed that the needs of non-Catholics were not reflected in the school policies adopted. He commented that:

> If one of the aims of the Roman Catholic Church in maintaining Catholic schools is to provide an educational environment in which pupils display a favourable attitude towards Christianity, this study places a caveat against the policy for compensating for falling rolls by recruiting into Catholic schools a higher proportion of non-Catholic pupils, even from Church going non-Catholic back-grounds.[101]

Francis's empirical data on Catholic schools suggests a disparity between current Catholic educational statements and practice in schools. He suggests that if the Church maintains its traditional position then it will need to reduce the number of school places. If the practice remains, there would have to be a modification of theory. This would lead to an alternative position which might possibly embrace a wider Christian perspective and foster a greater

ecumenical dimension in the provision of Christian schools.[102] The
bishops have allowed the admission of non-Catholic pupils since
they claim that the ethos of Catholic schools is often attractive to
parents outside the Catholic community.[103] Nevertheless, it is
recognised that the admission of non-Catholics may have negative
influences on the effectiveness of Catholic education and dilute
the religious ethos of the school. For this reason Cardinal Hume
has warned against haphazard admission policies which create
obvious problems such as altering the purpose and atmosphere of
the school.[104] Against this there are many within the Catholic
community who argue for a line of development involving broader
entry policies on the grounds that it is appropriate in Britain's
multi-ethnic society. Some even advocate an alternative form of
schooling, not exclusively Catholic, nor even Christian in nature.[105]
As one parish priest says:

> . . . the real problem seems to be not that Catholic schools can no
> longer fulfil the purpose for which they were founded — that of
> fostering a strong Catholic community — but rather that this aim
> in itself is no longer in tune with the challenge facing the Church
> in the modern world.[106]

Catholic schools generally stress a Christian-related criterion in
their admissions policies, which has the effect of restricting the
possibility of cultural and religious diversity. This point has been
taken up in a Church report entitled *Learning from Diversity*, published by the Bishops' Conference in 1984, which contained
recommendations on the problem of 'white' Catholic schools in
predominantly racially mixed areas. The report stressed the urgent
need for the Church to address itself to eliminating any racist
practices in admission policies. Curiously, there is no evidence in
the report that Catholic schools have ever discriminated on the
grounds of race. A High Court ruling of July 1991 found that Bishop
Challoner Catholic Girls' School in Stepney, east London, had
discriminated against two non-Christian children, one Hindu, the
other Muslim, in denying them places at the school. The problem
arose because the school had not formally agreed its admission
policy with the LEA under Section Six of the 1980 Education Act.[107]
The diocesan authorities and the governors appealed against the
decision and won their case in the Court of Appeal. The example,
whilst untypical, does reinforce the need for Catholic schools to
have justifiable admissions policies and procedures. There is a
number of inner City Catholic schools which have become multi-

faith communities and cannot have meaning on the basis of their 'shared Catholic beliefs', which the aims of the school would imply. The admission policies of these schools have rendered the title 'Catholic' somewhat redundant. The policies pursued by these governors have been of their own pragmatic making.

Government intervention, through legislation in respect of admissions, has nevertheless limited the powers of governors. Section 26(10) of the 1988 Education Reform Act establishes a 'standard number' for each school by which it is the duty of the school to admit up to that number if demand warrants it. This 'standard number' is taken to be the number of pupils admitted to the school in the year 1979 to 1980 and the Secretary of State for Education and Science alone, upon application from governors under Section 28 of the 1988 Act, has the power to alter this number. The implications for Catholic schools, as for all others, is that they must call back into use classroom accommodation no longer in use if this is needed to provide for the 'standard number'. Catholic schools might be required to admit non-Catholics not just to fill empty places, but to fill empty classrooms. During the passage of the Education Bill, the CEC campaigned to include a clause in the Bill to the effect that preserving the character of the school provided grounds for modifying the 'standard number' formula.[108] This attempt failed, but the final version of the legislation did mention the character of a school as being a matter for attention in agreeing admissions criteria. The full consequences for Catholic schools cannot be properly understood without making the link between admissions and the closely connected provisions in the 1988 Act, establishing new budgetary arrangements for schools under local management. A school's budget is directly related to the number of children it admits and a Catholic school may be driven by a need to survive and expand, rather than through a need to preserve the school's character.

Agreements on admissions criteria for Catholic schools are undertaken with the local education authority; when a dispute arises it is referred to the Secretary of State for Education and Science for a final decision. Such a dispute arose with St Anne's School in the local authority of Tower Hamlets in east London in 1989.[109] The local authority could not come to an agreement with the school over admissions and the school governors sent the matter to the Secretary of State who in turn referred it back for further discussion between the governors and LEA. At the centre of the issue was a dispute about the school's 'standard number' and the school's religious character. The authority claimed that the school was only two-thirds full and had 104 places which could be used for the 74 children (non-Catholics and largely new immigrant Bangladeshis) without schooling in that area. The school said that it was concerned about the preservation of its religious character and had already admitted 10% non-Catholics in accordance with diocesan advice. The authority threatened to refer the matter back to the Secretary of State and claimed that there were 267 empty places in the 11 Catholic schools in the authority whilst there were still children without schooling. In the event St Anne's School accepted larger numbers of non-Catholics. This example indicates how the Education Reform Act's ability to protect the character of Catholic schools is inadequate and thus a LEA may not only have different priorities from the Catholic authorities, but can have them implemented in Catholic schools.

Control

The control of education in England and Wales is commonly described as an administrative partnership, between central Government, LEAs and voluntary bodies. Much of the educational literature on governance focuses on central and local government control over schooling and assigns the voluntary bodies, mainly the Churches, a minor role in policy formulations. Michael Hornsby-Smith once characterised the strategies of Catholic decision-makers in the political process as 'playing the system' by which he meant:

> ... keeping a low profile, avoiding overt conflict and the antagonisms of other interests and sectors of the community and pursuing a policy of secret rather than open diplomacy.[110]

Today, in regard to Catholic educational policy, this observation is still generally appropriate. The Catholic Church in the last decade has campaigned openly and vigorously against many of the Government's policies on schools and colleges of education. They have attempted to preserve the 'partnership' involved in the dual system between the Church and State at the centre of which is the voluntary school. As described earlier, voluntary-aided schools are part-financed by their founding trust, by a religious order or diocesan commission. In return for these payments (15% of major capital and maintenance expenditure on the school buildings) the schools are granted a greater degree of freedom from LEA control than that given to county schools. This includes the freedom to teach within the framework of a particular set of religious beliefs. The founding bodies of voluntary-aided schools appoint a majority of the school's governors, who in turn appoint and employ the staff. Although voluntary-aided schools are allowed to set their own admissions policy, their guidelines for head teachers may not conflict with the overall policy of the Government or of the LEA. The Catholic sector, in partnership with the local authority, still attempts to retain a distinctive admissions procedure. Catholic schools are also classed in law as charities. Where other differences are known at all, it would seem that they are usually regarded as insignificant variations, of largely historical interest.

'Partnership' is also a concept that applies within the Catholic sector itself, in particular to the relationships between parents, governors and the trustees of the schools. Cardinal Hume has called for this local partnership to be regulated by legal safeguards especially when there are 'fundamental and irreconcilable differences of view on the part of parents, governors and Trustees.'[111] In a speech to the National Conference of Priests in September 1989, he called for a public Catholic campaign to secure legislation which would allow the trustees to dismiss governors who acted contrary to their policies and for the trustees to have the option of a veto over a Catholic school's application for grant-maintained status.[112] These safeguards, which he thought were necessary, are clearly directed towards protecting and strengthening the position of trustees in the local Catholic partnership. The Cardinal claimed that he was not opposed to grant-maintained schools in principle and that indeed there could well be a situation in which it would be desirable for Catholic schools to become grant-maintained. Consequently, a number of Catholic headmasters have reflected this support for grant-maintained schools in letters to the press.[113]

These examples indicate that there is a measure of uncertainty in the Catholic community about the powers of the trustees. The Church's relationship with LEAs has generally been supportive. This is despite the fact that most recent disputes in Catholic schools have been with LEAs and not with the Government. These local-authority disputes have concerned not only admissions, the appointment of teachers and transport questions, but have also involved disagreements over the provision of funds by local authorities for the training of governors in Catholic voluntary schools.

Nevertheless, Bishop Konstant in his presidential address to the North of England Education Conference in January 1991 said that he would regret the weakening of LEAs powers by the Government.[114] Continuing support for the diocesan and local education authority link would appear to be strong among the bishops. The Archdiocese of Westminster, for example, comments that:

> Although in recent years there has been some tension within certain areas of London as a result of political influence attempting to affect the conduct of Catholic schools, this has been minimal compared with the great benefits which have been derived from the partnership.[115]

The statement, however, went on to say that:

> ... it would not be the intention of the Trustees to dissolve such a partnership unless a serious threat to Catholic education as a whole were being made.[116]

Many diocesan education authorities have excellent relations with their local authorities and support the view expressed by the Archdiocese of Westminster. The success of Catholic links may be illustrated by the fact that the Church of England complained publicly that Sheffield Education Authority was discriminating against its schools whilst leaving Catholic ones untouched.[117]

The control exercised by the Catholic Church over its maintained schools has been significantly eroded by legislation. Some LEAs have used Government legislation and regulations effectively to threaten the continued existence of Catholic schools in their area. In discussing admissions it was clear that Government and local authority use of 'surplus places' in the maintained sector has serious implications for Catholic practice and policy. The use of the 'surplus places' issue has also direct bearing on two other important areas for the maintenance of a Catholic school system; namely free transport and diocesan reorganisation plans.

The Question of Free School Transport

Prior to the controversy over the clause in the 1980 Education Bill to withdraw transport assistance to children attending Church schools, Oxfordshire LEA in a review of transport policy attempted to restrict the amount of money it spent on denominational school transport.[118] This was resisted by the Archdiocese of Birmingham and the matter was ended by the defeat of the school transport clause in the Education Bill 1980.[119] In the following year, Croydon LEA refused to pay the travel costs of children attending denominational schools. The diocese appealed to the then Secretary of State for Education, Sir Keith Joseph, but he refused to intervene.[120] The diocese considered legal action against the authority, but decided not to take such action. In June 1990 Hertfordshire LEA also decided to withdraw support for transport to denominational schools on the basis that the authority would save an estimated £400,000 per annum. In the July of the same year Kent LEA were asked in a internally commissioned report to consider proposals which identified opportunities for achieving cumulative savings of over £1 million.[121] These included adopting a uniform approach to school transport based upon the principle of attendance at the nearest geographically appropriate school. The report also recommended that the authority should consult with the diocesan authorities concerning denominational school transport as this was an area where Kent, when compared with other LEAs, according to the report, applied 'excessive discretion' in its transport assistance to pupils. In the event, Kent did not proceed with its plan but other authorities are currently considering such plans and Bromley LEA has joined with Croydon in ceasing payments for school transport.

In the Hertfordshire case, which was a decision to withdraw assistance and substitute a £50 termly charge for each of the first two children in a family attending Church schools, the Archdiocese of Westminster sought the intervention of the Secretary of State for Education. The Education Secretary, Kenneth Clarke, announced in January 1991 that there were no formal grounds for intervention. He rejected the claim that Catholic schools were being discriminated against and said that parents who chose other schools had to pay the transport costs. He also rejected the claim by the Archdiocese that the proposed action by Hertfordshire was a precedent and cited the Croydon case.[122] Cardinal Hume in a letter to Mr Clarke argued that:

> It has to be a matter of policy whether the dual system is to continue to apply throughout the country or merely where the local authority is favourably disposed.[123]

As far as the Government was concerned, this was entirely a matter for the LEA; it evaded having to give a ruling on whether Hertfordshire acted unreasonably. The Archdiocese was dissatisfied by this and encouraged a Catholic comprehensive in Stevenage, John Henry Newman School, to register a dispute between the governors and the local education authority. Under Section 67 of the

Education Act 1944, any dispute between a voluntary school and
the local education authority must be resolved by the Secretary of
State. In another move, the school has called for an opt out ballot
with the full approval of the trustees, on the basis that with full
control over the budget the school could contribute to the transport
costs of pupils from low income families.[124]

It is interesting that a few months earlier, in May 1990, an article
appeared in the influential *British Journal of Educational Studies* on
this subject. It outlined in a study of school transport the reasons
why assistance for transport to denominational schools should
cease, or be severely curtailed, in the interests of the savings that
would be made by LEAs. In an interesting letter in response by
the Secretary of the CEC to what he considered to be an inaccurate
article, it is stated that:

> The common view of the law is that . . . there is an obligation to
> provide transport to the school attended if it is over walking
> distance, unless a place can be offered at a nearer school. Applied
> to Catholic schools, this has the effect that transport is an obligation
> unless there are surplus places in nearer county or other schools.[125]

It would appear from this that Catholics would pay their own
transport costs if their local LEA school had surplus places. Since
pupil rolls have fallen steadily in many secondary schools in the
1980s, this statement admits that LEAs have no obligation to help
children attending Church schools in the circumstances described
above. The same letter makes this clear when it ends:

> It is only when there are surplus places in schools that transport to
> Catholic schools may cease to be a matter of obligation.

Since most LEAs have surplus school places, they could classify all
assistance in transporting Catholic school children as concessionary free transport and could end this practice at their own discretion. A local authority could not end free transport if the Catholic
school was the nearest available school. The net effect on Catholic
school provision in country areas could be devastating, as Catholic
parents may no longer choose a Catholic school because of excessive transport costs. The Audit Commission, which has a duty to
point out inefficiencies in local government, has also subsequently
made clear that LEAs have no legal duty to pay for transport for
children whose parents opt to send them further afield than their
neighbouring schools and recommended the end to free transport
to denominational schools. The Commission said that:

Current arrangements for the transport of pupils from home-to-school are anachronistic. The laws which govern home-to-school transport were conceived for a society very different from that which exists today . . . The government's last attempt to reconstruct the home-to-school transport system in the 1980 Education Bill was rejected by Parliament. Development in the last decade underlines the need for a further attempt.[126]

This will no doubt strengthen the determination by an increasing number of authorities to reduce such spending which currently costs councils £280 million a year.

The CEC continues to dispute the claimed discretion of LEAs to end the traditional provision of free transport on the grounds that the existence of empty spaces in LEA schools does not of itself constitute suitable alternative arrangements for Catholic children. Here the CEC draws attention to the wording of the 1944 Education Act (Section 39(2)(C)), in particular to the phrase 'suitable arrangements'.[127] Alternative arrangements may require the provision of extra resources which must be made available by the local authority. The CEC goes on to argue that it may not be proper for the LEA to make such resources available to the county school and considers the position under pre-delegated and post-delegated budgets. Under pre-delegated budgets it will be necessary to set the extra resources against the savings on transport and any eventual savings at the school previously attended. The change of school may therefore involve duplication of facilities, at least initially; all, it is argued, in the cause of subverting parental preferences. Under the post-delegated budget it is not possible for the local authority to provide additional resources to make possible 'suitable arrangements', as the school budget is set from the previous year and allows for no contingencies. This legal and technical reasoning by the CEC may have some value in preventing the withdrawal of free transport in the short term, but it has no real weight for any long term consideration. Apparently, the law does not protect the traditional practice of local authority provision of free transport to children attending Catholic schools distant from their homes.

The Rejection of Diocesan Reorganisation Plans

The grounds given by the Secretary of State for Education and Science in recent years for refusing voluntary-aided status have been either that the local education authority objects to the proposed reorganisation plan or that there are surplus maintained school places in the area. In the case of Catholic schools, it has almost always been the latter. As discussed in Chapter Four, the diocese of Salford had its reorganisation plans rejected on the grounds that there were 'surplus places' in local LEA schools. In the same way, the Archdiocese of Birmingham's plans to replace an existing school which was declared structurally unsafe, were initially rejected by the DES. It has recently been calculated that over twenty-seven Catholic schools have had their plans for repairs and extensions rejected on the grounds that there are vacancies in nearby LEA schools.[128]

It was not because of any Catholic pressure that Baroness Cox introduced an Education Bill into the House of Lords in 1990 with a specific proposal (Clause Two) that placed an obligation upon the Secretary of State to 'take into account the need for a diversity of schools within the maintained sector in a particular area in order to satisfy parental demand and children's needs'.[129] This seemed to Baroness Cox to be the logical corollary of the requirements to give greater parental choice. The Bill was motivated by Baroness Cox's desire to see Government funding for Christian fundamentalist, Moslem, Jewish and other 'philosophically' grounded schools in the interests of parental choice. Whilst she contacted and sought support from the Church of England and a wide range of other bodies, no official approach was made to the Catholic Church for support.[130] This was despite the public statements made by Bishop Konstant in his presidential address to the North of England Education Conference, supporting the principle of schools for Muslims and other minority groups to be financed in part by the State.[131] In addition, the two most vocal supporters of the Bill, at least at the level of principle, during its Second Reading were Catholics — Lord Longford and the Duke of Norfolk.[132] The Bill had little hope of success and was withdrawn by Baroness Cox at the end of its Second Reading. Nevertheless, the discussion which it generated was revealing, not least for the issue of 'surplus places'.

The debate raised various questions about the attitudes of the partners in the control of education. Baroness Cox began the debate by speaking of the ideological hostility of many councils to admitting new voluntary-aided schools to the maintained sector.[133] This seemed to be confirmed when Baroness Blackstone, officially replying for the Labour party, stated that there was a good case to make all publicly maintained schools secular schools.[134] This prompted the intervention of Lord Longford, himself a Labour peer, to clarify that this was not official Labour Party policy.[135] The Bishop of Guildford put the Church of England position which was not to support the Bill in its present form, although he pledged his support in principle for religious minority schools.[136] The Lords addressed the technical question of 'surplus places' at some length, a matter which has not been publicly discussed by the House of Commons nor by its own Select Committee on Education. Lord Campbell of Alloway made the point that it was the Secretary of State for Education and Science who had the sole power to make decisions about applications for voluntary-aided status and that this was unsatisfactory.[137] He commented that there was no proper provision for making representation to the Secretary of State, nor did the Secretary of State have to give his reasons for his decision in writing and that it was not possible for the exercise of this discretion to be challenged in the courts by way of judicial review. The rules which govern the Secretary of State's decision are compiled by the Secretary of State himself and are that he takes the following into consideration; first, the overall need for school places in the area; second, the demand for a particular kind of school; third, whether the local education authority supports it; fourth, whether the school will be able to deliver the national curriculum; fifth, whether the premises are up to standard; sixth, whether the promoters can meet the expenditure; and seventh, whether there will be provision of equal opportunity for boys and girls. In the case of the diocese of Salford's plans, the Secretary of State rejected them on the basis of his first rule for consideration. The question of the religious demand and parental preference for a particular school type clearly takes second place to the eradication of 'surplus places' in the school system overall. This has led some Catholic dioceses to build Catholic schools because of the demand, without the normal 85% capital funding granted by central Government.[138] The same procedures are employed by the Secretary of State when he considers questions relating to admissions, transport and exception regulations for the national curriculum in Catholic schools. By contrast, whilst considering grant-maintained status applications, the Secretary of State is at the same time able to encourage such applications in line with his party's policy. The Secretary of State has the ultimate and sole power to make

decisions under the Education Reform Act 1988 over a wide range
of important issues in a Catholic school.

'Surplus places', however, do not appear to have been a consideration in the Government's sponsorship of City Technology Colleges and Grant-Maintained Schools.[139] Both are non-fee-paying
schools. The latter can be established by governors of all primary
and secondary schools who apply for the school to be run independently of the LEA. If they are backed by a ballot (or series of
ballots) that produces a simple majority of those parents who vote,
and provided the Secretary of State gives approval to the scheme,
a school may opt out; it will then receive a block grant directly from
the Department of Education and Science. The schools will be
required to account to the Secretary of State for their spending. It
is interesting that the first Catholic secondary school, Blessed
Hugh More in Lincolnshire, to apply for grant-maintained status,
with the support of the diocesan bishop and the only school to have
a 100% yes vote, was rejected on the grounds that the school was
not viable and therefore unable to implement the National Curriculum. It has been strongly argued by the Rev. John Ryan that the
Government's policies discriminate against Catholic schools because they tend to be smaller than LEA schools. He argued that
the 'flat rate mentality' whereby a standard sum of money is given
for each pupil in an annual allocation to each school, directly
threatens Catholic schools. He claimed that Catholic schools could
be tempted to attract more pupils in order to sustain a larger staff
and bigger budget and may in the process alter the ethos of the
school by an open admissions policy. He cited the example of the
disputes in Gwent and Hertfordshire between the LEAs and
Catholic governors as the consequence of Government policy. In
addition, he attacked LEAs for not taking account of the complementary responsibilities of the Church in maintaining voluntary-
aided schools. He expressed fundamental disquiet by saying:

> The dual system is intended to be a partnership but no partnership
> can work if one of the partners denies the legitimate status of the
> other.[140]

By attacking the local authorities, he clearly indicated that it is not
simply the Government's legislation which has undermined the
partnership, but the attitude of some LEAs. Much earlier, Saran,
in a case-study of local education authority decision-making in the
1960s found Catholic influence strong, with Roman Catholic councillors within each party group able successfully to exert pressure

on behalf of the Church by engaging in cross-party voting.[141] Two Catholic councillors in Gwent did exactly this over the threatened closure of St Alban's school in 1991, but the Catholic councillors in Hertfordshire, including the chairman of the education committee, did not. Reliance by the Church on the support of Catholic politicians and the Catholic community would appear less justified today.

Conclusion

Catholic educational policy, as espoused by the bishops, appears at first sight to be based upon the principles found in the post-conciliar documents of the Church. The actual policy consequences of these ideals, as understood and operated by the bishops, allow for significant gaps. At the episcopal level it is more appropriate to talk of a degree of disjunction between principle and policy in Catholic education. Whilst the bishops seek to encourage their ideals of schools as 'faith communities' which are 'inspired a by a single Christian vision', at the same time they devise policies which do not allow for the fulfilment of these ideals. Policies on admissions, for example, vary from diocese to diocese and from school to school and the admission of non-Catholics from a faith group defeats the principle of a 'faith community' inspired by a 'single Christian vision'. Nor do these policies attempt to address the increasing implications for the nature of Catholic schools in the admission of non-practising Catholics. Bishop Konstant, in a letter to the Bishop's Consultation on 'Catholic Schools and Other Faiths', has departed from previous positions on admissions in writing:

> It is not possible to determine, in any realistic way, what is the maximum proportion of non-Catholic pupils that can be accepted into a Catholic school without changing the religious nature of the school; there cannot be a hard and fast rule. Hence the notional limits are pragmatic guidelines. [142]

It is unclear whether the other bishops share Bishop Konstant's views on this matter.

The repeated statements of the bishops that the Catholic religion should permeate the whole curriculum have no foundation since their actual policies provide no methods for implementation. The recent interest shown by the Bishops' Conference in developing a Catholic dimension to the National Curriculum is an indication of

the attempt to incorporate these principles into some policy.
However, the last attempt at producing a distinctive Catholic
contribution to the curriculum failed because of a lack of will to
continue by the Catholic authorities in 1972. Many Catholic
schools, for all practical purposes, have either abandoned or been
unable to integrate religion into the wider curriculum. This is due
in part to the fact that the bishops, while having clear principles,
have been unable to articulate and enact a clear policy. In teacher
training and appointments the bishops appear to have no policy on
how to prepare teachers from universities for service in Catholic
schools. It can be concluded that the bishops have not pursued
policies which are tightly based on the principles of the post-conciliar education documents as understood by themselves in the
English and Welsh context. One serious constraint has been Government action, especially during the past decade.

The method of consultation by the Government has become one
principally of 'consultation by response'. By this means the Government simply makes a request for responses to its proposals. The
opportunity for the Church to take the initiative is small. In other
forms of negative consultation, the Government simply informs
the Church of what it intends; this was illustrated most clearly over
teacher training provision. In 1982 the Government issued a 'discussion paper' which threatened some teacher training colleges by
an omission in statistics — beside certain college names was placed
the word 'nil' for the number of students that institution could
admit in 1983.[143] Consultation by Church representation on Government committees has also been a feature of Government policy,
but it is not a method of consultation which the Government has
employed much recently. This is illustrated by the Government's
refusal to allow Church representation on a number of national
councils, such as the Further Education Funding Council, that now
fund many Catholic schools and colleges.[144]

Government legislation and regulations, together with the many
and varied actions and interpretations of LEAs and the courts, have
constrained the shape and scope of Catholic education policy. The
Secretary of State for Education and Science has since 1979 increasingly pursued centrally determined educational policies.
These policies are no longer based exclusively upon statute, but
on the considerable and unprecedented powers awarded to the
Secretary of State under the Education Acts of 1980, 1986, and
especially 1988. There are in reality no statutory guarantees which

allow governors of Catholic schools to control the religious ethos of their school through restrictions on their admissions policies. Both the 1980 and 1988 Education Acts have eroded this discretion. Despite the 'exception regulations' in the National Curriculum, which will always depend on the co-operation of the Secretary of State, the Government of the day could still impose subject content in schools which is unacceptable to the Catholic Church. The bishops have in their most recent statement shown increased concern at the place of religious education in the curriculum. The closure of Catholic colleges and the Government's policy not to consult with the bishops over their closure also show the direct constraints on Catholic policy. Diocesan disputes and problems with Bromley, Croydon, Gwent, Hertfordshire, Liverpool, Oxfordshire, Rochdale, Salford, Tower Hamlets, and other LEAs, which have all reached the national press, strongly indicate the type of pressures currently on Catholic education policies. Moreover, the Government's use of the 'surplus places' argument to reduce capacity in the education system as a whole has adversely effected the ability of diocesan authorities to plan provision with LEAs. In addition, calls from the right wing of the Conservative Party, at a senior level, for:

> A radical review of the disproportionate influence of the Church and charitable trusts in the administration of the educational system . . .[145]

directly threatens Church schools. These are constraints which arise not only from official Government, but also from within the Catholic community.

The secretary of the diocesan schools commission for the Diocese of Arundel and Brighton said in 1990 that the best defence for the Catholic school was its distinctiveness.[146] This raises the question of what this 'distinctiveness' should mean and whether it is desired by parents for their children. Problems and disputes between the parents and diocesan school commissions were not uncommon during comprehensive reorganisation in the late 1960s and 1970s. The use of certain principles, normally derived from outside the Church, by groups of parents and clergy can and do undermine diocesan policies. Grant-maintained schools can undermine the obligation on all Catholic schools, expressed at the Second Vatican Council, to work together. Bishops who have schools that have 'opted-out' of local authority control will need to accommodate them in some way that may involve a change of policy by the diocese. There have been instances where the local school community has usurped the powers of the diocesan trustees to appoint the governors. For example, the Archdiocese of Birmingham, in its bulletin to schools, was forced on two occasions to remind head teachers and governors that it was the diocesan commission that appointed foundation governors on behalf of the trustees.[147] A number of Catholics have different priorities from their diocesan bishop's policies and are intent on fulfilling them. Another example of the range of different priorities is the direct challenge made to the trustees of the Archdiocese of Southwark by a dismissed foundation governor who claimed that 'distant' and 'childless trustees' had no right to determine the education of children.[148] Tensions and conflict within the Catholic community itself exert a powerful influence over the final outcome of Catholic education policies, especially in their ultimate implementation.

Notes

1. Lawton, D., *Education, Culture and the National Curriculum*, Hodder and Stoughton, London, 1989, p. 30.
2. Walsh, P. , 'The Church Secondary School and its Curriculum' in O'Leary, P. (ed.), *Religious Education and Young Adults*, St Paul's, Slough, 1983, pp. 4–19.
3. Selby, D.E., *The Work of Cardinal Manning in the Field of Education*, University of Birmingham, PhD, 1974.
4. Holland, M.G., *The British Catholic Press and the Educational Controversy 1847–1865*, Garland Publishing, New York, 1987, p. 186.
5. Finan, J.J., *Struggle for Justice: A Short History of the Catholic Teachers' Federation*, published by the Catholic Teachers' Federation, London, 1976, p. 31.
6. *Catholic Education: An Educational Journal*, Catholic Education Council, (two editions were published in 1956).
7. Eagleton, T., 'Catholic Education and Commitment', in *Catholic Education Today*, Vol. 1, No. 1, January/February 1967, pp. 8–10.
8. Miss. N. Hodgson, a Vice-Principal of Newman College of Education, Birmingham, represented the Catholic Education Council on the Schools Council.
9. Humble, S. and Simons, H., *From Council to Classroom*, a Schools Council Publication, London, 1978. There are few references to Catholic schools in this evaluation of the SCHP, however, they are: pp. 49, 138, and 117–118.
10. Higgins, T., *Teaching About Controversial Issues in Catholic Schools*, Centre for Applied Research in Education, Occasional Publication, No. 7, 1979, p. 1.
11. *Ibid.*, p. 13.

12. *Hansard*, House of Commons, Vol. 397, Cols. 2360 ff, 10th March 1944.

13. *The School Curriculum*, Department of Education and Science, March 1981.

14. CEC, *Report 1980*, p. 11.

15. CEC, *Report 1980*, p. 11 ff.

16. *The Religious Dimension of Catholic Education*, Congregation for Catholic Education, Rome, 1988, section 100.

17. *Better Schools*, Government White Paper, 1985, para. 272.

18. Education Act 1986 (No 2) Section 19 (b).

19. *The Education Act (No 2) 1986 and Catholic Schools*, Catholic Education Council, 1986.

20. Department of Education and Science, Committee of Enquiry into the Education of Children from Ethnic Minority Groups, HMSO, 1985.

21. *The Education Reform Bill — A Commentary for Catholics*, Bishops' Conference, 1988, p. 11.

22. Robinson, T., *Distinctive Characteristics of Roman Catholic Secondary Schools*, University of Oxford, MSc, 1982.

23. Burgess, R. G., 'Five Items for the Policy Agenda in Church Schools', in O'Keeffe, B. (ed.), *Schools for Tomorrow*, Falmer Press, London, 1988, p. 170.

24. Wake, R., 'Catholic Education in Schools', *The Month*, July 1986, pp. 248–250.

25. Green, B., 'Church Schools in a Pagan Culture', *The Tablet*, 6th October 1990, Education Supplement, p. 1271 ff.

26. Bishops' Conference of England and Wales, 1987–88 various campaign papers distributed to parishes on the Education Reform Bill.

27. *The Education Reform Bill — A Commentary for Catholics*, Bishops' Conference, 1988. Also repeated by Cardinal Hume in his speech to the North of England Education Conference in January 1990 and reported in *Briefing*, 26th January 1990, Vol. 20, No.2.

28. *The Education Reform Bill — A Commentary for Catholics*, Bishops' Conference of England and Wales, 1988, p. 7.

29. Hackett, P., 'The Curriculum and the Governors', *The Month*, October 1983, pp. 341–344.

30. Kelly, P., *Catholic Schools*, Diocese of Salford, 1987, p. 10.

31. Reported in *Briefing*, March 1988, Vol. 18, No.6.

32. *Evaluating the Distinctive Nature of a Catholic School*, Department of Education and Formation, Bishops' Conference, second edition, 1990.

33. Hume, B., 'No Room for Religion', *The Times*, 13th January 1988.

34. *Evaluating the Distinctive Nature of a Catholic School*, 1990, *op. cit.*

35. *The Catholic School*, Congregation for Catholic Education, Rome, para. 33, 1977.

36. *Evaluating the Distinctive Nature of a Catholic School*, 1990, *op. cit.*

37. Hackett, P. , *op. cit.*

38. Between 1989 and 1991 the Bishops' Conference of England and Wales Department for Catholic Education and Formation produced a number of draft papers on the National Curriculum which included Health Education, Technology, Science, Mathematics, Economic and Industrial Relations and English. These papers have not been distributed to schools and therefore references to them in the text are to their draft forms.

39. *Ibid.*

40. *Ibid.*

41. Joint Pastoral Letter on Education of the Bishops' of England and Wales, January 1991, Bishops' Conference.

42. *Christianity in Religious Education Programmes*, Culham College Institute News, September 1989.

43. Morris, R. (ed.), *Central and Local Control of Education After the Education Reform Act 1988*, Longman, London,1990, p. 17. See especially Meredith, P., *Government, Schools and the Law*, Routledge, London, 1992, pp. 51–88.

44. Hurley, M.J., *Declaration on Christian Education — A Commentary*, Paulist Press, New Jersey, 1966, p. 19.

45. Beales, A.C.F., 'Struggle for the Schools', in Beck, G.A. (ed.), *The English Catholics*, Burns and Oates, London, 1950, p. 392.

46. Phillips, F.R., *Bishop Beck and Education*, Edwin Mellen Press, Leominster, 1990, p. 7.

47. CEC, *Report, 1957*, see also notes 102 and 108 in Chapter II.

48. *The Curriculum — A Christian View*, The National Society, London, 1989.

49. McClelland, V.A., 'Education', in Hastings, A. (ed.), *Modern Catholicism*, SPCK, London, 1991, p. 173.

50. Bishops' Conference Department of Education and Formation, Schools Committee Questionnaire Survey, 1990.

51. Hume, B., 'The Future of Catholic Schools', an address to Catholic headteachers in London, reported in *Briefing*, 30th September 1988, Vol. 18, No.19.

52. *Declaration on Christian Education*, Second Vatican Council, Catholic Truth Society, 1966, Section 8.

53. Hume, B., *op. cit.*

54. See *Minute Book of the Annual Meetings of Diocesan Inspectors*, 1875–1968 in two volumes and held at the offices of the Bishops' Conference in London.

55. *Ibid.*, Vol. I, p. 111, 29th April 1891.

56. *Ibid.*, Vol. I, p. 232, 19th and 20th May 1908.

57. *Ibid.*, p. 233 ff.

58. *Ibid.*, Vol. II, p. 57, 31st May 1933.

59. *Ibid.*, Vol. II, p. 135, 21st October 1959.

60. *Ibid.*, Vol. II, p. 195, 10th October 1968.

61. Gay, J., in McClelland, V.A. (ed.), *Christian Education in a Pluralist Society*, Croom Heime, London, 1988, p. 206.

62. CEC, *Report, 1985*, p. 5.
63. Arthur, J., 'Teachers in Need of Better Training', *The Universe*, 30th July 1989, p. 5. Burgess, R., 'Schools for the Nineties', *The Tablet*, 5th October 1991, p. 1206.
64. Bishops' Conference Department of Education and Formation, Schools Committee Questionnaire Survey, 1990.
65. *Minute Book of the Annual Meetings of Diocesan Inspectors*, Vol. II, 10th October 1968, p. 194.
66. *The Religious Dimension of Catholic Education*, Congregation for Catholic Education, Rome, 1988, sections 26 and 96.
67. *Memorandum on the Appointment of Teachers*, Bishops' Conference, 1974.
68. *Memorandum on the Appointment of Teachers*, Bishops' Conference, 1990.
69. CES, *Report 1993*
70. *Ibid.*
71. *Ibid.*, p. 157.
72. CEC, *Report, 1986*, p. 14 ff.
73. *Ibid.*
74. *Ibid.*
75. Letter of R.F. Cunningham, Secretary of the Catholic Education Council, to Diocesan Schools Commissioners, dated 29th January, 1988.
76. Bishops' Conference of England and Wales, *Statement on Education*, 1987.
77. Arthur, J., 'Teaching and Employment Conditions in Catholic Schools: Principles and Practice', *Law and Justice*, Hilary/Easter, 1995, No. 123/124, pp. 40–53.
78. Jones *v.* Lee and Another, *LGR*, 78 (1) 1979, p. 213ff.
79. *The Tablet*, 26th March 1994.
80. Arthur, J., *Ibid.*
81. *The Tablet*, 12th March 1994.
82. Wells, D., 'The Supply of Catholic Teachers for Catholic School', *Catholic Education Service*, London, 1994.
83. Bishops' Conference Department of Education and Formation, Committee on In-service, Evaluation and Appraisal letter to Heads and Diocesan Commissioners, dated November 1989.
84. Bishops' Conference Department of Education and Formation Committee on In-service, Evaluation and Appraisal, November 1989, B1.
85. *The Religious Dimension of Catholic Education*, Congregation for Catholic Education, Rome, 1988, section 1 and 43, and compare them with a speech by Cardinal Hume, reported in *Briefing*, 30th September 1988, Vol. 18, No.19.
86. Birks, P. L., 'Professional Appraisal in Catholic Schools', *The Month*, September/October 1990, pp. 408–413.
87. *Ibid.*

88. *Ibid.*
89. CES, Report 1993.
90. CEC, *Hanbook 1975.*
91. *Further Insights into Catholic Education*, Catholic Education Council, 1975, p. 21 ff.
92. *Ibid.*
93. CES, Report 1993.
94. Francis, L., 'Roman Catholic Secondary Schools', *Educational Studies*, Vol. 12, No. 2, 1986, pp. 119–127.
95. O'Keeffe, B. (ed.), *Schools for Tomorrow*, Falmer Press, London, 1988, p. 235.
96. Education Act 1980, Sections 6–9 and Schedule 2, see especially Section 8.
97. *The Education Reform Act 1988 and Catholic Schools*, Catholic Education Council, 1988, p. 15.
98. Roehampton Group, 'Admissions Policy in Catholic Schools', *The Month*, April, 1985, pp. 157–159.
99. See the various guidelines provided by diocesan schools commissions, for example the Archdiocese of Westminster in its booklet, *Our Catholic Schools*, of 1988 suggests a limit of 10% non-Catholic admissions. The reason why the Education Reform Act refers specifically to the ethos of a school in the matter of admissions was, as Baroness Hooper says 'to meet concerns expressed by the Churches about the effect that more open enrolments might have on the particular ethos of voluntary-aided and special agreement schools' House of Lords, Debates, Vol. 496, col. 1038, 10th May 1988. However, this addition to the Bill was little different from the substance and effect of section 6 (3) (b) of the Education Act 1980, it is rather cosmetic.
100. Arthur, J., 'Admissions to Catholic Schools: Principles and Practice', *British Journal of Religious Education*, Vol. 17, No. 1, 1994, pp. 35–45.
101. Francis, L., 'Are Catholic Schools Good for Non-Catholics?', *The Tablet*, 15th February 1986, Education Supplement No. 47, pp. 170–172.
102. *Ibid.*
103. *The Education Reform Bill — A Commentary for Catholics*, Bishops' Conference of England and Wales, 1988.
104. Hume, B., *Towards a Civilisation of Love*, Hodder and Stoughton, London, 1988, p. 111.
105. Sallnow, T., 'Truly Catholic Schools', *The Tablet*, 14.2.87. Judd, J. 'Schools with Open Doors', *The Tablet*, 14th February 1987. Catholic Commission for Racial Justice, Notes and Reports, No. 11, April 1982, *Catholic Education in a Multiracial Society*.
106. Green, B., *op. cit.*
107. Regina *v.* Governors of the Bishop Challoner Roman Catholic School and Another *Ex parte* C, Same v. Same, *Ex parte* P. (judgement 31st July 1991), *The Times*, Law Report, 6th July 1991, p. 28.

108. *The Education Reform Act and Catholic Schools*, Catholic Education Council, 1988, p. 16.

109. *TES*, 27th July 1990.

110. Hornsby-Smith, M.P. , *Catholic Education: The Unobtrusive Partner*, Sheed and Ward, London, 1978, p. 3.

111. Hume, B., Speech to the National Conference of Priests, reported in *Briefing*, 7th September 1989, Vol. 19, No. 18, p. 356.

112. *Ibid.*

113. *TES*, Letters, 8th February 1991 and reports in *The Universe*, 7th August 1988.

114. Konstant, D., Speech to North of England Education Conference, January 1991, reported in *Briefing* for 26th January 1991, Vol 21, No. 2.

115. *Our Catholic Schools*, Archdiocese of Westminster, September 1988, p. 19.

116. *Ibid.*

117. *TES*, 1st March 1991, p. 3.

118. Minutes of the Catholic Education Committee for Oxford — part of the Archdiocese of Birmingham Schools Commission Structures, 1979–1980.

119. *TES*, 4th January 1991, p. 1.

120. Education Bill, House of Lords, 1980

121. Advisory Centre for Education, Bulletin No. 36, 1st July 1990, p. 12.

122. *TES*, 4th January 1991, p. 1.

123. *Ibid.*

124. *Education*, 22nd March 1991, p. 233.

125. Letter of R. Cunningham, Secretary of the Catholic Education Council, to the editor of the *British Journal of Educational Studies*, dated 13th December 1990.

126. Thornthwaite, S., 'School Transport — The Need for Change', *British Journal of Educational Studies*, Vol. XXXVIII, No. 2, May 1990, pp. 133–143. See also *The Universe* , 23rd September 1990, and *TES*, 5th October 1990, p. 5, see especially The Audit Commission, *Home to School Transport: A System at the Crossroads*, HMSO, 1991, p. 7 and p. 33.

127. Letter of R. Cunningham, Secretary of the Catholic Education Council, to S. Thornthwaite, dated 30th January 1991. On 15th March 1991 the High Court ruled that free transport for children attending a school of their parents choice rather than their local education authorities, is not a legal right — see *The Times*, 16th March 1991.

128. *The Universe*, 23rd September 1990 and 27th October 1991. See especially 'Tories Infuriate Catholic Votes', *TES*, 7th February 1992, p. 1. Subsequent editions (*TES*, 14th February 1992, p. 2), indicate a reversal of DES policy on the issue before the calling of the General Election of April 1992.

222   The Ebbing Tide

129. Private Members Bill, Education (Amendment) Bill, House of Lords, 1991, Clause 2.
130. Interview with Baroness Cox at House of Lords on Monday 18th February 1991.
131. Konstant, D., *op. cit.*, and *TES*, 4th January 1991, p3.
132. *Hansard*, Vol. 526, Monday 4th March, 1991, House of Lords, Education (Amendment) Bill, Second Reading, col. 1247 ff.
133. *Ibid.*, col. 1248.
134. *Ibid.*, col. 1254.
135. *Ibid.*, col. 1255.
136. *Ibid.*, col. 1263.
137. *Ibid.*, col. 1270 ff.
138. In 1990 the Archdiocese of Birmingham opened a middle school, called Cardinal Newman, in Oxford which did not receive the usual 85% capital grant from the DES. The diocese built the school from its own funds very close to a joint Anglican/Catholic school.
139. This point is made very strongly in *Secondary Education in Gwent*, Archdiocese of Cardiff, 1990.
140. Ryan, J., 'Squeeze on Our Schools', *The Christian*, No. 22, p. 7, *The Universe*, October 1990.
141. Saran, R., *Policy-Making in Secondary Education*, Clarendon Press, Oxford, 1973, p. 201 ff, and pp. 252–253.
142. Catholic Schools and Other Faiths, A Consultation for the Bishops' Conference of England and Wales, Final Report, November 1994, p. 7.
143. Moyser, G (ed.), *Church and Politics Today*, T. and T. Clark, Edinburgh, 1985, p. 245.
144. *The Catholic Herald*, 12th July 1991.
145. *TES*, 19th April 1991, p. 4 carried a report on these proposals from the Carlton Club Political Committee, but it did not highlight the potential threat to Church schools. *The Observer*, 28th April 1991, p. 1 carried a front page headline entitled 'Top Tories Threaten Church Schools'. On May 5th 1991, *The Universe*, p. 5, informed its readers that a 'special adviser' to the Secretary of State for Education had told them that Church schools 'were not even an area that is being considered' for reform by the Conservative party. The *Catholic Herald* in an article and full editorial of 10th May 1991 thought otherwise. It is interesting to contrast this with a Debate in the House of Commons in 1982, Vol. 20, cols. 453–460. The Conservative Minister of Education commented 'Voluntary schools are one of the foundation stones of free society.' The whole debate was in support of voluntary schools.
146. Ryan, J., *op. cit.*
147. Archdiocese of Birmingham, Diocesan Schools Commission 1987 Newsletter, No. 11 p. 2 and No. 12 p. 10.

158. Various press reports, e.g. *The Independent*, 17th December 1990, *Catholic Herald*, 13th January 1991, and *The Universe*, 13th January 1991.

7

Models of Catholic Schooling

Introduction

The Church recognises that Catholic schools can fail to correspond to the principles of education which should be their distinguishing feature. The problem for most Catholic schools is to decide what principles they should follow. It is not surprising that a number of Catholic schools have pursued a line of development which is not in harmony with their founding principles. In effect their governors, parents and teaching staff have lost sight of the Christian principles which support the ideals of Catholic education, in order to legitimate their own ideas of what makes a Catholic school. Often in such schools, the principles and activities which link the school with the missionary and evangelising tasks of the Church have been largely disregarded. And yet Catholic schools cannot hope to remain 'Catholic' for long without constant attention to their reason for existing — which, as I have demonstrated already, is to establish aims and practices in education which accord with the central values of Church teaching and to identify with the Church's goals and mission. A Catholic school's aims are no less than its credal statement. The school's mission statement is a starting point, expressing the assumptions, beliefs, values and practices to which the institution is fully committed.

If a school describes itself as 'Catholic', the thrust and practice of that institution should explicitly aim to correspond to that description. Yet, whilst we may urge parents to send their children to Catholic schools because they are 'different', we sometimes find great difficulty in articulating the difference. The real issue is identifying the 'principles' which serve to guide our practice in Catholic education so that they become effective tools in fashioning the aims and policies that are adopted in Catholic schools. The Catholic school operates under the auspices of the Catholic

225

Church, and if it is to retain the support of that Church, it must remain Catholic in more than name. There needs to be a closer relationship between the Catholic school and the Church as Educator. This means close collaboration with the hierarchy, so that the standards for Catholic schools are derived from authentic Church teaching. This was a point which the Dutch bishops clearly stressed in their joint pastoral letter of 1977:

> What it means to be a Catholic is not something which each individual can reinvent for himself. The same is true for the Catholic school. It cannot decide for itself what it means to be Catholic.[1]

The interaction and implications of official Catholic education principles and policy with the actual practice of each diocese and school, and of national and local government legislation and regulations with the whole Catholic school system is extremely complex. To analyse how these elements constrain or affect Catholic educational policy and practice, it is useful to look at three models for the Catholic school and draw some policy conclusions from them. None of these models is necessarily exclusive, but by keeping them separate it is easier to illustrate the policy consequences of each for the Catholic community and the likely support they might receive from current educational legislation. These models are termed the 'dualistic', 'pluralistic' and 'holistic' and the following attempts to illustrate their characteristics and implications for the principle-policy perspective. First of all however, some mention of joint schools as a possible model must be made.

In 1993 there were eight joint secondary schools shared between the Church of England and the Catholic Church. This is a tiny proportion of schools and one which has not shown much sign of growing. They were introduced as a form of 'experimentation' and they have had their share of difficulties as described by Priscilla Chadwick.[2] The reason for their original foundation was not entirely positive, for most had been established as a result of the failure of existing Church schools or the inability of one or both Church bodies to provide a Church school except as a joint school. They remain a possible model for the future as Cardinal Hume commented: 'Christian ecumenical schools have broken new ground and may well be a significant indication of a way forward.'[3] The evidence would suggest that joint schools are tolerated by the Catholic Church when the alternative is no Catholic education at all in a particular place. In spite of Cardinal Hume's comments about the possibility of their being 'a way forward', one bishop, whose joint school failed to compete for Catholic places with neighbouring Catholic schools, announced in February 1993 that he intended to withdraw, leaving the school to its Anglican foundation.[4] Parents who choose a Catholic school for their child do so because they want an education that takes place within a given perspective, that of the Catholic Faith. When one considers that many Anglicans and other Protestants have an understanding of Christian education which is altogether closer to the 'holistic' model than that advocated by many 'progressive' Catholics, there is obviously potential for renewed ecumenical discussion on the possibility of further joint schools in an education system which is suspicious of absolute commitment, antagonistic to religious nurture and which encourages a liberalising relativism.

The Dualistic Catholic School

The first model, here called 'dualistic', distinguishes education from religion both conceptually and practically. Terry McLaughlin refers to this model of a school as the 'dual function' school.[5] The underlying principle is that although the Catholic school is a single institution, it conducts two separate activities within itself. The 'dualistic' model separates the secular and religious aims of the school — not only in its teaching, structures and practices, but also in the minds of its pupils. On this model there are two realities set together — one specifically Christian and the other secular. Religious education, school assemblies, school liturgy and religious events in general are viewed as having little or no relevance to, for example the teaching of science or preparation for examinations. The Catholic ethos of the school is seen as something additional. The 'dualistic' school does not assume that a majority of children come from believing families and are themselves believers. It might make attendance at liturgical celebrations voluntary. The policy implications of this type of school model are clear.

First, on admissions, potential applicants may or may not be expected to accept the additional religious 'package'. Whilst admissions criteria may still give Catholics priority, on this model admissions would be more open, often as a result of a pragmatic, rather than a consciously religious, stance. Non-Catholic pupils could also be admitted without adapting existing school policies. Second, the 'dualistic' model emphasises the appointment of Catholic teachers for religious education, but not necessarily for other subjects. Training Catholic teachers is thus limited to the

preparation of teachers of religious education. Third, there is no
real attempt to view the teaching of secular subjects as contributing to the Catholic vision of life. In the teaching of religious
education within the school, there is a separation between catechesis and religious education. This corresponds to the approach
adopted by the National Project for secondary religious education,
as described in Chapter Three. In fact, religious education as a
catechetical activity had come under attack from a number of
religious education teachers as early as the late 1970s, especially
in the pages of *The Tablet*. In the number dated 30th August 1980,
Geoffrey Turner, a religious education teacher at Trinity School,
Leamington Spa, took as his starting-point an understanding of
catechesis as by definition offered to those who had made a free
decision to be Christians, and had freely sought instruction in their
faith. Since amongst pupils there was a wide range of religious
commitments, or none, the Catholic school could not be called a
'Christian community' without qualification. The aim of religious
education in a Catholic school was merely to make pupils aware of
the 'religious dimension' of life so that they could make their own
judgements. Similar thinking was pursued, in the 22nd November
1980 number of *The Tablet*, by David Jackson, the head of religious
education at Cardinal Heenan High School, Leeds. He felt that
both catechesis and evangelisation were inappropriate in the
Catholic classroom. These views substantially prepared the way for
the 'dualistic' approach in Catholic schools.

Whilst the 'dualistic' model is not official Catholic policy, it is
characteristic of current practice in a number of Catholic secondary
schools. Government policy and legislation does not threaten this
type of school. Since the start of the National Curriculum, current
teacher training courses and local authority policies and practices
on admissions are all acceptable on this model, there arise few
conflicts with national or local government for schools which adopt
it. Schools conforming to this model merely share in the general
problems which face all schools, such as the shortage of certain
types of subject teachers and the lack of educational resources.
There is no attempt, in this model, to integrate religious faith and
secular culture. Often, the provision of excellent pastoral care is
seen as the crucial consideration. The 'dualistic' approach to education prepares the ground for the second model — here called the
'pluralistic' Catholic school.

The Pluralistic Catholic School

The 'pluralistic' model is based on the assumption that all single-faith schools offer an educational setting which is narrow and divisive. It is argued that such schools fail to prepare children for life in a diverse and 'pluralistic' society. This model rejects as inadequate the idea of a school as being inspired by a single vision of faith because such an idea is too prescriptive — constraining the freedom of the child to make up his or her own mind. However, while the 'pluralistic' model objects to the permeation of Christian principles, it nevertheless advocates the application of multi-cultural and multi-faith principles to all aspects of a Catholic school's education programme and structures. This is clearly illustrated by a Church report *Learning from Diversity*:

> ... education for a diverse society is not a 'subject' which is 'taught', in the sense that history or geography are disciplines conveyed in specific lessons, rather it is an approach which must permeate all aspects of school life. If this definition is to be applied in our schools and colleges then it will require both personal and institutional changes.[6]

Since many cultures are inextricably linked to particular faiths, this school model would involve accepting other faiths into Catholic schools. Catholic teachers would be obliged by natural justice to enable pupils to sustain and develop their own culture and faith. This model concludes that only in attending to the full diversity of religious faith and commitment within a school, will the Catholic Church be provided with an indication of the right approach to adopt in education. On this model, the Catholic school would cease to be an evangelising and catechising community and there would be little explicit identification with the goals and mission of the Catholic Church. The Catholic school would cease to be confessional. The 'pluralistic' model might even view the Catholic school in certain contexts as a recipe for social division.

The implications for policy are many and varied. First, there would be an open admissions policy, which would encourage pupils of many cultures and faiths to apply to the school. Catholic schools situated alongside multi-faith communities might come to the conclusion that the traditional view, emphasising the education of Catholic children by Catholic teachers, is no longer realistic, and seek instead to serve the wider community. They might see in this an opportunity to educate all pupils for a pluralist society, and even seek some form of partnership arrangement on admissions with

other local faith communities. Some view this type of Catholic
school as an 'environment of faith'; but since we do not know the
religious commitments, if any, of the 96,000 non-Catholic pupils
in Catholic schools, it cannot be said that these pupils will all have
definite faith identities able to contribute to the building up of an
'environment of faith'. In practice, a 'pluralistic' school would
simply open its doors to the local community.

Second, teachers would be appointed who were committed to
promoting cultural and religious diversity, their Catholic creden-
tials might be of secondary consideration. There would be a strong
case for the appointment of teachers of other faiths as role models,
since the central point of a 'pluralist' school is the 'affirmation of
the individual and of the collective faith identities of all its pupils'.[7]
Religious education teachers would have to reflect the varied
backgrounds of the pupils by teaching about all religions, with none
being placed in a superior position. The curriculum would follow
the National Curriculum, but there would be an attempt to permeate it with a multi-faith perspective, and there would be emphasis on dialogue between faith groups within the school. Such a
school would not in general conflict with Government policy, since
open admissions and appointments would be seen as matters for
the governors. The curriculum that arises in such a school might
conflict with government policy, but this would not be due to any
Catholic elements in its composition. The 'pluralistic' model completely rejects a catechetical approach in the classroom, and their
would be no attempt to evanglise non-believers. Religious education would not presuppose religious belief, or non-belief. The
Catholic chaplain in such a school would find it difficult to operate
according to the role outlined for him in the 1979 Bishops' Conference Memorandum on School Chaplains. This memorandum
says that the Catholic chaplain in a Catholic school must be 'an
evangelist' and must 'stimulate individuals and groups within the
school to live a Christian life of prayer and action'. The 'pluralistic'
school would take full account of the secular and pluralist social
context, and would resemble the LEA school in many respects.
There are a number of Catholic schools which have a majority of
pupils from other faiths and cultures. Normally this occurs as a
result of the school attempting to become more viable, rather than
because of the existence of an explicitly multi-cultural or multi-
faith policy.

The Holistic Catholic School

The 'holistic' Catholic school attempts to form policies which follow post-Vatican II principles, viewing the school as an educational setting within which a critical synthesis should occur between culture and the Catholic religious vision. In claiming to be Catholic, the school commits itself to pursuing the meaning, values and truths specific to the Catholic faith. On this model, the Catholic school does not merely provide that which other schools fail to provide, nor is its purpose to be a shelter from the world. Rather it seeks to establish a partnership with parents in being the seed ground for the apostolic mission of the Church; for as the Church's *Declaration on Christian Education* says:

> . . . the Church, like a mother, is obliged to provide an education which can inspire the whole of their [children's] lives with the spirit of Christ.[8]

This model views the Catholic school as being inspired by the unifying vision of Christ, and as being integrally bound up with the work of the Church, which gives it its special character, a character which resides in the possibility of teachers, pupils and parents uniting as a community around a Catholic conception of school life inspired by the Gospel and the Church. The Catholicity of the school depends on there being a body of people whose lives are deeply imbued by the Catholic faith, and who are therefore able to bring the light of Christ into every aspect of school life.

On this model the Catholic school, together with the family and parish, may be seen as one of the principal constitutive elements of the Church's life. Such a school would explicitly share the aims of the Church and would enjoy a special relationship with the local diocesan bishop, who is the focal point of the local Church and the guarantor of its unity. As Pope John Paul II said of the Catholic school:

> Its work is seen as promoting a faith-relationship with Christ in whom all values find fulfilment, but faith is principally assimilated through contact with people whose daily lives bear witness to this.[9]

Consequently, there need to be specific policies for admissions, appointments and the school curriculum designed to incorporate these principles.

The 'holistic' model would entail that admissions be controlled, in order to safeguard the religious character and identity of the school. Most Catholic schools publish admissions policies which

give priority to Catholics and which define Catholics as those who
have been baptised and, perhaps, confirmed in the Catholic faith.
No reference is normally made to 'practising' or 'non-practising'
Catholics, but some schools founded on the 'holistic' model would
seek to check that parents were at least attempting to bring their
children up as practising Catholics. This is often done by asking
the parish priest whether or not the parents and their child attend
Sunday Mass. The 'holistic' model does not exclude non-Catholics,
but it does limit their number; non-Catholics would only be
admitted if there was a shortage of Catholics applying to the school.
Non-Catholic pupils who are admitted would need positively to
support the school's character and life, and their parents would
need to demonstrate that they agree with the model of education
being operated in the school. The limited amount of research as
yet conducted into admissions to Catholic schools indicates that a
number of schools are adopting this admissions policy. In one
research project, a number of head teachers strongly emphasised
the criterion of Christian faith for admission to Catholic schools,
and one head teacher said he would only accept non-Catholic
Christians on the condition that they 'should be baptised and
supportive of the aims of the school. They should be prepared to
take part in religious education lessons and services in the school.'[10]

The 'holistic' model assumes that appropriately trained Catholic
teachers will be available, and it gives priority to the employment
of teachers who are practising Catholics and who share the ideals
at work in the school. Teachers would be employed by the governors
who could guarantee consistency and continuity in the presentation of the Catholic faith. Governors would also seek to appoint
teachers, of all subjects, who have completed a course in Catholic
religious studies, and they would endeavour to provide appropriate
courses in religion for their existing staff. The head teacher would
be concerned about staff development in specifically Catholic
ways, would encourage and facilitate faith-sharing, and would have
an expectation that the teacher should witness to the Catholic
Faith in and out of school. Head teachers themselves would have
very specific responsibilities with regard to the religious identity
and life of the school. This is well illustrated in a memorandum
approved by the Westminster Council for Diocesan Affairs in 1989
entitled 'Description and Responsibilities of a Head teacher of a
Catholic School'. The memorandum details the three principal
responsibilities of the Catholic head teacher. First, they should

thoroughly understand the nature and purpose of Catholic education. Second, they should establish and sustain the Catholic identity of the school, and safeguard the Church's teaching day-to-day.
Third, they should be leaders of a Catholic community comprising
parents, teachers and pupils. On this model, the head teacher
could never be a non-practising Catholic.

In the curriculum, there is an attempt to understand each
subject from the Catholic perspective. This means that the secular
curriculum will be, as far as possible, imbued with Catholic beliefs
and values. Those who are appointed to teach, whether they are
Catholic or not, will be expected to give priority to this principle.
Pre-evangelisation, evangelisation and catechesis are all integral to
this model. The school's purpose is to assist both growth in faith
through sound catechesis and growth in learning through sound
theology. The school will play a part in confirming the religious life
of those pupils who already have an active Catholic life and faith,
and will attempt to strengthen or challenge those whose commitment
to Catholic life is either less secure or practically non-existent. Like
the 'dualistic' model, this model holds that there are two aspects
to the Catholic school, one shared with the Church and the other
shared with secular culture. But they differ fundamentally because
the 'holistic' model holds that these two aspects are in reality never
formally separated in the life of the school. The 'holistic' approach
is concerned with the transmission, from generation to generation
of the Catholic faith and culture — its beliefs, values, character
and norms of conduct — within a Catholic educational setting. It
aims for a deep interior acceptance of the Catholic faith, so that as
the pupil matures, they accept it as true and freely use it to guide
their conduct.

It is this model of the Catholic school which receives most
approval by the Church's teaching, yet it is the one which appears
most threatened. The five main Education Acts of 1980, 1986,
1988, 1992 and 1993, and the government's continuing educational
policies and regulations, make it difficult for the Catholic Church
to regulate its school admissions policies, teacher training and
curriculum content. The 'holistic' model is the one which the
bishops have officially supported in negotiations with government
bodies. It has resulted in a whole range of legal documents, secured
in order to protect Catholic education within the dual system. The
Trust Deeds of Catholic schools normally specify that their purpose
is the promotion of the Catholic religion within a given area. The

1944 Education Act linked these provisions in trust deeds to the duties of governors when it made it the legal duty of foundation governors to preserve and develop the character of the school as outlined in the trust deed. In addition, instrument and articles of government for individual Catholic schools normally repeat these provisions, and some even specify that foundation governors must be practising Catholics. Teachers' contracts in Catholic schools further place a duty on teachers to have regard to the Roman Catholic character of the school. It should therefore be difficult for Catholic schools to promote a pluralist model of education.

The years which have passed since Vatican II have shown how easy it is for Catholic schools, which were virtually all founded on the 'holistic' model, to become 'dualistic' or 'pluralistic'. Gradually, indeed imperceptibly, without conscious decisions on the part of the diocesan authority and without change in the trust deed, a 'Catholic' school can be transformed into something very different. It seems that some foundation governors need to be reminded of their legal responsibility to ensure that the trust deed is not simply respected, but implemented. This could be secured by the trustees if they changed the articles and instruments of government for each Catholic school, so that governors were obliged by law to report formally to the trustees each year on the progress they were making in implementing the provisions in the trust. The trustees could also issue, from time to time, a statement of principles and policies on Catholic education for the guidance of governing bodies. This would ensure a degree of accountability to the Catholic community.

Catholic primary schools still largely follow the holistic model, although a number have pursued a similar course to many secondary schools. In contrasting Catholic primary and Catholic secondary schools, three major differences can be highlighted. First, 90% of pupils in Catholic primary schools are Catholic and the number is rising; in Catholic secondary schools the proportion is only 60 per cent and the number is declining. The proportion of Catholic teachers in Catholic primary schools is 86 per cent whilst in Catholic secondary schools it is only 59 per cent and declining. Second, the National Project's *Weaving the Web* religious education programme in secondary schools excludes catechesis, whilst its religious education programme for primary schools, *Here I Am*, is seen as 'complementary' to catechesis, encouraging pupils to deepen their knowledge of the Catholic faith. Third, the Catholic primary school receives greater support from parish priests, who visit them more often than Catholic secondary schools. Consequently, the 'dualistic' and 'pluralistic' models are largely operative in Catholic secondary schools. In order to illustrate how a Catholic secondary school might come to displace its original aims and pursue 'dualistic' or 'pluralistic' approaches in education, the following scenario is presented. Although this scenario does not represent any single school, many of the policies and approaches which it outlines have been adopted by a number of Catholic secondary schools.

How St Michael's Was Changed

1960

The school is opened with a celebration of Mass and the reservation of the Blessed Sacrament in the school chapel. The school is established as an 11–16 secondary modern boys school by the Diocese, with the bishop and some senior clergy of the diocese acting as the trustees. The school serves the Catholic community in the heart of a City which comprises six parishes. Whilst the school has no formal admissions policy, it only recruits pupils from Catholic families in the area. The religious education programme in the school is essentially catechetical in content and approach.

1965

After five years the school has a total intake of 700 boys, who are all Catholic. The proportion of Catholic teachers is 87%. The aims of the school, which are published, make it clear that the school serves the Catholic community. All six parish priests encourage parents to send their children to the school.

1967

School is re-designated as a comprehensive school in line with diocesan policy. There is also speculation about a merger with the local convent school, a girls' 11–18 school. The sisters who are the trustees of the girls' school resist diocesan pressure to merge the two schools, as do the parents of the convent school.

1970

Convent school is closed and formally merged with the boys school creating a school of 1,450 pupils. Some Catholic parents remove their daughters from the school and send them to other Catholic schools or to the local LEA grammar school. However, most girls remain in the new school. The proportion of Catholic pupils in the school is 97% of the total.

1974

The number of Catholic teachers in the school falls to 75%. A roof leaks in the school and each of the six parishes is asked to contribute to repairing the roof. They do so willingly.

1975

First mention at a governors' meeting of the problem of non-practising Catholics in the school. Governors resolve only to admit practising Catholics as far as possible.

1977

The proportion of non-Catholic pupils in the school has risen to 10%. Catholic families appear to be moving out of the City to the suburbs, and the diocese has opened a new Catholic secondary school which is proving to be more popular with Catholic parents.

1979

The governors discuss admissions and resolve to give priority to baptised Catholics — whether practising or not. The fifth of the governors' criteria states that the school will admit non-Catholics if the parents specifically seek a Catholic education for their children. The proportion of non-Catholic pupils rises to 15% and of non-Catholic staff to 35%. The Head of Mathematics successfully applies for the deputy headship; he is a divorced Catholic.

1981

The school is redecorated and afterwards the crucifixes which once hung on classroom walls are not replaced. The chaplain is unable to spend more than three hours in the school each week as he has a busy parish to run. A physics post is given to a non-Catholic, because the Catholic candidate was not as well qualified. A decision is made by the headteacher to abandon job advertisements in the Catholic press, because it does not result in a large field of applicants.

1983

The first lay Chairman of Governors is elected and the number of priests on the board is reduced, mainly because many priests have indicated to the bishop that they are too busy in their parishes to be members.

1984

A Liturgy Committee is formed by the head teacher to organise voluntary prayer groups and retreats for pupils. The 'Hail Mary', 'Glory Be' and other specifically Catholic prayers, once said each morning in every form room, have been abandoned, and only the 'Our Father' is said at assemblies in deference to the non-Catholic pupils. Religious assemblies are conducted only twice a week, because their is no space each morning for the whole school, which now numbers 1,700. The proportion of non-Catholics has risen to 30% and the Diocese has published suggested admissions criteria to the effect that schools should attempt to limit admissions of non-Catholics to 15%. Some governors are concerned, but two newly elected parent governors, neither of whom is Catholic, support the school's present admissions policy.

1985

The end-of-term school Mass is now made voluntary by the Liturgy Committee with the approval of the head teacher and governors. Masses which have hitherto been said in school on feast days are abolished and the school starts one hour later on feast days to allow pupils to attend Mass in their parish if they want. A weekly voluntary Mass is retained, but it takes place outside school hours. Class Masses decline from this time on. Staff organise retreats at the diocesan retreat centre and take with them a chaplain of their choice, one seen as more in tune with young people.

1986

The head teacher and senior management draw up a mission statement which does not mention the word 'Catholic'. Instead, terms such as 'Christian' and 'Gospel values' are prominent. The local parish priest objects to this mission statement, but the governors approve it. They consider grant-maintained status, but decide against it, principally because it would upset the LEA, with which the governors wish to co-operate, especially in the provision of in-service courses. None of the staff is registered on courses at the diocesan centre for religious education or has attended any of the recent one-day conferences organised by the centre on Catholic education.

1987

There is a diocesan inspection of the school which congratulates the staff on the excellent provision of pastoral care, but suggests that more Catholic pupils should be recruited to the school. The proportion of non-Catholic staff has increased to 45% and the number of non-Catholic pupils has reached 40%.

1988

Form prayers have ceased in classes, as some members of staff felt that they were 'divisive'. The religious education department has a new head who seeks to exclude explicit catechetical approaches to religious education teaching. The number of pupils in the school has declined to 1,400 and admissions continue falling. The school begins to recognise and unofficially to celebrate non-Christian religious festivals.

1989

The head teacher retires and the governors advertise for a new head. The advert includes the following sentence: 'Governors seek head teacher who is a thinking Catholic with experience of a multi-cultural environment and who has the vision to develop this successful school in a multi-faith City'. The new appointee is a progressive Catholic who pledges to open the school's doors to the wider community. Some governors strongly object to her appointment, but a small majority vote for her. One of her first actions is to set aside a room for the use of the small number of Muslim pupils in the school who wish to pray during the school day. A few non-Catholic parents have requested that their children be excused from any Catholic services in the school, and the head teacher agrees to this.

1990

A school development plan is drawn up which changes the aims and mission statement of the school. All reference to catechesis is dropped, service to the local community is emphasised, as are justice and peace, and the school mission statement explicitly refers to the fact that the school now offers its service to the wider community in the City. The head teacher wishes to recruit larger numbers of pupils in order to expand the curriculum offered in the sixth-form and is under pressure to do so by the local education authority. Religious education is made voluntary for the sixth-form. The governors approve the mission statement. The local parish priest informs the bishop of his concerns about the direction of the school.

1992

The proportion of Catholic teachers is now 50%, and the proportion of non-Catholic pupils has risen to 55% since the new head has been successful at recruiting more pupils — the decline in overall numbers has been reversed. A religious education programme which is strictly non-catechetical is enthusiastically introduced by the head teacher and religious education department. Two parents complain about the new syllabus, and the head responds by telling them that the bishop has approved the syllabus for use in all Catholic schools in the diocese. A major re-building programme is undertaken, with the diocese providing over £200,000. The head teacher organises a day conference on the school mission. Most staff are either non-Catholic or non-practising Catholics, but nevertheless contribute their ideas to what the religious mission of the school should be. Few teachers mention doctrine or worship as being important in the educational context. Contact with the six parishes which once served the school is practically non-existent. Some staff are unsure about what role the Church has in schooling. The diocese is in deficit because of its capital debts on schools, it raises a special levy from parishioners and increases the proportion of money it takes from Sunday Mass collections in an effort to maintain the current level of expenditure on Catholic schools.

1994

The governors are informed by the head teacher that the proportion of non-Catholic pupils is actually more than 55%, since there had been an error in collecting the information; the true figure is 70%. The chaplain has abandoned the weekly voluntary Mass. The diocesan school commission writes to the Chair of Governors asking him to restore the proportion of Catholic pupils as indicated in the diocesan report. The Chair responds that the school is very popular with local people, that it is inspired by Jesus's command that we should offer our service to the marginalised in society, and that the school seeks to avoid being a bastion of white supremacy and therefore promotes anti-racist policies. The Chair also refers to the fact that the school has won a number of curriculum awards and is fully supported by the local community, and that the local education authority views the school as one of the best it maintains in the City.

1995

The head teacher resigns to take up a post in a larger non-Catholic school, and the governors advertise the post. One of the applicants short-listed is one of the existing deputy heads, who has since remarried. Some local parish priests are alarmed at the possibility of a divorced and remarried Catholic being appointed head teacher, and complain to the bishop. The bishop replaces a number of foundation governors in order to restore a more traditional Catholic approach to the school's governance. Conflict follows, since the new governors seek to rejuvenate the school as an agent of mission to the Catholic community, whilst the parent and community governors view the school as an agent of mission for the whole community. A petition is presented by parents to the bishop, demanding the removal of the new Catholic governors who they say are interfering in a successful school for the sake of divisive and outmoded ideology. Local politicians and the press support the parents. One local priest writes to the head teacher to point out that he feels that since the school community is now overwhelmingly non-Catholic in composition, the school is therefore *de facto* non-Catholic.

1996

The bishop is pressured into removing two of his foundation governors and replacing them with governors acceptable to the staff and parents of the school. After a number of governor meetings the remarried deputy head fails to be appointed head teacher, but the governors increase his salary and appoint him first deputy. The new head teacher has not taught in a Catholic school for some years, but is eager to continue the policies of his predecessor. The school chaplain discovers that the chapel has been used for music lessons and careers interviews. Without protest from parents, staff or governors, he decides to remove the Blessed Sacrament from the school premises.

A small number of Catholic secondary schools and colleges in England have followed a similar pattern to 'St Michael's'. The question is whether they are still Catholic institutions in anything more than name. There are excellent reasons why Catholic schools should be involved in inter-faith dialogue; for the Catholic school being a resource to the local community; for serving the poor in an area; and for being more ecumenical. Many good Catholic schools already do these things, others should follow them. The developments at 'St Michael's' went beyond this. The implication is that the policies followed by the senior management at 'St Michael's' were pluralist and therefore somehow more tolerant and generous to the wider community. However, genuine tolerance of differences is by no means assured by a pluralist model of Catholic schooling. As Peter Donovan argues, pluralism is coercive for it does not allow others simply to be themselves. As he says:

> To play the pluralist game properly, parties are expected to countenance quite radical reinterpretations and amendments being made to their own positions as well as those of others. Pluralism presupposes liberalism, which involves compromise, accommodation, and the dismantling of distinctive traditional convictions. The common features and agreed truths it purports to arrive at, though embracing a wide range of viewpoints, are in fact simply reinforcements for the political and economic interests of a dominant ideology. [11]

Catholic schools are not meant to be pluralist communities in this way. Peter Hastings, writing in *The Tablet* on 11th February 1989, pleads for policies on Catholic schools to be based on 'fact not fantasy'; and yet the Bishops' Consultation on 'Catholic Schools and Other Faiths' feels able to make a number of important and radical draft policy recommendations for Catholic schooling, despite the absence of any statistics on the number of children belonging to other faiths who attend Catholic schools in England and Wales.[12] Catholic schools are not intended to be multi-faith communities, nor are they equipped to be so.

Conclusion

Whilst the Church recognises that Catholic schools will differ, it maintains that there are general principles which reflect the universality of the Church that must form the basis of a Catholic education. Catholic schools cannot simply abandon principles in order to capitulate to existing realities for this would be tantamount to betraying a child's baptismal right to an education in the faith. One of the basic criteria by which a Catholic school must be evaluated is the role the Catholic faith plays in its community — in parents, pupils and teachers. The 'holistic' Catholic school attempts to form policies which follow post-Vatican II principles, viewing the school as an educational setting within which a critical synthesis should occur between culture and the Catholic religious vision. It is in this way that the Catholic Church contributes something distinctive to the public debate on education. Catholic schools which depart from the ideals contained in the 'holistic' model of education inevitably move away from the official teachings and policies of the Catholic Church in England and Wales and those of the Universal Catholic Church.

The adoption and promotion of the 'holistic' model does not entail a retreat into the safety of orthodoxy in order to protect one's beliefs against the threat of the modern world. There is no such retreat for the Catholic. Nevertheless, some may view such a model of schooling for Catholics as 'ideological enclosure', as a form of tribalism, or even as displaying attitudes of exclusion for fear of contamination by other forms of religion.[13] This reading of the model would be wrong, for what must be remembered is that Catholic schools are intentionally confessional institutions where committed teachers and pupils reflect the life of the wider community of faith. It should therefore be quite legitimate to assume the Catholic faith in Catholic schools. Afterall, as Hulme reminds us, secular education is largely dominated by liberalism, which has 'an ideological confessional character of its own'.[14]

It will be clear from previous chapters that each of these models has implications for the relations of the Church with government and local education authorities. The 'dualistic' model most readily provides a basis for peaceful coexistence with secular authority, which it does not challenge except peripherally. Should the Church decide to return to a 'holistic' model for its schools, which denies the instrumental and achievement-orientated ethos of contemporary education practice, it might be involved in major political clashes. This could be the case especially if the Labour Party were in power, many of whose members and supporters are hostile in principle to denominational education. Any decision to restore the 'holistic' model would have to be taken in full awareness of such consequences. In addition, the Catholic community needs to consider that it costs around seven million pounds to build a new secondary school of which a diocese would contribute £750,000. This is a great sum of money for any diocese, and should in itself force the Catholic community to question the wisdom of investing so much finance in Catholic schooling. The Archdiocese of Cardiff's 1995 Pastoral Congress and Synod looked at the matter in the following way:

> That the maintenance of our Catholic Schools, both primary and secondary, is necessary for the development of the Faith is a proposition that must be continually examined and tested. Many experi-

enced people think we should withdraw from secondary spheres and some from the primary sphere also. Our schools are clearly only a means to an end and their success in Christian formation must determine their priority in the allocation of resources. A debate about the future of our schools must be opened and the criteria for assessing success must be carefully and prayerfully worked out.[15]

Notes

1. *Education: The Responsibility of All*, Pastoral Letter of the Dutch Bishops, 11th January 1977.
2. Cf. Chadwick, P. , *Schools of Reconciliation*, Cassell, London, 1994.
3. Hume, B., *Towards a Civilisation of Love*, Hodder and Stoughton, London, 1988, p. 111.
4. Chadwick, P. , *op. cit*, p. 56.
5. McLaughlin, T.H., *Parental Rights in Religious Upbringing and Religious Education within a Liberal Perspective*, University of London, unpublished PhD, 1990, p. 212. These ideas are identical to the ones proposed by De Ferrari, T.M. 'American Catholic Education and Vatican Council II', *Catholic Educational Review*, Vol. LXIII, No. 8, November 1965, pp. 532–541.
6. *Learning from Diversity*, Bishops' Conference of England and Wales, 1984.
7. *The Catholic School and Other Faiths*, Consultation of the Bishops' Conference of England and Wales, Final Draft Report, 1994, p. 22.
8. *Declaration on Christian Education*, Second Vatican Council, Catholic Truth Society, London, 1966, Section 3, p. 6.
9. The Pope in Britain: Collected Homilies and Speeches, St Paul Publications, Slough, 1982, Speech at St. Andrew's College, Glasgow to teachers and students.
10. Arthur, J., 'Policy Perceptions of Headteachers and Governors in Catholic Schooling', *Educational Studies*, Vol. 19, No. 3, 1993, pp. 275–288.
11. Donovan, P. , 'The Intolerance of Religious Pluralism', *Religious Studies*, Vol. 29, No. 2, 1993, pp. 217–230.
12. 'Catholic Schools and Other Faiths', Final Draft Report of Bishops' Conference of England and Wales, Consultative Group, 1994.
13. Hull, J., *What Prevents Christian Adults from Learning*, SCM Press, London, 1985.
14. Hulme, E., *Education and Cultural Diversity*, Longman, London, 1989, p. 18.
15. Archdiocese of Cardiff Pastoral Congress and Synod — Final Reports from Task Groups, Lent 1995, p. 40.

8

Conclusions

Catholic schooling in England and Wales has had a remarkable history. Before and after each of the major Education Acts of 1870, 1902, 1944 and 1988, the Catholic Church has conducted a campaign for its own vision of education. Two principal claims were made in these campaigns: that parents have an inalienable right to decide whether or not their children should be brought up and educated in accordance with their religious beliefs; and that political and social equity demand that the State recognise this parental right and materially assist it by the provision of denominational schools. Both these claims are now enshrined in the 1983 Code of Canon Law. After 1902, the Church's educational campaigns focused, not on the rights of Catholic schools to exist, but on the need for a greater share of national and local resources to be made available for the voluntary Catholic effort in providing schools. By the 1950s, parental wishes were clearly interpreted by the courts as subordinate to central and local government policy. It was established that the wishes of parents, in regard to their choice of a denominational school, were to be balanced against the general educational policy of the local education authority, together with considerations of cost. Since the 1960s, Catholic education has become increasingly problematic, with attention focused on two central areas: the educational principles which should shape the aims and objectives of Catholic schools; and the nature, development and direction of Church influence over Catholic schools within the maintained sector. The first area concerns the identity of Catholic schools, the second concerns the Church's role in achieving and sustaining that identity.

So far as the identity of Catholic schools is concerned, the Church has a continuing interest in teaching an explicit philosophy of education which reflects her long-standing belief that true education aims at the formation of the human person in the light

of their final end. There does appear to be no agreement, no unity
of purpose among Catholics in education on the necessary means
to achieving this end. Fragmentation has occurred within the
Catholic community and has produced the uncertainty and tension
reflected in recent litigation. Whilst these cases have pinpointed
some specific organisational and management issues, there are
many other tensions and problems surrounding the identity of the
Catholic school system. In reality there has been a disjunction
between principle and policy in Catholic education. The practice
of many governors and head teachers, partly under pressure from
influential parents, has in many important respects departed from
the teaching of the Catholic Church. Two conclusions may be
drawn. First, the bishops have expressed considerable support for
official Catholic principles, but have been entirely weak in developing practical educational policies which incorporate and apply
those principles. Second, the Catholic community has not been
united on a clear post-Vatican II framework for Catholic education.

Consequently, a number of competing models of Catholic education have arisen in Catholic schools. The three models of Catholic schooling that I have oulined all have their defenders. The
'holistic' model views educational activities in a Catholic school as
aspects of a whole, and seeks to provide a clear set of educational
principles and policies. In the 'dualistic' model there is no real
attempt to derive these principles from an elaborated Christian
theological position and so the 'dualistic' model substantially prepares the ground for the 'pluralistic' model. This model seeks
co-operation in education between people of different beliefs,
without any explicit appeal to specificlly Catholic principles. For
those who adhere to the 'pluralist' model, it is thought to be
counter-productive to attempt to develop an educational policy on
religious grounds, this may inhibit co-operation with others. Those
who adopt this approach appear to think that the ends of Catholic
education can be achieved without reference to Catholic doctrine.
Neither the 'dualistic' model or the 'pluralistic' finds much support
in the Conciliar and post-Conciliar documents. I would argue that
the documents of Vatican II overwhelmingly support the 'holistic'
model of Catholic education. They provide a statement of philosophy and goals which express the holistic principles to which the
Catholic school should be committed.

There are policy implications for Catholic schools resulting from
these holistic principles. The first is that the content of Catholic

education should be infused with Catholic principles. But, as I have argued, modern curriculum theories and models, such as the National Curriculum, cannot address the specifically religious nature of Catholic schools. There is a lack of curriculum theories and programmes which deal exclusively with Catholic schools. There is a conspicuous lack of reflection on the goals which underpin the Catholic school system. Educational philosophy, psychology, management, curriculum theory, and policy studies have all developed in the mainstream of educational research, to the neglect of the Catholic dimension in education. The Church has made few attempts to develop any of the major trends in education along Catholic lines, nor has it given any incentive to educational research from a Christian perspective. As a result, it has been easier for many to question the justification for a separate Catholic school system. Many within the Church feel that too broad a conception of what is to count as Catholic schooling results in a loss of distinctiveness, while others feel that too narrow a conception is divisive. Some Catholics would argue for a line of development which involved the closure of many Catholic schools in order to concentrate resources on parish catechetics and adult Christian education. Others would argue for alternative educational strategies, such as joint or ecumenical schools, although these approaches appear to have been ruled out by the bishops.

The main objections in England and Wales to the Catholic school can be reduced to five. First, that general schooling can and should be separated from religious formation. Second, that Catholic schools are relics of a 'siege mentality'. Third, that they are divisive in a pluralistic society. Fourth, that they contradict the spirit of ecumenism. Fifth, that they consume time, effort, and money that might be better spent in other ways. Curiously, the majority of these objections appear to have originated from within the Catholic community itself. The bishops have largely rejected these criticisms, but have offered no systematic defence of the ideal of the Catholic school which they attack.

The problem of the authority of the Church in achieving and sustaining the identity of Catholic schools raises serious questions about who within the Church should have genuine control over them. The bishop has authority in theological matters within the Catholic community, but since the Church rejects the separation of religion from secular subjects in education, the question of where the scope of the bishop's authority ends is pertinent. The

parallels between 1847 and 1988 are worthy of attention. In 1847
the Privy Council desired lay control of schools, and inserted a
management clause into each school's trust deed, which threatened the growing clerical control of education. The bishops sought
to guard against binding agreements, with the secular authorities,
that served to protect rebellious laymen who held positions of
authority in Catholic schools from the control of the Church as
detailed in Canon Law. Conflict between the Privy Council and
the Church was therefore inevitable. In 1988 the government once
again attempted to increase the power and authority of governing
bodies, mainly composed of lay people, and reduce the influence
of trustees, all of them clerics. The government employed arguments substantially similar to those used in 1847, largely to the
effect that the laity can still defer to the authority of the Church
in spiritual matters. And just as they did in 1847, the bishops found
this argument wholly unsatisfactory. It is also doubtful if school
governors can, in civil law, effectively defer to an outside authority
on issues of management, such as the diocesan bishop, even if the
bishop is acting as a trustee.

Catholic schools have developed and exist today because many
within the Catholic community continue to desire a Catholic
education. The formulation of Catholic education policy continues
to be clerically-dominated. This tradition of a clerically-controlled
education system began in the early nineteenth century. The
insecurity of Irish immigrants, facing racial and religious discrimination, led them to invest their future mainly in the hands of the
clergy. For this reason Catholic schools have traditionally operated
under the auspices of priests and Religious Orders in the Catholic
Church. The role of diocesan education commissions was confirmed and reinforced with the increasingly centralised method of
financing schools which emerged after the 1944 Education Act.
Parochial schools looked increasingly to diocesan organisations for
financial, legal and planning assistance, and local education
authorities looked to diocesan schools commissions for a contribution to some overall policy strategy for Church schools. This
increased the influence of the diocese and lessened the influence
of the parish, and meant that many Catholic secondary schools
served an ever larger number of parishes. Whilst educational developments have changed fundamentally since 1950, the basic
demand of the bishops, that they should be responsible for Catholic schools within their diocese has remained unchanged. This

demand involves direct episcopal influence on the character and management of the schools. Since the management of schools is not a matter of doctrine, it does not fall under the ordinary teaching authority of the bishops. It is the responsibility of the bishops to protect and preserve the Catholic identity and character of schools which bear the name 'Catholic'. It is the bishop, and he alone, who has the authority to sanction the use of the title 'Catholic' by any institution within his diocese. Therefore, maintaining the Catholic ethos of a school is often equated with maintaining control over it. This role of the bishop is not accepted unreservedly by some members of the Church, and this has resulted in considerable dissent from official policy.

The respective roles of the parties concerned in Catholic education, and the relationship between them, require much clearer definition. These parties include the central government, local education authorities, the trustees of voluntary schools, the governors, the head teachers and the parents. Procedures, rights and remedies, moreover, could be much better tailored to specifically Catholic educational concerns. In addition, provision needs to be made for redress, in particular for parents, by recourse to administrative proceedings at diocesan level rather than in the civil courts. The Government's educational legislation of the 1980s, concerned primarily with provision and control of schools, has contributed little to the establishment of a well-defined and finely balanced partnership between the trustees of schools and governors. This has led to conflict and confusion. The basic problem concerns the individual rights of parents as against those of the whole Catholic community. Central Government favours the former over the latter, and this clashes with the Church's support for the rights of the whole community in determining the future direction of Catholic schools. Although Church teaching has always accorded parents a primary role in education, they have been effectively excluded from Church policy-making structures. The Church has shown itself to be rather sensitive to Governmental reforms which in any way diminish clerical control over the schools.

Whilst the Education Acts of 1967 and 1975 increased financial relief for voluntary schools, primarily as a consequence of Catholic pressure, the attitude of successive governments toward the voluntary sector has steadily changed. By the late 1970s a number of Catholic Colleges of Education were closed, notwithstanding the protests of the bishops. The government also announced plans to change the composition of governing bodies to allow for greater parental representation. These plans were eventually to include voluntary-aided schools as well, despite the fact that they had been excluded from the *Taylor Committee's* remit as a direct result of Catholic pressure. In particular, in the negotiations leading to the Education Act of 1980 the Catholic authorities found the government completely impervious to the Church's claims. Despite the Church's earlier success in blocking the government's attempt at abolishing concessionary and free transport to children, the Education Act of 1980 began the formal erosion of the rights of the Church within the 'dual system'. The Education Act of 1980 legislated on the rules for admission to all schools by forcing them to publish 'defensible' admission policies. The Education Act of 1986 (No. 2) encouraged the idea of real 'parental choice', and voluntary schools had formally to agree details of their admission policies with their local education authorities. The 1988 Education Reform Act introduced a 'standard number' for admissions to be determined by the DFE, and left the final decision over admissions, in disputed cases, within the voluntary sector to the discretion of the Secretary of State. On the curriculum, the Education (No. 2) Act of 1986 stated that voluntary-aided schools should have regard to the local authorities' curricula, whilst the 1988 Act completely removed curriculum control from the voluntary school. The Education Act of 1986 appeared to confirm the right of trustees to dismiss governors who opposed diocesan education policy, but the courts have interpreted this to mean that the character and management of a Church school are not the responsibility of the trustees and that they cannot dismiss governors on the grounds of opposition to diocesan education policy.

The use of a school's religious identity in the operation of its admission policy, and the provisions of Section Seventeen of the 1988 Act which allow voluntary-aided schools to have some control over the content of the curriculum are both dependent on the discretion of the Secretary of State for Education. Even the provision in the Act, that the trustee must give written permission before a voluntary grant-maintained school can change its character, seems unsure — especially since the Secretary of State has power to change the wording of a trust deed if he feels it is appropriate 'in consequence of a change of character' initiated by the governors or parents. At local level, Catholic schools have, as a result of falling rolls, been forced to use LEA staff redeployment schemes, effectively reducing the ability of the voluntary-aided school to function independently with regard to appointments. The Act also allows diocesan reorganisation plans to be rejected on criteria produced by the Secretary of State, leaving the Catholic community without recourse to judicial review. Diocesan plans for reorganisation have already been rejected as a result of the 'surplus places' argument, which constitutes a threat to the whole basis on which the 'dual system' is founded. The provision of free transport by LEAs is increasingly being withdrawn, and the government refuses to intervene. Many local councils treat voluntary-aided schools no differently from county schools and this may explain why some Catholic schools have opted-out of local authority control.

The Further and Higher Education Act 1992 has removed all sixth-form colleges from LEA control, and has also removed 'spiritual and moral' aims from the provisions of the curriculum to be offered the 16–19 age range. In addition, the Act provides for religious education on a voluntary basis within sixth-form colleges. These provisions have serious consequences for Catholic voluntary-aided sixth form colleges, and the bishops opposed them without success. The Education Act of 1993 excludes the Catholic Church from any formal representation on the national education quango which the Act established. All these examples demonstrate the erosion of the legal rights of voluntary-aided status and the powers of trustees. The 'concessions' which the government made to the Catholic authorities were minimal. The decline in the political importance of the bishops was illustrated by their failure to secure important amendments to this legislation. The consensus in the Catholic community necessary for the bishops to claim political significance has been eroded. The bishops lacked the power to mobilise their communities for a protracted struggle, and it is doubtful whether the Catholic community could be mobilised on behalf of the 'dual system' itself. Some would argue that it is simply not possible for the Church to advocate specific education policies on management or administration, as this involves taking sides on political matters and would threaten the unity of the Church. Nevertheless, there was an observable convergence between Church and Government in the dispute over comprehensive schooling in the 1960s. In the 1980s the Conservative Party's education policy has promoted competition between schools, the autonomy of individual schools, and the promotion of free-market ideas, in order to distribute scarce resources in the field of school-

ing. All of these policies have been applied in one form or another
in Government action or legislation. The bishops have consistently
opposed these policies. Yet these policies have combined with
changes in the Catholic community and have effectively limited
the scope and authority of the bishops, in making a significant
contribution to schooling within the maintained sector.

It would be wrong to suggest that the Church's problems in
providing Catholic schools are altogether the responsibility of
government, whether local or national. Changes in perceptions and
practices within the Catholic community itself have also reduced
the ability of the bishops to implement the official principles of
Catholic education. Schools which have adopted open admission
policies, contrary to diocesan advice, have pursued their own
pragmatic understanding of what makes a Catholic school distinctive. In many cases they have come to function as LEA schools in
all but name. The Catholic Church in England and Wales has
become more caught up in the drama of national life, and many of
its religious interests and priorities in education have been substantially replaced by secular concerns. Catholic schools have as-
pired to become more like LEA schools, only the teaching of
religion seeming to differentiate them. The Catholic community
is not united around a common Church policy, and in many cases
individual Catholics involved in schooling are simply unaware of
Church teaching in education. Despite official principles, based on
theological thinking and papal teaching, many Catholics approach
issues on educational policy with an underlying and flexible prag-
matism. Attention is still focused on the maintenance and expansion of Catholic schools. It would appear that the Church's
educational pronouncements bring together a particular policy and
a general educational principle. This approach assumes that the
connection between the two is clear to all. The changing educational priorities of teachers, governors and parents have involved
considerable compromises with LEAs over appointments and admissions in order that Catholic schools survive even if their *raison
d'être* disappears. The idea of a monolithic national educational
structure with consistent religious aims for Catholic schools is a
myth. Within the education system, the Church still occupies a
prominent structural position, both proprietorial and managerial,
and the bishops still have a great deal of patronage over schools
concentrated in their hands. This is a position which the bishops
seem willing to defend. The Catholic Church's thinking about

education policy seems to amount to no more than a determination to maintain the status quo.

Further research is urgently required into Catholic education and it should be directed at producing a clear definition of the goals of Catholic educational policy, especially with regard to how effective this policy has been in achieving these goals. This will require a detailed study of the historical development of Catholic educational policy, especially at the level of the individual diocese. In addition, it is important that research focuses on the question of how Catholic educational structures reflect the basic educational ideals found in Church teaching. In all these areas it is essential that research be planned in relation to the beliefs, values, goals and norms derived from official Catholic documents on education. This is important, since many influential writers on education do not accept that religious beliefs should form any part of the debate on education.

The arguments in support of current Catholic education policy vary enormously, with the principal argument, in the absence of any other, being an appeal to the inherited wisdom of established practice. However, this idea of 'established practice' is misleading: practice has changed radically since the 1960s. As regards the future, the alternatives are clear. The bishops might act decisively, formulating a clear model of Catholic schooling which they are prepared systematically to promote, if necessary against considerable resistance from within the Catholic schools system. This, of course, implies a programme of mobilisation within the Catholic community of support for the Church's teaching. As Pope John Paul II's encyclical letter, *Veritatis Splendor* of 1993, states:

> It falls to them, [the bishops] in communion with the Holy See, both to grant the title 'Catholic' to Church-related schools . . . and, in cases of a serious failure to live up to that title, to take it away.

But, if the bishops, as seems likely, are not willing or able to face the difficulties which such a policy would undoubtedly involve, the gradual deliquescence of Catholic schools, which began in the 1960s, will continue until at least in the secondary sector, they become institutions practically indistinguishable from those under LEA control. There are those, both inside and outside the Church sector, who would welcome such an outcome.

Note on Sources

The main difficulty for any study of Catholic education is to overcome the paucity of scholarly critical literature in the area. Volumes specifically on Catholic education tend to be descriptive rather than analytical. In the period since 1965 there have been only six volumes addressing some aspects of Catholic education policy and these are of varying quality. In 1968 two collections of essays were published, one edited by Philip Jebb, *Religious Education: Drift or Decision*, and the other by Bernard Tucker, *Catholic Education in a Secular Society*. In 1971, Anthony Spencer, as a member of the Catholic Renewal Movement, published his critical account of *The Future of Catholic Education in England and Wales*. The Association of Religious in Education held a symposium in 1974 which was edited by Nichols under the title *Theology of Education*. In 1978 Michael Hornsby-Smith published a collection of his sociological papers as *Catholic Education: The Unobtrusive Partner* and in 1988 Josephine Egan published her doctorate, on religious attitudes of pupils in Welsh schools, as *Opting Out: Catholic Schools Today*. Apart from these six volumes there have only been a number of edited volumes on theology, education or Catholic life which have included a chapter or two on Catholic education. In particular the volume of essays edited by Alan McClelland, as *Christian Education in a Pluralist Society* (1988) is worth mentioning, as is Adrian Hastings's *Modern Catholicism* (1991).

The general lack of secondary source material hinders the attempt at filling in the historical, political and philosophical background, which is essential in indicating the state of available knowledge. There is, by comparison, a relatively large collection of volumes on 'Christian Education' both in Britain and America. Catholic periodicals and newspapers are an invaluable source of information. Articles in the *Tablet*, especially since the relaunch of its educational supplement in 1975 (previously the *Tablet* had a weekly section entitled 'Education Notes'), the *Month*, the *Clergy Review* (now *Priests and People*), the *Universe*, the *Catholic Herald*, and a whole host of other journals and newspapers, Catholic and non-Catholic, are worth consulting and are listed in the bibliography of this book. Theses, especially at doctoral level, also yield material of great interest. Government reports and papers are of limited value as they seldom address directly the question of Church schools. For example *Better Schools*, a government White Paper published in 1985, has only one brief reference to denominational schools. By far the most important source is the varied educational documentation within the Church.

Among the published primary sources are the minutes of the Catholic Poor School Committee and the records of the annual meetings of the National Board of Diocesan Religious Education Inspectors, both established in the nineteenth century. These are invaluable in examining the growth of the Catholic maintained school system and help to throw light on present trends. At the offices of the Catholic Education Service (CES) in London a vast collection of relevant papers, reports, minutes, pamphlets, booklets, statistics, handbooks, and letters exist. Unfortunately, this collection has never been indexed. It is worth mentioning the house journal of the CES — *Catholic Education* — *An Educational Review*, which was published for only three years 1956–59, but contains useful material. In addition, J. Winstanley, as Secondary Education Adviser to the CES, produced a series of booklets variously called *Insights into Catholic Education* throughout the 1970s which were based on seminars about Catholic education policies and practice. The statistics kept by the CES on Catholic schools are unrivalled and the yearly reports contain the minutes of CES meetings.

Public papers of the Bishops' Conference of England and Wales also provide useful source material. In 1987 the bishops advisers at the Conference offices produced campaign literature against the 1987 Education Reform Bill. They have also produced other materials on teachers' in-service training and teacher appraisal. Reports of the Conference include the only major report on Catholic education in the period, *Signposts and Homecomings* of 1981. *Easter People* and the materials for the National Pastoral Congress in Liverpool in 1980 are also worth mentioning. The speeches of bishops and extracts from their pastoral letters are often printed in *Briefing*, which is the bulletin of the Bishops' Conference and is produced by Catholic Information Services. A final source from the Bishops' Conference is the publications of their religious education advisers. Worthy of mention are the books and articles by Kevin Nichols and by his successors in the position of religious education adviser to the bishops. Whilst these volumes tend to be on religious education, they provide some information on Catholic educational principles and policy. At diocesan level there is a wealth of information, much of it confidential and apparently unorganised at present. There is a strong case for these papers to be made available to researchers in education.

Conventional Catholic sources include handbooks, reports and minutes of the meetings of various bodies in Catholic education. Principally these are the Catholic Teachers' Federation, the Conference of Catholic Secondary Schools and Colleges, the Association of Religious in Education, the Laity Commission, the National Council for the Lay Apostolate, the Catholic Union of Great Britain, the National Conference of Priests, and the Newman Association. All have contributed to the process of evaluating the major trends in Catholic educational policy development since 1965. Naturally, the publications of the Vatican are also essential to an understanding of Catholic principles in education and therefore the Code of Canon Law, the publications of various Congregations, and statements of individual bishops serving the congregations in Rome are useful. The following bibliography contains almost all of the principal books and articles on policy issues concerning Catholic schooling and education in England and Wales.

Bibliography

Alexander, W.P. & Taylor, G., *County and Voluntary Schools*, Councils and Education Press, London, 1977.

Allies, M. H., *Thomas William Allies*, Burns and Oates, London, 1907.

Alves, C., 'The Christian Formation of Children', *Catholic Education Today*, March–April 1968, Vol. 2, No. 2, pp. 13–16.

Angus, L.B., *Continuity and Change in Catholic Schooling*, Falmer, London, 1988.

Arbuckle, G.A., 'Racism, Multicultural Education and the Church — Implications of the Swann Report', *Clergy Review*, Vol. LXX, No. 12, December 1985, pp. 431–440.

Arthur, J., 'Church Schools in Search of a Philosophy', 2.4.89, 'Classrooms Without Catholic Teachers', 9.4.89, 'The Threat to Catholic Schools', 16.4.89, a series of three articles in the *Catholic Herald*. Also in the *Sower*; 'Worship in the School Community', Vol.7, No. 4, 1984, pp. 17–18, 'Catholic Schools — Rhetoric or Reality', Vol. 11, No. 4, 1988, pp. 13–14, and 'The Problem with Multi-Faith Catholic Schools', Vol. 12, No. 1, 1988, pp. 26–28.

Arthur, J., 'Searching for Identity in Catholic Education', *Priests and People*, May 1990, pp. 169–172.

Arthur, J., 'Communicating the Faith in Catholic Schools', *The Allen Review*, No. 8, Michaelmas, 1992, pp. 20–26.

Arthur, J., 'Policy and Principles of Catholic Education in England and Wales since the Second Vatican Council 1965–1990', DPhil, *University of Oxford*, 1992.

Arthur, J., 'The Catholic School and its Curriculum', *British Journal of Religious Education*, Vol. 14, No. 3, 1992, pp. 157–168.

Arthur, J., 'Catholic Responses to the Education Reform Act: problems of authority and ethos', *British Journal of Religious Education*, Summer 1991, Vol. 13, No. 3, pp. 181–189. Republished in *Christian Perspectives on Church Schools: A Reader* by Francis, L., and Lankshear, D., (eds.), Gracewing, Leominster, 1993, pp. 1 78–189.

Arthur, J., 'Policy Perceptions of Headteachers and Governors in Catholic Schooling', *Educational Studies*, Vol. 19, No. 3, 1993, pp. 275–288.

Arthur, J., 'Parental Participation in Catholic Schooling: A Case of Increasing Conflict', *British Journal of Educational Studies*, Vol. 42, No. 2, June 1994, pp. 174–190.

Arthur, J., 'An Historical Perspective on Catholic Educational Policy', *The Allen Review*, No. 10, Hilary, 1994, pp. 22–26.

Arthur, J., 'Trusteeship and the Governance of Roman Catholic Voluntary Aided Schools', *Law and Justice*, Hilary/Easter, No. 120/121, 1994, pp. 3–11.

Arthur, J., 'Admissions to Catholic Schools: principles and practice', *British Journal of Religious Education*, Vol. 17, No. 1, 1994, pp. 35–45.

Arthur, J., 'The Ambiguities of Catholic Schooling.' *Westminster Studies in Education*, Vol. 17, 1994, pp. 65–77.

Arthur, J., 'Teaching and Employment Conditions in Catholic Schools: Principles and Practice', *Law and Justice*, Hilary/Easter, No. 124/125, 1995, pp. 40–53.

Arthur, J., 'A Catholic Policy on Teachers', *Educational Management and Administration*, Vol. 23, No. 4, 1995, pp. 254–259.

Arthur, J., 'Government Education Policy and Catholic Voluntary-Aided Schools 1979–1994, *Oxford Review of Education*, Vol. 21, No. 4, 1995, pp. 447–456.

Arthur, J., 'Church Colleges in the FE Sector: The Erosion of Trust', *Education and the Law*, Vol. 7, No. 4, 1995.

Arthur, J. and Gaine, S., 'The Relationship between Religious Education and Catechism in Catholic Theory and Practice', in Francis, L. (ed.) *Research in Religious Education*, Gracewing, Leominster, 1996 (forthcoming).

Aspin, D.N., 'Church Schools, Religious Educators and the Multi-Ethnic Community', *Journal of Philosophy of Education*, Vol. 17, 1983, pp. 229–240.

Augustine, P.C., *A Commentary of the New Code of Canon Law*, London, 1921.

Avalos, B., *A New Man for New Times: A Christian Philosophy of Education*, Sheed and Ward, New York, 1962.

Ball, W., and Troyna, B., 'Resistance, Rights and Rituals: denominational schools and multicultural education', *Journal of Education Policy*, Vol 2, No 1, 1987, pp. 15–25.

Barker, G.D., *A New Guide for Church Governors*, SPCK, London, 1948.

Barnes, A.S., *The Catholic Schools of England*, Williams and Norgate, London, 1926.

Barry, M.J., *A Cost Analysis of the Provision of Catholic Sixth Form Education in South Glamorgan*, MEd, University of Cardiff, 1985.

Bates, D.J., *The Nature and Place of Religion in State Education 1900–1944*, University of Lancaster, PhD, 1976.

Bauch, P., 'On the Importance of Catholic Schools', *Todays Catholic Teacher*, Vol 17, April 1986.

Baum, W., Vatican Report on Catholic Education: 1983 Synod of Bishops, *Origins*, 17th November 1983, pp. 391–395.

Baum, W., Letters to Cardinal Hume, *Briefing*, Vol. 19, No. 16, August 1989.

Battersby, W.J., 'What is Catholic Education?', *Catholic Education: An Educational Review*, Vol. 4, March 1958, pp. 1–8.

Beales, A.C.F., *Religious Education in England, Past, Present and Future*, Sword and the Spirit, London, 1943.

Beales, A.C.F., *The Catholic Schools Crisis of 1950*, Catholic Social Guild, London, 1950.

Beales, A.C.F., 'The Future of Voluntary Schools', in *Looking Forward in Education* by A.V. Judges (ed.), Faber and Faber, London, 1955.

Beales, A.C.F., 'The Free Churches and the Catholic Schools', *Catholic Teachers Journal*, Vol. 1, No. 3, July 1958, pp. 8–9.

Beales, A.C.F., 'Jacques Maritain', in *The Function of Teaching* by A.V. Judges (ed.), Faber and Faber, London, 1959.

Beales, A.C.F., *The Tradition of Catholic Education*, Catholic Education Council, 1963.

Beales, A.C.F., *Education Under Penalty*, London University Press, 1963.

Beales, A.C.F., 'The Schools Debate', *Catholic Education Today*, Vol. 1, No. 1, March/April 1967, pp. 11–13.

Beales, A.C.F., 'The Education Act of 1870 and the English Catholics', *Catholic Education Today*, Vol. 4, No. 4, July–August 1970, pp. 4–7.

Beales, A.C.F., 'Parental Rights in Education: the English Record since 1944'., *Catholic Education Today*, Vol. 7, No. 2, March–April 1973, pp. 4–7.

Beck, G.A. (ed.), *The English Catholics*, Burns and Oates, London, 1950.

Beck, G.A., 'The Schools Question: How We Stand', *The Clergy Review*, October 1951.

Beck, G.A., *Religion in Education*, Catholic Truth Society, London,1954.

Beck, G.A., *The Cost of Catholic Schools*, Catholic Truth Society, London, 1955.

Beck, G.A., 'Counting the Cost', *The Dublin Review*, Winter 1956, pp. 147–155.

Beck, G.A., 'How the 1953 Education Act Took Shape', in *Catholic Education: An Educational Review*, No. 3, December 1957, pp. 2–31.

Beck, G.A., 'Faith and Prejudice — Rights of Religious Parents', *Times Educational Supplement*, 5th July 1957, p.973.

Beck, G.A., *Progress Report*, Catholic Education Council, London, 1963.

Beck, G.A., 'Comprehensive Schools', *Times Educational Supplement*, 8th May 1964, p.1250.

Beck, G.A., *The Reorganisation of Secondary Education*, Catholic Education Council, London, 1964.

Beck, G.A., 'The Rights of Parents', an address at the Second Vatican Council, *Catholic Teachers Journal*, Vol. 8, No. 2, March–April 1965, p.8.

Beck, G.A., 'Point of View', *Catholic Teachers Journal*, Vol. 9, No. 1, January–February 1966, p.45.

Benedictine Monks of Solesmes: *Education: Papal Teachings*, St. Paul, Boston, 1979.

Benson, P.L., 'What Are the Religious Beliefs of Teachers in Catholic Schools ?', *Momentum*, Vol. XIV, No. 1, February 1985.

Belich, R., 'Teachers and Teaching: What Makes Catholic Schools Different', *Momentum*, Vol. XV, No. 3, September 1985.

Bell, D., 'Have Catholic Colleges a Future?', *Clergy Review*, April 1973.

Bereen, V.C., *Administration and Parent Perception of Real and Ideal Parent Involvement in Selected Catholic Schools*, PhD, Fordham University, 1976.

Best, A.E., 'Education and its Aims', *Scottish Educational Studies*, Vol. 1, No. 1, June 1967, pp. 40–47.

Birks, P.L., 'Professional Appraisal in Catholic Schools', *The Month*, September/October 1990, pp. 408–413.

Bishop, B., 'Catholic Schools: Changes and Problems', *Clergy Review*, January 1973, pp. 53–56.

Blanchette, C.A., *Social Justice: Mandate and Dilemma for Roman Catholic Religious Education in the Light of the Second Vatican Council*, PhD, Boston College, 1979.

Blum, V.C., *Catholic Education: Survival or Demise?*, Argus, Chicago, 1969.

Blundell, M.J., 'The Reorganisation of Catholic Schools', *Education*, No. 127, 14th January 1966, pp. 61–64, 21st January 1966, pp. 133–134.

Boffa, C.H., *Canonical Provisions for Catholic Schools*, Catholic University of America, Washington D.C., 1939.

Bottomley, F., 'Catholics and the Aims of Education', *The Month*, July 1973.

Bottomley, F., 'New Directions for Catholic Education', *Clergy Review*, Vol. LVIV, No. 1, January 1974, pp. 42–52.

Boxer, C., 'The Social Dimension of Catholic Education', *Catholic Education Today*, Vol. 2, No. 1, January–February 1968, pp. 13–14.

Boyer, E.L., 'Communicating Values: The Social and Moral Imperatives of Education', *Momentum*, Vol. XVII, No. 3, September 1986.

Boyle, J.D., 'Education: The Catholic Contribution', *The Month*, November 1963, pp. 281–289.

Boys, M.C., *Educating in Faith*, Harper and Row, San Francisco, 1989.

Boys, M.C., 'Curriculum Thinking from a Roman Catholic Perspective', *Religious Education*, Vol. 75, No. 5, 1980, pp. 516–527.

Brady, B.J., *The Congregation for Catholic Education, the Catholic School and the Thought of Jacques Maritain*, Columbia University, EdD, 1979.

Brannigan, J.J., *The Teaching of Religion in Catholic Schools*, Catholic Truth Society, London, 1960.

Brennan, J., 'Catholic Headteachers in the Community', *The Month*, May 1987.

Bristow, S.L., 'The Impact of Falling Rolls on English Church Schools', *British Journal of Religious Education*, Vol. 8, No. 3, Summer 1986, pp. 161–167.

Broderick, M., *The Catholic Schools in England*, Catholic University of America, Washington, 1963.

Brothers, J., *Church and School*, LUP, 1964.

Brothers, J., 'Grammar School versus Parish', *Clergy Review*, Vol. XLVII, 1963, pp. 566–575.

Brothers, J.B., *Grammar School Education as a Factor of Change in the Social Structure of Roman Catholicism*, University of Liverpool, PhD, 1961/1962.

Brungs, R.A., 'Catholic Education and the Family', *Communio.*, 4(Fall), 1977.

Burgess, R.G., *Experiencing Comprehensive Education: A study of Bishop McGegor School*, Methuen, London, 1983.

Butterworth, R., *The Structure of Catholic Lay Organisations*, University of Oxford, DPhil, 1959.

Buetow, H.A., *The Catholic School*, Crossroad, New York, 1988.

Burgess, R.G., 'Five Items for the Policy Agenda in Church Schools', in O'Keeffe, B (ed.), *Schools for Tomorrow*, London, Falmer Press, 1988.

Cannon, C., 'The Influence of Religion on Education Policy 1902–1944', *British Journal of Educational Studies*, Vol. 12, May 1964, pp. 143–160.

Capaldi, G.I., 'Pluralism, Religious Education and Catechesis', *Clergy Review*, Vol. LXIX, No. 2, 1984 pp. 52–59.

Caperon, J., *Church Schools and their Governing Bodies*, University of Oxford, MSc, 1983.

Carmody, B., 'A Context for the Catholic Philosophy of Education', *Lumen Vitae*, Vol. 36, No. 1, 1981, pp. 45–62.

Carrigan, D., *The Catholic Teacher Colleges 1850–1960*, PhD, Catholic University of America, 1961.

Carroll, H.F., *Parish School Board Involvement in Policy*, Fordham University, PhD, 1984.

Cashman, J., *The 1902 Education Act and Roman Catholic Schools*, University of Keele, PhD, 1985.

Catholic Bishops' Conference Of England And Wales:
  Statement on the Appointment of Teachers, 1959.
  Teaching the Faith, 1973.
  Memorandum on the Appointment of Teachers, 1974.
  Statement on Catholic Education, 1975.
  The Empty School, Education 1978 (Laity Commission) 1978.
  Statement on Catholic Schools, 1978.

Principal Documents of the National Pastoral Congress, 1980.

Catholic Education in a Multi–Cultural Society, 1982.

Review of Structures and Procedures, 1983.

Learning from Diversity — Catholic Media Office, 1984.

Evaluation and Appraisal, 1987.

Statement on Education, 1987.

Evaluating the Distinctive Nature of Catholic Education — Committee for Inservice, Servicing Roman Catholic Schools, 1988.

The Education Reform Bill: A Commentary for Catholics, 1988.

Campaign Literature on the Education Reform Bill 1988.

Catholic Education Service — New Structures 1990.

Joint Pastoral Letter for Education Sunday January 28th 1991.

A Series of Development Materials for Catholic Schools (3 packs).

Catholic Schools and Other Faiths (Draft Final Report, Unpublished) 1994.

Annual Meetings of Diocesan Inspectors from 1875.

Catholic Education Council Publications:

Annual Reports of the Council 1905–1989.

Memorandum on the Present Problems of Voluntary Schools, 1959.

A Report of the Committee to Study the Crowther Report, Handbook 1960.

Schools Throughout the World, Handbook 1967.

The Nature and Character of Catholic Education, Conference Papers 1967.

Insights into Catholic Education, 1972–3 Seminars.

Further Insights into Catholic Education, 1973–74.

Further Insights into Catholic Education, 1975.

Insights into Catholic Education, Statement 1977.

Memorandum to the Sacred Congregation for Catholic Education in Rome, 1980.

The Education Act 1980 and Catholic Schools 1981.

The Education Act (No2) 1986 and Catholic Schools 1987.

The Education Act 1988 (ERA) and Catholic Schools 1988.

Catholic Information Services — Briefing:

'Catholics and the General Election', 3rd June 1983, Vol. 13, No. 16.

'Catechetics — The Future', 5th March 1977, Vol. 7, No. 8.

'Bishops Concerned About Catholic Education', 16th December 1983, Vol. 13, No. 40.

'Religious Education in a Diverse Society', 1st May 1987, Vol. 17, No. 9.

'The Core Curriculum', 2nd October 1987, Vol. 17, No. 19.

'Catholics and the General Election', 29th May 1987 Vol. 17, No. 11.

'The Education Reform Bill — Hidden Dangers', 13th May 1988, Vol. 18, No. 10.

'Education Reform Bill', 8th July 1988, Vol. 18, No. 14

'The Future of Catholic Schools', 30th September 1988, Vol. 18, No. 19.

'The Crisis for Catholic Schools', 4th August 1989, Vol. 19, No. 16.

'The Education Bill 1992', 22nd April 1992, Vol. 23, No. 8.

'Catholic Colleges', 7th July 1994, Vol. 24, No. 8.

Catholic Newspapers and Periodicals:

Allen Review, Ampleforth Review, Catholic Education Council Annual Reports and bi-annual Handbooks, Catholic Education: An Educational Review 1956–1958, Catholic Encyclopedia, Catholic Education Today 1958–1980, Catholic Herald, Catholic Information Services — Briefing, The Catholic School, Catholic Teachers Journal 1958–1966, Christian Order, Clergy Review (now Priests and People), Concilium esp World Catechism on Inculturation No 204, Communio, Downside Review, Dublin Review, The Furrow, Herder Correspondence, Law and Justice, Lumen Vitae — International Review of Religious Education, The Month, New Blackfriars, L'Osservatore Romano, Religious Life Review, Recusant History, Seminarium, Slant, Spode House Review, The Sower, Sword and the Spirit, The Tablet especially the following Educational Supplements; 5/8/78, 11/11/78, 30/8/80, 22/11/80, 30/5/81, 26/6/82,19/2/83, 8/10/83, 18/2/84, 26/5/84, 6/10/84, 16/2/85, 15/2/86, 14/2/87, 30/5/87, 10/10/87, 28/5/88., Thirty Days, The Universe, The Way.

Catholic Teachers' Federation:

Catholic Non-Selective Education — A Report of the Secondary Committee in *Catholic Teachers Journal*, Vol. 4, No. 5, September 1961, pp. 23–25.

Where we Stand, 1975.

Catholic Schools — A Vision and a Hope, 1983.

Chadwick, P., *Schools of Reconciliation: Issues in Joint Roman Catholic-Anglican Education*, Cassell, London, 1994.

Cloud, D., *The Catholic School and its Function*, The Old Palace, Oxford University Chaplaincy, Paper No 6, 1962.

Cluderay, T.M. (ed.), *The Catholic Teacher*, Catholic Teachers' Federation, London, 1967.

Congregation for Catholic Education:

The Catholic School 1977.

Lay Catholics in Schools — Witnesses to Faith 1982.

The Religious Dimension of Catholic Education 1988.

Conrad, J.F., 'A Theological Rationale for Catholic Schools', *Notre Dame Journal of Education*, Vol. 3, No. 4, Winter 1973, pp. 310–317.

Conway, P.H., *Principles of Education: A Thomist Approach*, Thomist Press, Washington D.C., 1960.

Corbett, A., 'Catholics at School', *New Society*, 28th November 1968, pp. 792–794.

Corcoran, T., 'The Catholic Philosophy of Education', *Studies*, Vol. XIX, 1930, pp. 199–210.

Cosgrove, J., 'Threat to Catholic Schools', *The Month*, October 1982

Cramer, J., 'Academic Freedom and the Catholic Church', *Educational Record*, Vol. 67, No. 2–3, Spring/Summer 1986.

Crecco, R., 'The Role of the Priest in Our Catholic School', *Priests and People*, September 1983, pp. 34–38.

Cronin, K., 'The Catholic Tradition of the Arts in Education', *Catholic Education: An Educational Review*, Vol. 1A, July 1956, pp. 1–21.

Cross, E.J., 'Catholic Means Comprehensive', *Catholic Education Today*, Vol. 7, No. 3, May–June 1973, pp. 11–12.

Crowley, J.J., 'Secondary Education', *Catholic Education: An Educational Review*, No. 2, March 1957, pp. 1–16.

Cruickshank, M., 'The Denominational School Issue in the 20th Century', *History of Education*, June 1972, pp. 200–213.

Cruikshank, M., *Church and State in Education*, Macmillan, London, 1963.

Cunningham, A., 'Catholic Schools and Ideology', *Catholic Education Today*, Vol. 3, No. 1, January–February 1969, pp. 16–17.

Cunningham, R., *Teacher Supply*, Catholic Education Council, 1961.

Cunningham, R., 'Point of View', *Catholic Teachers Journal*, May–June 1966, Vol. 9, No. 3, pp. 6–7.

Cunningham, R., *The Present and Future Situation in Catholic Education*, Catholic Education Council, 1967.

Cunningham, R., 'Catholic Schools: some aspects of their Development', *Dublin Review*, No. 518, Winter 1968–69.

Cunningham, R., *Catholic Education — 25 Years Review*, Catholic Education Council, 1975.

Cunningham, R., *Catholic Direct Grant Schools*, Catholic Education Council, 1974.

Cunningham, R., *The Catholic Schools System in England and Wales*, Catholic Education Council, 1987.

Cunningham, R., 'The Education Reform Act 1988', *Law and Justice*, No. 104/105, 1990, pp. 39–46.

Cunningham, W., *The Pivotal Problems of Education: An Introduction to the Christian Philosophy of Education*, Macmillan, New York. 1949.

Dawson, C., *The Crisis of Western Education*, Sheed and Ward, London, 1961.

Dawson, C., 'The Study of Christian Culture as a means of Education', *Lumen Vitae*, Vol. V, No. 1, 1950.

Dearden, R.F., 'Philosophy of Education 1952–1982', *British Journal of Educational Studies*, Vol. XXX, No. 1, 1982, pp. 57–71.

De Houre, F., translated by E.B. Jordan, *Catholicism in Education*, Benziger, New York, 1934.

Dent, R., *Faith of Our Fathers — Roman Catholic schools in a multi-faith society*, City of Coventry, Education Department, 1989.

De Rosa, G., 'The Catholic School and Scholastic Pluralism', *L'Osservatore Romano* (English version), May 11th 1978, p.528.

Dillon, T. and Guest, J., 'A Nottingham Conference on Catholic Schools', *Clergy Review*, Vol. LXIX, No. 6, 1984, pp. 222–225.

Donahue, J.W., 'A Vatican Salute to Catholic Lay Teachers', *America*, October 30th 1982, pp. 251–252.

Donohue, J.W., *Critique of Recent Literature in Catholic Philosophy of Education*, in Proceedings of the Annual Conference of the Philosophy of Education Society, 1967.

Donohue, J.W., *Thomas Aquinas and Education*, Random House, New York, 1968.

Donohue, J.W., *Catholicism and Education*, Harper and Row, London, 1973.

Donovan, J.D., *The Academic Man in the Catholic College*, Sheed and Ward, New York, 1964.

Donovan, G.F., *Workshop on Vatican II: Its Challenge to Education*, Catholic University of America, Washington D.C. 1967.

Dulles, A., *The Communication of the Faith and its Content*, National Catholic Educational Association, Washington D.C., 1985.

Dummet, A.M. and McNeil, J., *Race and Church Schools*, Runnymeade Trust, 1981.

Duplass, J.A., 'The Marginal Difference in Catholic Education', *Religious Education*, Vol. LXX, No. 3, 1975, pp. 278–288.

Dyson, A.O., 'The Church's Educational Institutions', *Theology*, Vol. 80, July 1977, pp. 273–279.

Eagleton, T., *'The Bending of a Twig'*, *Slant*, Vol. 1, Spring 1965.

Eagleton, T., 'Catholic Education and Commitment, *Catholic Education Today*, Vol. 1, No. 1, January/February 1967, pp. 8–10.

Earl, W.J.H., '1944 Education Act — Forty years On', *British Journal of Religious Education*, Vol. 6, No. 2, Spring 1984, pp. 88–92.

Eckersley, H.P., 'Catholic School: A Pause for Thought', *Clergy Review*, Vol LXII, No 2, 1987, pp. 74–76.

Eckoff, M.A., 'Speaking of Standards and Expectations in Catholic Goals', *Momentum*, Vol. XV, No. 4, December 1984.

Eckersley, H.P., 'Catholic School: A Pause for Thought', *Clergy Review*, Vol LXII, No 2, 1987, pp. 74–76.

Education: 'Who Employs the Voluntary Head?', 7th March 1980, four articles on 'Church and School', 1959 and after: Vol. 118: 620–623, 684–687, 749–752, 798–904. October 20th – November 10th 1961, and 'Catholic Schools Under Threat', 172, July 1988. 'C.T.S.s and Catholics', 171, January 1988. 'Catholics and Religious Education', 170, December 1987.

Egan, J., *Opting-out: Catholic Schools Today*, Gracewing / Fowler Wright, Leominster, 1988.

Egan, J., *An Evaluation of the Implementation of the Principles of Catholic Education in the Comprehensive Schools of Wales*, University of Wales, Cardiff, PhD, 1985.

Egan, J., and Francis, L.J., 'School Ethos in Wales: the impact of non-practising Catholic and non-Catholic pupils on Catholic secondary schools', *Lumen Vitae*, Vol. 41, No. 3, 1986, pp. 159–172.

Elvin, L., *Religious Education 1944–1984*, George Allen and Unwin, London, 1966.

Enright, P., 'A Future for Catholic Colleges of Education', *Catholic Education Today*, Summer 1978.

Enright, P., 'Christian Philosophy of Education', *Catholic Education Today*, Vol. 9 No. 4, July–August 1975, pp. 3–5.

Erickson, D., 'Differential Effects of Public and Sectarian Schooling on the Religiousness of the Child', in Argyle, M., (ed.), *The Social Psychology of Religion*, RKP, London, 1962.

Esty, J.C., 'The Public Purpose of Non-Public Education, *Momentum*,Vol. XV, No. 3, September 1984.

Evans, J.W., 'Has the Catholic Intellectual a Future in America ?', *Sociology of Education*, Winter 1965, pp. 150–163.

Evennett, H.O., *The Catholic Schools of England*, CUP, Cambridge, 1944.

Exeler, A., 'Faith and Education', in K. Nichols (ed) *Voice of the Hidden Waterfall: essays on Religious Education*, St. Paul Publications, Slough, 1980.

Fahy, P.S., *Faith in Catholic Classrooms*, St. Paul, Victoria, 1992.

Feheney, J.M., 'Towards Religious Equality for Catholic Pauper Children 1861–1868', *British Journal of Educational Studies*, Vol. 31, No. 2, June 1983, pp. 141–153.

Finan, J.J., *Struggle for Justice: a short history of the Catholic Teachers Federation*, CTF, London, 1976.

Fletcher, B.A., *Some Essentials of Christian Education*, Catholic Education Council, 1967.

Fletcher, G., 'Priests and School Government', *The Month*, (15) June 1982, pp. 202–203.

Fletcher-Campbell, F.J., *The Christian School*, University of Oxford, MSc, 1984.

Flynn, M., *Some Catholic Schools in Action*, Australian Catholic Information Office, Sydney, 1975.

Flood, B., *The Catholic National Building Office*, Catholic Education Council News Bulletin No. 11, 1965.

Foley, A., et al. 'Meeting the Religious Needs of Non-Catholic Students in Catholic Schools', *Momentum*, February 1981, pp. 22–23.

Foster, J., 'The Culture of Feelings: A New Stage in Catholic Education and Formation', *The Clergy Review*, November 1962.

Francis, L.J., 'Roman Catholic Secondary Schools: falling rolls and pupil attitudes', *Educational Studies*, Vol. 12, No. 2, 1986, pp. 119–127.

Francis, L.J., 'Are Catholic Schools Good for Non-Catholics?', *The Tablet*, Educational Supplement No. 47, 15th February 1986.

Francis, L.J., and Egan, J., *Catholic Schools and the Communication of Faith* Catholic School Studies, Sydney, 1987.

Francis, L.J., 'Measuring Attitudes Towards Christianity Among 11–16 Pupils in Catholic Schools in Scotland', *Educational Research*, Vol. 31, No. 1, February 1989, pp. 65–68.

Francis, L.J., and Egan, J., 'The Catholic School as 'Faith Community' — An Empirical Inquiry', *Religious Education*, Vol. 85, No. 4, 1990, pp. 588–603.

Francis, L.J., and Lankshear, D.W., (eds.) *Christian Perspectives on Church Schools*, Gracewing, Leominster, 1993.

Freire, P., *Pedagogy of the Oppressed*, Penguin, London, 1972.

Gaine, M., and Nichols, K., 'The Dual System', *Catholic Education Today*, September–October 1971, Vol. 5, No. 5, pp. 4–9.

Gaine, M., 'The Development of Official Roman Catholic Educational Policy in England and Wales', in P. Jebb., (ed.), *Religious Education*, London, 1968.

Gallagher, D., and Gallagher, I., *The Education of Man: The Educational Thought of Jacques Maritain*, Notre Dame University Press, 1967.

Gallagher, J., 'Parents' Right to Educate', *Homilitic and Pastoral Review*, No. 76, December 1975, pp. 29–32.

Gallagher, J., *Our Faith, Our Schools*, Bishops' Conference of England and Wales, 1988.

Gallagher, J., *Catechesis in Roman Catholic Tradition: Recent Trends and Issues*, University of Liverpool, MEd,1986.

Gallagher, W., 'Priests as Partners in the Catholic School Apostolate', *Momentum*, December 1976, pp. 25–26.

Garone, G.M., 'The Catholic School: A Commentary', *L'Osservatore Romano*, (English version), July 28th 1977, p.487.

Gerard, D., *Roman Catholic Opinion*, Catholic Truth Society, London, 1980.

Gill, R., 'Sociology of Christian Education', *Catholic Education Today*, Vol. 9, No. 4, July–August 1975, pp. 2–3.

Glass, C., 'The Case for the Denominational School', *Catholic Education Today*, Vol. 5, No. 3, May–June 1971, pp. 4–7.

Glover, D., *Roman Catholic Education and the State: A Sociological Analysis* University of Sheffield, PhD, 1979.

Glynn, W.T., *Aims and Objectives of Catholic Education*, Catholic Teachers' Federation, London, 1980.

Greeley, A.M., McCready, W.C. and McCourt, K., *Catholic Schools in a Declining Church*, Sheed and Ward, Kansas City, 1976.

Greeley, A.M. and Brown, W.E., *Can Church Schools Survive ?*, Sheed and Ward, New York, 1970.

Grist, A., 'Britain's First Ecumenical Comprehensive', *Comprehensive Education*, Summer 1976, pp. 11–13.

Gus, J., 'The Gospel, The State and Education Rights, *New Black-friars*, Vol. 70, No. 830, September 1989.

Hackett, P., 'Curriculum Matters: Catholic and Secondary Considerations', *The Month*, June 1981.

Haldane, J., 'Religious Education in a Pluralistic Society', *British Journal of Educational Studies*, Vol. 34, No. 2, June 1986, pp. 161–181.

Haldane, J., 'Metaphysics in the Philosophy of Education', *British Journal of the Philosophy of Education*, Vol. 23, No. 2, 1989, pp. 171–184.

Haldane, J., 'Chesterton's Philosophy of Education', *Philosophy*, Vol. 65, No. 251, January 1990, pp. 65–80.

Hamilton, C.D., *Theory of the Roman Catholic Church in Support and Control of Education*, PhD, Florida State University, 1965.

Hanlon, K., 'A Survey of Religious Education in Roman Catholic Secondary Schools in England and Wales', *British Journal of Religious Education*, Vol. 11, No. 3, Summer 1989, pp. 154–162.

Hartley, F., *The Diocesan School Commission and the Reorganisation of Catholic Secondary Education in Birmingham 1972–1976*, MEd, University of Birmingham, 1983.

Haughton, R., 'Schools, de-schooling and Education for a Future', *New Blackfriars*, Vol. 53, 1972.

Hastings, P., 'SOS for Catholic Schools', *The Tablet*, 6th February, 1991, pp. 196–197.

Hawker, J., 'Arousing the Beginnings of Faith', *Momentum*, February 1982, pp. 28–30.

Hawker, J., *Catechesis in the Catholic School* Washington D.C., National Catholic Educational Association, 1985.

Heenan, J., Pastoral Letter on Education of 8th September 1972 Archdiocese of Westminster, reprinted in *Catholic Mind*, March 1973.

Hennessey, M., 'Catholic Educational Policy', *Slant*, Vol. 6, March 1970.

Hickey, J., 'The Christian Community', *Catholic Teachers Journal*, Vol. 9, No. 4, July–August, 1966, pp. 6–8.

Higgins, A., 'The Catholic School Humanities Project', *Catholic Education Today*, Vol. 4, No. 2, March–April 1970, pp. 20–21.

Higgins, A., *Teaching About Controversial Issues in Catholic Schools*, Centre for Applied Research in Education, Occassional Publications No. 7, 1979.

Hirst, P.H., 'Morals, Religion and the Maintained School', *British Journal of Educational Studies*, Vol. 14, No. 1, 1965, pp. 5–18.

Hirst, P.H., 'Christian Education — A Contradiction in Terms', *Learning for Living*, Vol. 11, No. 4, 1972, pp. 6–10.

Hogan, P., 'The Question of Ethos in Catholic Schools', *The Furrow*, November 1978.

Holland, M.G., *The British Catholic Press and the Educational Crisis 1847–1865*, Garland Publishing, New York, 1987.

Hollis, C., 'The Education of Catholics', *Catholic Teachers Journal*, Vol. 9, No. 6, November–December 1966, pp. 4–5.

Hornsby-Smith, M.P., 'Education: A Continuing Process', series of three articles in *Catholic Education Today*, Vol. 8, No. 2, March–April 1974, pp. 4–6.

Hornsby-Smith, M.P., 'Religious Attitudes of Catholic Adolescents', *Catholic Education Today*, Vol. 9, No. 2, 1975.

Hornsby-Smith, M.P., *A Feasibility Study of the Roman Catholic Community in England*, Final Report, Social Science Research Council, London, 1975.

Hornsby-Smith, M.P. and Petit, M., 'Social, Moral and Religious Attitudes of Secondary School Students', *Journal of Moral Education*, Vol. 4, June 1975, pp. 261–272.

Hornsby-Smith, M.P., 'Are Catholic Schools a Waste of Money ?', *Catholic Education Today*, July–September 1976, Vol. 10, No. 3, pp. 2–3.

Hornsby-Smith, M.P., and Lee, R., *Roman Catholic Opinion: A Study of Catholics in England and Wales in the 1970s*, London, 1980.

Hornsby-Smith, M.P., *Catholic Education: The Unobtrusive Partner*, Sheed and Ward, London, 1978

Hornsby-Smith, M.P., *Roman Catholics in England and Wales*, CUP, 1987.

Hornsby-Smith, M.P., *The Changing Parish*, Routledge, London, 1989.

Hornsby-Smith, M.P., *Roman Catholic Beliefs in England*, CUP, 1991.

Houtart, F., 'Conflicts of Authority in the Roman Catholic Church', *Social Compass*, Vol. 16, No. 3, 1969, pp. 309–325.

Howie, G., *The Educational Theory and Practice of St. Augustine*, RKP, London, 1969.

Howie, G., *St. Augustine on Education*, Henry Regne, Chicago, 1969.

Howson, J., 'Report on Headteacher Turnover in Roman Catholic Schools in England and Wales', Unpublished Paper, Oxford Brookes University, School of Education, 1989.

Hudden, J., 'Catholic Comprehensive School: Model of the Church', *Catholic Education Today, Vol. 2, No. 3,* May/June 1968, pp. 12–14.

Hume, B., 'Threat to Catholic Schools', *Briefing*, 22nd January 1988, Vol. 18, No. 2.

Hume, B., *Towards a Civilisation of Love*, Hodder and Stoughton, London, 1988.

Hume, B., 'The Future of Catholic Schools', an address to Catholic Headteachers, 19th September 1988, reported in *Briefing*.

Hume, B., 'Catholic Schools Today, an address to the National Conference of Priests, 5th September 1989, reported in *Briefing*.

Hume, B., 'Building Bridges — A Vision for Education', Presidential Speech to the North of England Education Conference, 3rd January 1990, reported in *Briefing*.

Hume, B., 'Recapturing the vision' an address to the conference on the Future of Post-16 Education in Catholic Schools and Colleges, 27th June 1991, reported in *Briefing*.

Hume, B., An address to the Catholic Secondary Headteachers in the Archdiocese of Westminster, 19th September 1991, reported in *Briefing*.

Hume, B., An Address to the First National Conference on Catholic Education, 13th July 1992, reported in *Briefing*.

Hunt, T.C., et al. *Religious Schools in America: A Selected Bibliography* Garland Publishing, New York. 1986.

Huot, D., *Denominational Schools as a Problem in England and Wales 1940–1959*, DPhil, University of Oxford, 1961.

Hurley, M., *Declaration on Christian Education*, Paulist Press, Glen Rock, New Jersey, 1966.

Hurley, M., 'The Declaration on Christian Education', *Homiletic and Pastoral Review*, Vol. 66, December 1965.

Jamison, C., 'Catholic Schools Under Fire', *Priests and People*, August–September 1991, pp. 293–296.

Jebb, P., *Religious Education: Drift or Decision?*, Darton Longman and Todd, London, 1968.

Johnson, L., 'The Training of Catholic Teachers', *Clergy Review*, April 1973.

Jones v Lee and Another *LGR* 78 (1), 1979, p2134f.

Kealey, R.J., *Curriculum in the Catholic School*, Washington D.C., National Catholic Educational Association, 1985.

Kelly, F.D., 'Ecumenical Issues within Christian Education', *Journal of Ecumenical Studies*, Vol. 18, No. 4, 1981.

Kelly, M.F. and Doyle, J.R., '*Deus Inter Alia*', *Catholic Education: An Educational Review*, No. 2, March 1957, pp. 39–44.

Kelly, P., *Catholic Schools*, Diocese of Salford, 1987.

Kelly, S.E., 'The Voluntary Schools in Four Lancashire Boroughs 1903–1968: A Study in Policies and Provision', *Journal of Educational Administration and History*, Vol. 3, No. 2, June 1971, pp. 42–52,

Kerr, J., 'Catholic Schools in Scotland', *New Humanist* 88, October 1972, pp. 240–241.

Kienel, P.A., *The Philosophy of Catholic Education*, Whittier, California,1978.

King, N., 'Denominational Schools in a Multi-Racial Society', *Catholic Education Today*, Vol. 8, No. 4, July–August 1974, p.6.

Kitching, J., *Roman Catholic Education from 1700–1870*, PhD, University of Leeds, 1966.

Knight, P., 'The Case Against Church Schools', *New Humanist*, April 1973, pp. 484–486.

Knox, I., 'R.C. Miller and his Theory of Christian Education', *Notre Dame Journal of Education*, Vol. 5, No. 4, Winter 1974, pp. 313–332.

Kolesnik, W.B. and Power, E.J., *Catholic Education: A Book of Readings*, McGraw Hill, New York, 1965.

Konstant, D. *et al*, *Signposts and Homecomings*, Bishops' Conference, 1981.

Konstant, D., Presidential Speech to the North of England Education Conference, *Briefing*, 24th January 1991, Vol. 21, No. 2.

Koob, C.A., *What is Happening to Catholic Education ?*, National Catholic Educational Association, Washington D.C., 1966.

Koob, A.C., 'Making Smooth the Way for Lay Leadership', *Momentum*, Vol. XV, No. 2, May 1984.

Lannie, V., 'The Teaching of Values in Public, Sunday and Catholic Schools', *Religious Education*, Vol. LXX, No. 2, 1975.

Laplante, R.L., 'Catholic Religious Education in Canada', *British Journal of Religious Education*, Vol. 11, No. 3, Summer 1989.

Lawlor, M., 'Catholic Education', *Slant*, Vol. 2, No. 2, May 1966.

Leavey, M.C., *Religious Education, School Climate and Achievement*, PhD, Australian National University, 1972.

Lee, J.M., *The Purpose of Catholic Schools*, Washington D.C., National Catholic Educational Association, 1968.

Lee, J.M., *Catholic Education in the Western World*, University of Notre Dame, Washington, 1967.

Leeson, S., *Christian Education*, Longman, London, 1947.

Leetham, C., *Catholic Education*, Catholic Social Guild, London, 1965.

Leetham, C., *Post Conciliar Thoughts on Catholic Education*, Catholic Education Council, 1969.

Little, L.C., *Bibliography of Doctoral Dissertations in Character and Religious Education*, University of Pittsburgh, 1960.

Lombaerts, H., 'Evangelisation of the School Milieu', in Three Parts, *The Sower*, Vol. 7, No's. 2, 3, and 4, 1983.

Loughran, G., 'The Rationale of Catholic Education', in R.D. Osborne, R.J. Cormack, and R.L. Miller (eds.) *Education Policy in Northern Ireland*, Policy Research Institute, Belfast, 1987.

Losoncy, L.J., *Towards a more Democratic Theory of Roman Catholic Education in the U.S.A.*, PhD, Wayne State University, 1971.

Lundy, M.A., *Adult Catechesis in the Roman Catholic Church in Britain since the Second Vatican Council*, PhD, University of Manchester, 1990.

Lunn, A., 'Point of View', *Catholic Teachers Journal*, Vol. 9, No. 5, September–October 1966.

McBrian, R., 'A Case for Catholic Education', *Commonweal*, January 21, 1977, pp. 41–44.

McBride, A.A., *The Christian Formation of Catholic Educators*, National Catholic Educational Assocation of America, Washington D.C., 1981.

McBride, A.A., 'The Nature of the Church and its Educational Mission', *Notre Dame Journal of Education*, Vol. 3, No. 4, Winter 1973, pp. 293–296.

McCann, M.M., 'Catholic Schools and a Democratic Model of Administration', *Notre Dame Journal of Education*, Vol. 3, No. 4, 1973, p.318 ff.

McClelland, V.A., *Cardinal Manning*, OUP, 1962.

McClelland, V.A., 'The Protestant Alliance and Roman Catholic Schools 1872–1874', *Victorian Studies*, December 1964, Vol.8, No. 2, pp. 173–183.

McClelland, V.A., *Roman Catholics and Higher Education 1830–1903*, PhD, University of Sheffield, 1967/68.

McClelland, V.A., *English Roman Catholics in Higher Education*, Clarendon Press, Oxford, 1973.

McClelland, V.A., 'The "Free School" Issue and the General Election of 1885: A Denominational Response', *History of Education*, Vol. 5, No. 2, 1976, pp. 141–154.

McClelland, V.A., 'School or Cloister? An English Educational Dilemma 1794–1889', *Pedagogica Historica*, Vol. 20, No. 1, 1980, p. 108 ff.

McClelland, V. A., 'Educating for Life', *The Month*, October 1984.

McClelland, V. A., (ed.), *Christian Education in a Pluralist Society*, Croom Helm, London, 1988.

McClelland, V.A., "Sensus Fidelium': The Developing Concept of Roman Catholic Voluntary Education in England and Wales', in Tulasiwicz, W. and Brock, C., *Christianity and Educational Provision in International Perspective*, Routledge, London, 1988, pp. 61–88.

McClelland, V. A., *'Education' in Modern Catholicism : Vatican II and After*, (ed.) A. Hastings., SPCK, London, 1991.

McClelland, V. A., 'A Commitment to Crisis: The Witness of the Catholic School', *The Sower*, September 1992, pp. 9–11.

McCuskey, N.G., *Catholic Viewpoint on Education*, Doubleday, New York, 1962.

McDermott, E.J., *Distinctive Qualities of the Catholic School*, National Educational Association of America, Washington D.C., 1985.

McEwan, H.G., 'The Catholic Schools', *Scottish Education Journal*, Vol. 59, 25th November 1976.

McGettrick, B.J., 'Catholic Education in Scotland', *Scottish Educational Review*, Vol. 16, No. 2, November 1984, pp. 134–139.

McGucken, L.J., *The Philosophy of Catholic Education*, The America Press, New York, 1957.

McGucken, W., *The Catholic Way In Education*, Bruce, Milwaukee, 1934.

McGucken, W., 'The Philosophy of Catholic Education', in *Philosophies of Education* part 1 chapter 6, by N.B. Henry, (ed.), National Society for the Study of Education, Chicago, 1942.

McHugh, D., 'The 1992–1993 Education Bill', *The Sower*, April 1993, pp. 7–8.

McKeown, M., 'The Paradoxes of Catholic Education', *The Furrow*, November 1982, Vol. 33, No. 11, pp. 680–685.

McKinney, M.B., 'Parental Leadership in Vataican II Church', *Momentum*, Vol. XV, September 1984.

McLaren, P., 'Making Catholics: The Ritual Production of Conformity in a Catholic Junior High School', *Journal of Education*, Vol. 168, No. 2, 1986, pp. 55–77.

McLaren, P., 'Schooling for Salvation: Christian Fundamentalism's Ideological Weapon of Death', *Journal of Education*, Vol. 169, No. 2, 1987, pp. 132–139.

McLaughlin, R., *The Liberty of Choice: Freedom and Justice in Education*, Liturgical Press, Collegeville, 1979.

McLaughlin, T.H., 'Parental Rights and the Religious Upbringing of Children', *Journal of Philosophy of Education*, Vol. 18, No. 1, 1984, pp. 75–84.

McLaughlin, T.H., *Parental Rights in Religious Upbringing and Religious Education Within a Liberal Perspective*, PhD, University of London, 1990.

McLean, G.F., *Philosophy and the Integration of Contemporay Catholic Education* Catholic University of America Press, Washington D.C., 1962.

McLean, G.F. (ed.), *Catholic Thought: An Annotated Bibliography of Philosophy* Frederick Ungar, New York, 1967.

McManus, W., 'The Future of Catholic Education', *Notre Dame Journal of Education*, Vol. 2, No. 1, 1971, pp. 44–53.

McPolin, A., 'The Catholic School Today', *Catholic Education Today*, Vol. 6, No. 3, May–June 1972, pp. 17–18.

Maclure, S., 'Forty Years On', *British Journal of Educational Studies*, Vol. 33, No. 2, June 1985, pp. 117–134.

Mahoney, E.J., *Questions and Answers*, Burns and Oates, London, 1944.

Malone, V., 'Priests in School', *Clergy Review*, Vol. XLVI, 1961, pp. 513–24.

Malone, R.J., *The Roman Catholic School as Faith Community: Educational Developments and Theological considerations*, ThD, Boston College, 1981.

Manno, B.V., 'Lay Involvement in Catholic Schools', *America*, October 27th 1984, pp. 246–247.

Manno, B.V., 'Catholic School Education: Providing Leadership in the Educational Reform Movement', *Living Light*, October, Vol. 25, No. 1, 1988, pp. 7–12.

Marique, P., *The Philosophy of Christian Education*, Prentice-Hall, New York, 1939.

Maritain, J., *Education at the Crossroads*, Yale University Press, 1961.

Maritain, J., *The Aims of Education*, Yale University Press, 1964.

Marmion, J.P., 'Christian School, Pagan Curriculum: Results Unsatisfactory', *Priests and People*, Vol. 3, No. 7, July–August 1989.

Marmion, J.P., 'Catholic Tradition in Education', *Clergy Review*, July 1986.

Marmion, J.P., *Cornelie Connelly's Work in Education 1848–1879*, PhD, University of Manchester, 1984.

Martin, C., *Christian Aims in Education*, Leicester IVP, 1985.

Marr, P., 'Denominational Schools: some implications from ARCIC 1', *One in Christ*, Vol. 25, 1989.

Mathew, D., *Catholicism in England: the Portrait of a Minority, its Culture and Traditions*, Eyre and Spottiswoode, London, 1955.

MaxwelL-Collins, J., 'Catholic Education: Modifications, Merger, Metamorphosis', *Journal of Christian Education*, Vol. 15, No. 1, 1972, pp. 18–25.

Michel, G.J., 'Parent Participation in Catholic Schools', *Catholic Education Today*, Vol. 11, No. 1, January–March 1977.

Miller, R.C., *The Theory of Christian Education In Practice*, Religious Education Press, Birmingham, (U.S.A.), 1980.

Milroy, D., *Catholic Secondary Education — An Appraisal*, January 1987, Committee of the Conference of Catholic Secondary Schools.

Miranda, E.O., 'Some Problems with the Expression Christian Education', *British Journal of Religious Education*, Vol 8, No. 2, Spring 1986, pp. 94–102.

Mullaney, H., *The Catholic School and its Curriculum*, Catholic Education Council, April 1967.

Murdick, O.J., 'Religious Freedom and Vatican II', *Religious Education*, Vol. LXXI, No. 4, 1976, pp. 416–427.

Murdick, O.J., 'Toward a Philosophy of Catholic Education', *Today's Catholic Teacher*, February 1984.

Murphy, J., *Church, State and School in Britain 1800–1970*, RKP, London, 1971.

Murphy, J., *The Religious Problem in English Education*, LUP, 1959.

Mutschler, M.J., *Effective Catholic Schooling: An Organisational Analysis*, PhD, Fordham University, 1985.

National Catholic Educational Asoociation of America, Keynote Series: *1. History of U.S.A. Schools; 2. Public Relations; 3. Government and Administration; 4. Moral Development; 5. Parent, Parish and School; 6. Teacher; 7. Curriculum; 8. Catechetics; 9. Methods of Teaching; 10. Development of Students; 11. Research; 12. Pre-Service and In-Service Education; 13. Code of Ethics.*

Neuwien, R.A., *Catholic Schools in Action*, Notre Dame University, 1966.

Newman Association: *Reflections on Education*, London 1968.

Nichols, K., *The Basis of Catholic Education*, Catholic Education Council, 1969.

Nichols, K., 'Christianity, Humanism and Education', *Catholic Education Today*, Vol. 6, No. 5, September–October 1972, pp. 4–7.

Nichols, K., 'The Future of the Dual System', *Clergy Review*, May 1973.

Nichols, K., 'Towards a Theology of Education', *The Tablet*, Educational Supplement, No. 25, 1973.

Nichols, K., *Theology and Education*, St Paul, Slough, 1974.

Nichols, K., *Cornerstone*, St Paul, Slough, 1978.

Nichols, K., *Orientations*, St Paul, Slough, 1979.

Nichols, K., 'Taking Stock of the Catholic School', *The Tablet*, Educational Supplement, No. 39, 1983.

Nordberg, R.B., 'Curricular Integration in Catholic Education', *Religious Education*, Vol. 82, No 1, 1987, pp. 127–142.

Nott, M., *Partnership in Peril: the presssures at work on the dual system of state maintained education in England and Wales in a decade of change — 1976–1986*, University of Birmingham, MEd, 1987.

Nowell, R., 'How Necessary are Our Schools?', *Herder Correspondence*, Vol. 5, No. 10, October 1968, pp. 295–299.

Nuttgens, D., 'The Neglected Third', *Catholic Education Today*, Vol. 4, No. 6, November–December 1970, pp. 4–6.

O'Brien, J., 'Parents and Education', *Catholic Education: An Educational Review*, No. 1, 1956, pp. 8–37.

O'Brien, R., *The Nature of the Catholic School and its Function in the Modern World*, Catholic Education Council, London, 1959.

O'Brien, R., *An Act in Time*, Catholic Education Council, London, August 1959.

O'Brien, R., *The English Education System and Some Present Problems*, Catholic Education Council, London, 1959.

O'Connor, M., 'Touching Faith and the Future', *The Guardian*, 26th June 1984, p.11.

O'Gorman, K., 'Catholic Identity Crisis', *The Tablet*, 10th October 1987.

O'Gorman, K., 'The Inspection of Catholic Schools', *The Sower*, April 193, pp. 5–6.

O'Keeffe, B., *Faith, Culture and the Dual System*, Falmer Press, London, 1986.

O'Keeffe, B., (ed.), *Schools for Tomorrow*, Falmer Press, London, 1988.

O'Leary, D., *Religious Education and Young Adults*, St Paul, Slough, 1983.

O'Leary, M., *The Catholic Church in Education*, Burns and Oates, London, 1943.

O'Malley, F., 'Education of Man: A Discussion of Education at the Crossroads by J. Maritain', *The Review of Politics*, Vol. 6, January 1944.

O'Neil, M., *New Schools in a New Church: Towards a Modern Philosophy of Catholic Education*, Collegeville, St. John's University Press, 1971.

Pattison, R., *An Examination of the political and legislative background to the development of Catholic elementary education in the 20th century*, PhD, University of Leeds, 1968.

Pavey, G.S.A., *The Influence of the Doctrine of Orginal Sin on Education and Practice*, University of Leeds, PhD, 1957.

Peers, F.G., 'Philosophy of Education in Catholic Colleges', *Catholic Teachers Journal*, Vol. 9, No. 6, November–December 1966, pp. 19–20.

Pennock, M., 'The Heart of the Catholic School', *Momentum*, May 1980.

Phillips, F.R., *The Consolidation of Catholic Education Policy in England and Wales 1950–1959*, PhD, University of London, 1979.

Phillips, F.R., *An Investigation into the Development of Catholic Education Policy in England and Wales from 1944–1949*, University of London, MA, 1964/65.

Pollard, J.E., 'Why We Do What We Do: A Reflection on Catholic Education in Catholic Schools', *Living Light*, Vol. 25, No. 2, January 1989, pp. 103–111.

Pope John Paul II, *The Catechist*, Franciscan Herald Press, Chicago, 1980.

Pope John Paul II, *Sources of Renewal*, Collins, London, 1980.

Pope John Paul II, *The Role of the Family in the Modern World*, St Paul's, Boston, 1981.

Pope John Paul II, *Catechesis in Our Time*, Encyclical 1982.

Pope John Paul II, 'What is the Value of Catholic Education?', *Origins*, Vol. XIII, No. 23 1983.

Pope John Paul II, 'Pope Defends Catholic Schools', *The Tablet*, 7/6/84.

Pope John Paul II, 'The Gospel is the Soul of the Catholic School', in *L'Osservatore Romano*, Vol. XVII, No. 29, July 16th 1984.

Pope John Paul II, 'The Catholic School', in *The Pope Speaks*, Vol. 31, December 28th 1985.

Pope John Paul II, 'Address to Parents, Teachers and Students on the Role of the Catholic School in Modern Society', *The Pope Speaks*, Vol. 30, Winter 1985.

Pope Pius XI, *The Christian Education of Youth*, Rome, 1929.

Preiswerk, M., *Education in the Living World: A Theoretical Framework for Christian Education*, Orbis Books, Marynoll, New York, 1987.

Purnell, A.P., 'Alienated Youth and the Faith', *The Month*, October 1983, pp. 338–340.

Purnell, A.P., *Our Faith Story*, Collins, London, 1985.

Rafferty, K., 'The Theory of Education', *Catholic Education Today*, Vol. 6, No. 5, September–October 1972, pp. 5–7.

Rausch, T.P., *The Roots of the Catholic Tradition*, Michael Glazier, Wilmington, 1986.

Reck, C., *Vision and Values in the Catholic School*, National Catholic Educational Association, Washington, D.C., 1986.

Redden, J.D. and Ryan, F.A., *A Catholic Philosophy of Education*, Bruce, Milwaukee, 1957.

Regina *v.* Trustee of Roman Catholic Diocese of Westminster, ex parte Mars, *LGR*, 86, 1987, p. 507 f.

Regina *v.* Westminster Roman Catholic Diocese Trustee, ex parte Andrews, (not reported) see *The Independent*, 27th July 1989, p. 9.

Regina *v.* Governors of the Bishop Challoner Roman Catholic School and Another ex parte C, Same, ex parte P. (not reported) see *The Times*, 6th July 1991, p. 28.

Rhymer, J., *Family, School and the Church*, University of Edinburgh, Theology Paper, 1984.

Richards, N.J., 'Religious Controversy and School Boards', *British Journal of Educational Studies*, Vol. XVIII, No. 2, June 1970, pp. 180–196.

Rickett, B., 'Our Schools Are We Satisfied With Them?', *Clergy Review*, April, 1950.

Riessen, Van H., 'Freedom of Choice in Education in the Era of the Industrial Arts', *Catholic Education: An Educational Review*, Vol. 3, December 1957, pp. 32–46.

Robinson, J., 'Local Authorities and Schools Opting Out — The Minister's Role Reviewed', *Law and Justice*, Trinity, 1991, pp. 18–27.

Robinson, T., *Distinctive Characteristics of Roman Catholic Secondary Schools*, University of Oxford, MSc, 1982.

Roehampton Papers: 1. 'Admissions', *The Month*, May 1985; 2. 'Catholicity', *The Month*, April 1986; 3. 'Higher Education', *The Month*, January 1985; 4. 'Higher Education', *The Month*, May 1984; 5. '16–19 Education', *The Month*, January 1984.

Rudden, J., 'The Catholic Comprehensive School: Model of the Church', Vol. 2, No. 3, *Catholic Education Today*, May–June 1968, pp. 12–14.

Rossiter, G.M., 'The Need for a "Creative Divorce" between Catechesis and Religious Education in Catholic Schools', *Religious Education*, Vol. 77, No. 1, 1982, pp. 21–40.

Rummery, G., *Catechesis and Education in a Secular Society*, Dwyer, Sydney, 1975.

Rummery, R.M., *An Examination of the Concept Catechesis as a Traditional Description of Roman Catholic Religious Education*, PhD, University of Lancaster, 1972/73.

Ryan, M.P., *Are Catholic Schools the Answer?*, Holt, Rinehart and Winston, New York, 1964.

Sacks, D., *The Religious Issue in Education 1902–1914 in England and Wales*, University of New Mexico, 1961.

St John, H., 'Autonomy in Catholic Education', *Blackfriars*, October 1943.

Schiefen, R.J., *The Organisation and Administration of Roman Catholic Dioceses in England and Wales in the mid-nineteenth century*, University of London, PhD, 1970.

Selby, D.E., *The Work of Cardinal Manning in the Field of Education*, University of Birmingham, PhD, 1974.

Selby, D.E., 'The Catholic Teacher Crisis 1885–1902', *The Durham and Newcastle Research Review*, Vol. 37, Autumn 1976, pp. 33–47.

Shaw, R. (ed.), *Trends and Issues in Catholic Education*, Citation Press, New York, 1969.

Shelton, H.S., 'Religion in Schools', *The Political Quarterly*, Vol. 16, 1945.

Shields, T.E., *Philosophy of Education*, Catholic Education Press, Washington, 1921.

Shuster, G.N., *Catholic Education in a Changing World*, Holt, Rinehart and Winston, New York, 1967.

Simon, S.D., 'The Education Bill', *The Political Quarterly*, Vol. 15, 1944.

Smith, R.A.L., *The Catholic School and the Social Order*, Longman, London, 1943.

Smith, T.H., *The Traditional Philosophy of Religious Education: An Enquiry into the application of the Philosophy of St. Thomas Aquinas to the Teaching of Religion*, PhD, University of London, 1953/54.

Socialist Education Association, *The Dual System of Voluntary and County Schools*, Manchester, 1981.

Spencer, A.E.C.W., 'Tasks of Catholic Educational Research', *Catholic Education Today*, Vol. 1, No. 4, July–August 1967, pp. 12–15.

Spencer, A.E.C.W., 'An Evaluation of Roman Catholic Educational Policy in England and Wales 1900–1960.', in P, Jebb (ed.), *Religious Education*, London, 1968.

Spencer, A.E.C.W., 'PTAs in Catholic Schools', *Catholic Education Today*, Vol. 3, No. 2, March–April 1969, pp. 17–23.

Spencer, A.E.C.W., 'Catholic Education in a Changing World', *Catholic Education Today*, Vol. 2, No. 6, November–December 1968, pp. 18–19.

Spencer, A.E.C.W., *The Future of Catholic Education in England and Wales*, Catholic Renewal Movement, London, 1971.

Sullivan, J., 'Education and the State', *Catholic Teachers Journal*, Vol. 9, No. 1, January–February 1966, pp. 26–27.

Sullivan, V.M., *The Second Vatican Council Implications for Education*, University of Liverpool, MEd, 1969/70.

Stafford, F.J., 'Reflections on Catholic Education', *Origins*, Vol. 28, No. 2., 1982, pp. 63–64.

Storey, A., 'Teaching the Faith', *Clergy Review*, January 1968.

Swarbrick, M.A., *The Roman Catholic Interest in State Aided Elementary and Secondary Education in England and Wales 1902–1936*, University of Lancaster, PhD, 1985.

Sweeney, M.V., *The Laity in Catholic Education*, Catholic Education Council, Handbook, 1968, pp. 162–63.

Teese, R., 'The Political Function of the Administration of Catholic Education in France', *Journal of Education Policy*, Vol 4, No 2, 1989, pp. 103–114.

Thornthwaite, S., 'School Transport — The Need for Change', *British Journal of Educational Studies*, Vol. XXXVIII, No. 2, May 1990, pp. 133–143.

Torjussen, P., *Catholic Social Theory and the Democratic Organisation of the School*, University of Leeds, MEd, 1968/69.

Travis, M.P., 'The Ecclesial Mission of the School', *Today's Catholic Teacher*, September 1976, pp. 8–10.

Travis, M.P., *Doctoral Dissertations on Catholic Schools 1976–1987*, National Centre for Research, in Total Catholic Education, Washington D.C., 1989.

Tucker, B. (ed.), *Catholic Education in a Secular Society*, Sheed and Ward, London, 1968.

Vaille, S.J., *Catholic Education*, National Catholic Educational Assiociation, Ohio, 1968.

Veale, J., 'The Christian School', *Studies*, Vol. 59, Winter 1970, pp. 385–95.

Veverke, F., 'The Ambiguity of Catholic Educational Separatism', *Religious Education*, Vol. 80, No. 1, 1985, pp. 64–100.

Walsh, K., 'The School as a Community of Faith', *The Month*, June 1978, pp. 188–193.

Walsh, P., 'The Church Secondary School and its Curriculum', in O'Leary, D. (ed.), *Religious Education and Young Adults*, St Paul's Publications, Slough, 1983.

Wake, R., 'Catholic Education in Schools', *The Month*, July 1986.

Ward, L.R., 'Maritain's Philosophy of Education', *The Review of Politics*, Vol. 40, No. 4, October 1978, pp. 499–513.

Ward, M.R.A., *Patterns of Administration in Diocesan School Systems*, Catholic University of America Press, Washington D.C., 1957.

Warren, M., *Faith, Culture and the Worshipping Community*, Paulist Press, New York, 1989.

Watt *v.* Kesteven County Council, 1, *Q.B.*, 408 f, 1955.

Webster, D., 'A Spiritual Dimension for Education', *Theology*, Vol. LXXXVII, No. 721, January 1985, pp. 11–21.

Wells, D., 'The Supply of Catholic Teachers in Catholic Schools', Catholic Education Service, London, 1994.

Wenham, J., *The School Manager in Denominational Schools*, St Anselm's Press, London, 1892.

Whitehead, M., 'The Changing Face of Catholic Independent Schools', *Aspects of Education*, Vol. 35, 1986, pp. 63–72.

Whitehead, M., 'Briefly, and in Confidence': Private Views of Her Majesty's Inspectors of English Catholic Elementary Schools, 1875', *Recusant History*, Vol. 20, No. 4, October 1991, pp. 554–562.

Williams, J.S., *The Origin and Development of Roman Catholic Education in the Heads of the Valley Region*, University of Wales, MEd, 1974.

Woodhall, R., 'Educational Priority Areas: Towards a Christian Policy', *Catholic Education Today*, Vol. 4, No. 5, September – October 1970, pp. 4–8.

Wright, R., 'Pagans, Catholics and Christians', *Ampleforth Review*, Spring 1989, Vol. XCIV, Part I, pp. 36–39.

Yzermans, V.A., (ed.), *Pope Pius XII and Catholic Education*, Grail, St Meinrad, 1957.

Index

academic emphasis 58, 61, 197
admissions 173, 186, 198–204, 205; 19th cent. 18; 1970s 103–4, 105, 146; 1980s 112–14; and equality 123; erosion of autonomy 103–4, 233, 250; models of 227, 229–30, 231–2; principle/policy disjunction 213; 'standard number' 203–4, 250; supply and demand 198–9, 231; and viability 119–21, 128, 198, 212, 230, 252; *see also* non-Catholic children; non-practising Catholics; parents (choice of school); *and under* ethos
adult education 1, 65, 125, 247
aided schools *see* voluntary-aided schools
aims *see* goals
Allen, Cardinal William 10
Allies, Thomas 35
Anglican Church: access to state schools 29, 36, 122; claim for additional aid (1955) 33; and Education Bill (1990) 211; and free transport 110; joint schools 121, 122, 198–9, 247, 226–7; and National Curriculum 186; in 19th century 11, 12–13, 19, 35; schools 23, 122, 206,)(16th–17th century 10, 123, (transferred to State sector) 20, 29, 35

anthropology, Catholic 52, 78
appointments *see under* teachers
Arundel and Brighton, Diocese of 215
Audit Commission 208–9
authoritarianism 58, 74, 78, 137, 197
authority: Church, and identity of Catholic schools 247–9; dissent over 70, 71, 78, 91–2, 165; grant-maintained status and 115–17, 119; *see also under* bishops

Baker, Kenneth, MP 114
baptisms, number of 92, 103–4
Barry, Dom Patrick 104
Baum, Cardinal 80, 149, 159
Beales, Arthur 97, 100, 144
Beck, Archbishop G.A. 30, 32, 37, 63, 141, 185; and finance 93, 94, 95–6, 97
Bedford 194–5
behavioural sciences 81
Benevolent Society of St Patrick 11
Bible; Authorised Version 12–13, 13–14, 35
Birch, Bishop, of Ossory 141
Birks, Peter 197
Birmingham, Archdiocese of 10, 16; admissions 201; comprehensive reorganisation 144–5;